BELIEVING
CASSANDRA

▼

BELIEVING

CASSANDRA

AN OPTIMIST LOOKS
AT A PESSIMIST'S WORLD

Alan AtKisson

CHELSEA GREEN PUBLISHING COMPANY

WHITE RIVER JUNCTION, VERMONT

TOTNES, ENGLAND

Graphs in chapter 3 are adapted from Brown, et al., *Vital Signs 1999* (New York: W.W. Norton, 1999); Meadows, Meadows, and Randers, *Beyond the Limits* (White River Jct., Vt.: Chelsea Green, 1992); Redefining Progress, 1998; and "Human Development Report 1994" (United Nations Development Programme), with data from "World Development Indicators 1999" (World Bank).

Text designed by Dede Cummings Designs.

Chelsea Green books are available for course adoptions and organizational purchases. For special quantity discounts, please contact the national sales manager at the address below.

Printed in the United States of America.
03 02 01 00 99   1 2 3 4 5
First printing, September 1999

Printed on acid-free, recycled paper.

Library of Congress Cataloging-in-Publication Data
AtKisson, Alan, 1960–
    Believing Cassandra : an optimist looks at a pessimist's world
/ Alan AtKisson.
    p. cm.
Includes bibliographical references and index.
ISBN 1-890132-16-0 (alk. paper)
1. Environmental policy. 2. Environmental protection. 3. Human
    ecology. I. Title.
GE170 .A85 1999
363. 7 -- dc21   99-37784
                                                          CIP

Chelsea Green Publishing Company

P.O. Box 428

White River Junction, Vermont 05001

telephone (800) 639-4099

www.chelseagreen.com

CONTENTS

Part 1
CASSANDRA'S DILEMMA

The astonishing tale of a small book called The Limits to Growth, *and the mystery of how a computer model called "World3" shook the foundations of the real World, and then was promptly forgotten.*

Wherein we trace the development of humanity's growing awareness of certain very dangerous global trends, and how it came to pass that the warnings about these trends were mostly ignored, leading up to the tragic story of a political prince named Al Gore who shied away from his own gift of prophecy.

P a r t   2

REINVENTING THE WORLD

There is absolutely no inevitability
as long as there is a willingness to contemplate
what is happening.

—MARSHALL McLUHAN

▼

We need not want
what we are the middle of.

—JAMES BERTOLINO

ACKNOWLEDGMENTS

WRITING A BOOK MAKES one very aware of the extent to which one's life is supported on a web of relationship. I cannot say with certainty which thoughts in these pages are mine, and which should be credited to my colleagues and friends. I have attempted to give credit where it is due, but a complete catalog of my gratitude would fill the remainder of these pages.

This book owes its existence to Donella ("Dana") Meadows, who encouraged me to write it. She made the initial invitation to write a short summary of *Beyond the Limits*—a book I had long admired, along with its precursor, *The Limits to Growth*. The "summary" idea grew by strange fits and starts into this more wide-ranging project, and Dana cheered me on all the way. She also read the manuscript and offered a great many helpful corrections and suggestions. For all her help, encouragement, teaching, and friendship over the years, I am everlastingly grateful.

At several key stages of this book's development, Dennis Meadows offered guidance by means of short comments with long-lasting, beneficial impacts. His editorial input was also very valuable. I owe much of my understanding of systems to his excellent teaching as well.

As the founders of the Balaton Group, Dana and Dennis together created the remarkable international network that has provided me with a feeling of inexhaustible wealth in the form of friendship, experience, learning, cross-cultural understanding, and mutual support. I drew heavily on this Group's storehouse of knowledge and passionate commitment in the course of writing this book, as I do in many areas of my life. To Dana and Dennis, and to all the Group's members, I feel a separate and special debt of gratitude.

To Robert Gilman I make a deep bow of appreciation. Robert gave me the opportunity of a lifetime: the chance to edit the magazine he founded, *In Context*. Some of the core ideas in this book were introduced to me by Robert, and by all the contributors to *In Context*, where I served as editor from 1988 to 1992. I also bow to the memory of Robert's partner and my friend, Diane Gilman.

John A. (Jay) Harris provided the financial support, through a grant to the Sustainability Institute, that made the writing possible, as well as numerous helpful suggestions. I am very thankful.

Too much credit cannot be given to the staff of Chelsea Green Publishing—especially my editors, Jim Schley and Ian Baldwin, and publisher Stephen Morris—for skillfully nurturing this project from initial concept, through some very rough early stages, all the way through to final copyediting. Their steadfast faith in the project, and their insightful design hints, helped me bring it to completion on time. Jim Schley's meticulous attention to language and style helped greatly. Rachael Cohen both proofread the text and improved it in other ways. No writer could ask for better editorial partners.

Other early readers and commentators included Michael and Margi Baldwin, Paul Hawken, Chrissie Bascom, Margo Baldwin, Carola Lott, Hannah Silverstein, and Melita Rogelj. Their comments helped focus the text in critical ways, and I very much appreciate the gift of their time and reflection.

Diana Wright helped greatly with the research, as did the librarians at Dartmouth College. The researchers at Worldwatch Institute and the World Resources Institute, on whose published work I relied extensively, deserve the applause and gratitude of the world itself.

I doubt that this book would have been completed in this millennium were it not for the time I spent at the Mesa Refuge writer's retreat in Point Reyes Station, California. Many thanks to Peter Barnes and Leyna Bernstein for creating such a beautiful and supportive environment. Family and friends who opened their homes (and hotel rooms) in my quest for a quiet place to think and write included Hank and Kathy Collins, Bob and Carolyn Meadows, Anton and Zaga Rogelj, Peg AtKisson and Joel White, Lawrence Molloy, Lee Hatcher, and Russ "Rick" Jones, owner of the coolest seaside inn in Playa del Carmen, the Blue Parrot.

And to Melita, who listened, encouraged, prodded, inspired, and stuck with me through every phase of this project's wild life, I cannot begin to express my appreciation.

August, 1999   *Rodine, Slovenia and New York, New York*

A Note on Usage

A FEW TERMS USED IN THIS book could invite misunderstanding, so I provide my working definitions here.

"Earth" means the entire planet, third out from the Sun.

"World" means the human world, the sum total of human beings, their systems, cultures, and technologies.

"Nature" means the living systems of the Earth, together with the non-living systems on which life depends.

Once introduced, these words are capitalized throughout the text wherever there is a need to distinguish these definitions from other common usages. For example, in common usage, "world" can some-times mean planet, and sometimes people. The word "earth" can some-times mean soil. And "nature" can mean a set of qualities, as in "human nature."

Two other capitalized words, "Growth" and "Development," are introduced at the end of chapter 1, and they are subsequently capital-ized when used to refer to those specific definitions.

Quotations are left as their authors wrote them, with their capi-talization schemes untouched.

Notes are gathered at the back of the book. I have keyed the notes to the relevant passages in order to avoid the distraction of superscript numbers in the text itself.

Finally, an observation about using this book. In these pages the reader will find an introduction to global trends, global computer models, problems in the global environment, solutions for the global economy, and the tales of a global traveler. But the book is intended to be translated into local languages, local ideas, local actions. Please use *Believing Cassandra* in whatever way will help you to improve your corner of the World.

PROLOGUE

BEAUTIFUL CASSANDRA was the youngest daughter of the last King of Troy. The god Apollo fell in love with her, but she refused him. To win her affections, he made a proposal: If she agreed to love him, he would give her the gift of prophecy.

Cassandra accepted the bargain, and she was graced with the ability to see the future. But she could not bring herself to love Apollo after all. Apollo was filled with outrage. Though Cassandra's gift could not be taken back, the god revenged himself in the most cruel way imaginable. He begged her for a single kiss, and she consented. When their lips touched, Apollo breathed into Cassandra's mouth in such a way that no one would ever believe her prophecies.

Cassandra was thus doomed to a life of despair. She could see the dangers threatening others, but she could not prevent them. Cassandra warned the Trojans that the Greeks were about to attack, and she cried out to warn them that soldiers were hidden inside the Trojan Horse. But her warnings went unheeded. Troy collapsed under the Greek on-slaught.

Captured, she was taken back to Greece. Her reputation as a seer came with her, as did Apollo's curse. "What do you know about the fu-ture?" they taunted her. She foretold a palace murder, and her own death, and that both would happen before sundown. The Greeks scoffed.

Before the end of the day, everything came to pass exactly as Cas-sandra had foreseen—but in the long run, it all turned out far better than anyone could have imagined. . . .

PART 1

CASSANDRA'S DILEMMA

CHAPTER 1

When Worlds Collapse

Every man takes the limits of his own field of vision for the limits of the world.

—ARTHUR SCHOPENHAUER

Faster, faster, until the thrill of speed overcomes the fear of death.
—HUNTER S. THOMPSON

AT THE VULNERABLE age of nineteen, I read a small paperback book called *The Limits to Growth*. No other book would influence my life so greatly, though I could barely understand its message at the time. Had I been able to comprehend it thoroughly, I might have laid down my head in the library and wept. At the same time, had I been granted a vision of where my interest in the book and its central message would ultimately take me, I would have been overcome with amazement.

The Limits to Growth deserves a place on the list of "the most controversial books of the twentieth century," right up there with James Joyce's *Ulysses*, Madonna's *Sex*, and Salman Rushdie's *The Satanic Verses*.

Its publication in 1972 ignited a firestorm of international discussion and debate. The book's authors—Donella ("Dana") Meadows, Dennis Meadows, Jørgen Randers, and William H. Behrens III, with Dana as the principal writer—were part of a young team of scientists (average age twenty-six) from the Massachusetts Institute of Technology. They had spent two years programming a computer to act as a model of the entire world. The future of that simulated world—they called it "World3," because it was the third in a series of attempts to create a global computer model—did not look good. In scenario after scenario, when humanity's wildly accelerating growth in population, resource use, and pollution was left unchecked, World3 collapsed. No simulated improvements in technology could prevent simulated catastrophe. Humanity's swelling billions would consistently overshoot Planet Earth's capacity to feed, support, and employ them. Then they would start dying off, as their agriculture began to fail and their industrial production crashed. Without decisive action to bring growth under control, and quickly, collapse always came within one hundred simulated years.

That word "collapse" gives the impression of suddenness and finality, but these researchers were predicting neither a sudden nor a final apocalypse. In fact, they were not predicting anything at all. They were simply analyzing the existing trends, programming the computer to project these into the future, and reporting on the results. The statistical collapse that consistently occurred was more like a swift slide than a mad plummet, more swan dive than cannonball. The little line on the graph representing human population would keep rocketing up until it reached the stratospheric level of 12 or 15 billion people, then it would turn over and start heading down to ground zero just as rapidly. The same thing happened to the lines for food production and industrial output. There was an odd gracefulness to the shape of the curves coming out of the computer, an eerie mathematical beauty that masked the horror of their meaning.

It is mercifully difficult to imagine living through a global collapse of the kind portrayed by World3's symbolic line graphs. Over the course of a generation, some combination of horrific disasters—famine, disease, widespread slow-motion poisoning caused by pollution, vicious wars fought over dwindling resources by unemployed and desperate young men, and last but not least, astonishing natural disasters fueled by climatic change—would combine to kill off quite a few billion people. Nothing remotely like this has ever happened to humanity on the global scale. The closest examples might be the Black Plague in medieval Europe, or the mind-numbing carnage of this century's world wars. But even these were limited in scope, mere circus sideshows by comparison.

And that's just the fate of humanity. Although World3 did not overly concern itself with the ultimate effects on Nature and its web of complex ecosystems, one can easily discern, reading between the lines on the old printouts, the eventual collapse of evolution as well. A world full of desperate and impoverished people is a world emptied of swordfish, rainforests, and panda bears. A collapse, if it occurred, would take so many species with it that Nature would have to spend 5 to 10 million years rebuilding its storehouse of diversity.

And yet, life would go on. There would still be humans, and other species, albeit far fewer of both. "Collapse" does not mean the end of the world, the end of Nature, or the end of anything, really, except perhaps industrial civilization, together with thousands of species, billions of people's lives, and humanity's collective innocence about three fundamental laws of Nature. First, when it comes to population growth, what goes up exponentially must stabilize, or it will crash down. Second, with regard to forests and fish and other resources, what gets used too rapidly and too thoughtlessly will ultimately cease to exist. And finally, as for waste and pollution, what gets dumped—into the water, land, or air—spreads out, hangs around, and creates havoc for generations to come.

None of these are desirable outcomes for the human project known as global civilization. Yet these are the terrors consistently produced by World3, given certain assumptions about where the real world had been and where it was currently headed.

World3, its creators knew, was flawed. There were certain to be gaps of ignorance, errors of calculation, problems of interpretation. Estimates made to fill holes in the data were probably inaccurate. But since the whole point was to imitate, as closely as possible, the likely behavior of the real world, the consistent *pattern* of the model's results—rapid growth to the point of overshoot, followed by collapse—was rather disturbing. It almost didn't matter whether the inevitable estimates were optimistic or pessimistic: Collapse was the perennial outcome. Prodded by their funders, the World3 creators began to feel they had an important message to deliver to the citizens of the real world, in the form of a warning, which they attempted to deliver. Aided by a generous promotional budget and savvy media work, the image of a computer pronouncing on humanity's fate made big headlines. Unfortunately, the message was garbled in the transmission.

▲▼▲

The authors of *The Limits to Growth* did not think of themselves as prophets. They were just hotshot academics, playing with a new toy in a new field: computer-based models of dynamic systems. They had plenty of backing from a prominent internationalist forum known as the Club of Rome and from the Volkswagen Foundation. They were protégés of Jay Forrester, the brilliant founder of their new science, and they had done their mentor proud by taking his breakthrough ideas about stocks and flows, feedbacks and delays, and creating the most ambitious mathematical copy of the world that anyone had ever seen.

To accomplish this, they built smaller models of subsystems of the world—population, agriculture, resources, industrial production, and pollution—and then linked them together. The object was to see how various trends affected each other: how rising pollution levels, say, might eventually speed up death rates, and how that in turn might affect the food supply. World3 was an attempt to mimic, using differential equations and feedback loops, the famous dictum of John Muir that "everything is hitched to everything else in the universe."

The real world—let's call it the World—is far more complex than World3, or any of its successors. The World consists of systems within systems within systems. It also includes such wild-card elements as political scandals, breakthrough inventions, and renegade dictators. The World includes the beauty of Mozart and fine architecture and the Bolshoi Ballet, as well as the tawdriness of Atlantic City on a slow Monday night. The World is more than just people, culture, machinery, and the movements of capital, though it includes all of those, together with human qualities like courage and vanity and greed. The World, to dig deeply into its origins in Old English, is "the age of man." Or, since "man" is thought to be an old word for "consciousness," the World is "the age of consciousness." No one could presume to build a model of *that*.

But the beauty of World3 lies in the math. Barring cosmic intervention, a population growing at 2% per year always doubles in thirty-five years, unless something happens to change that growth rate. This is undeniably, unalterably true, whether it happens in World3 or in the World—or on Mars, for that matter. So a computer model like World3 cannot be discounted simply for being a model, because math is the link between the computerized fiction and the flesh-and-blood reality. Math makes the rules in both Worlds. The computer simply automates the task of calculating numbers, while compressing time: In World3 (and its successors), you can watch a hundred years flash by in a few seconds. In the World, a hundred years takes one hundred real years—and if you don't like what happens, you can't push "Reset" and start over. In World3, numbers representing human populations go up and down, just as they do in the real World, but without the attached drama of real human lives, with all their joys and sorrows. The potential avoidance of foreseeable, real sorrows is what makes World3 worth contemplating.

What happens in World3 is not exactly a forecast; it is, you might say, a parallel reality. In that alternate reality, the unrestrained expansion of people and their stuff makes everything go haywire, and civilization collapses sometime in the middle of the twenty-first century. Does that mean the real World is doomed to the same fate? Not necessarily. Unlike the virtual citizens of World3, real human beings have the power to become aware of danger, and to change course in order to avoid it. Our World is, after all, "the age of consciousness," a feature decidedly lacking in the computerized version.

But despite its toy-truck qualities, World3 teaches us something of devastating importance: If unrestrained growth continues in the real World, a future collapse is certainly possible, and maybe inevitable. The mathematics of growth are driving us ever more rapidly toward the limits of the Earth's capacity to provide resources and absorb wastes. There are enormous challenges to be overcome, but we can overcome them, so long as we exercise that distinguished quality of consciousness to its fullest extent. It's a question of choice.

This was the message that the young authors of *The Limits to Growth* tried to deliver. They were seriously and politely received into the halls of power, and their message was echoed around the World via the media. Their arguments were considered by some of the greatest minds of the day. Many, especially those in the Club of Rome, praised and publicized their work. But the young authors were quite naive about the ways of power, politics, and publicity. They mistook open doors and smiling faces for acceptance, and it came as a rude surprise when they were viciously attacked by their peers, their work was vilified in the American press, and most painfully, their message was subsequently ignored.

Today, we live in a World of swelling populations concentrated in the poorest regions, disappearing fish and fresh water resources, declining food production per capita, global financial turmoil, increasingly desperate migration (often caused by natural or environmental disaster), rising conflict over land and resources, toxic pollution affecting nearly every living organism, and a dangerously changing climate caused by the ever-increasing emissions from our cars, power plants, and factories. "Growth," meaning the number of human beings and how much stuff they use up and discard, shows a few modest signs of slowing down, but at nothing like the pace required to avert far worse catastrophes than the ones already being suffered by the poorest and most vulnerable in places such as Bangladesh and Honduras. We are not yet living in the global collapse envisioned by World3, but some of that computer model's downward-plunging curves are beginning to look frighteningly similar to patterns in some parts of the World, and to our own possible and increasingly probable future. In some areas, including climate, we appear to have already passed the point of no return; we can no longer prevent the changes we have already set in motion.

But according to the common wisdom among people who still vaguely remember it, *The Limits to Growth* was a provocative but flawed book whose "predictions" turned out to be "wrong."

▲▼▲

Carmel, California
Late summer 1981

I am driving with my friend Martin down the coast to visit Ansel Adams's house. The great nature photographer won't be home, but his assistant is an old friend of Martin's. We'll have the run of the place.

Martin was one of my professors in college, and he taught a course in Ecoscience that made a huge impression on me. He was an odd duck—always wore short pants and suspenders, and talked with a slight, inauthentic British accent—but he was passionate about this topic. We read books on population, ecology, and the growing impact of technology on the environment. We read The Limits to Growth *and* Small is Beautiful.

That's why I'm having such a hard time understanding why Martin, a geologist, has now gone to work for an oil company, helping them to find new deposits of fossil fuel.

On arrival, Ansel's actual house proves to be a bit dull, but then John, the assistant, takes us down to the cove. This isn't just any spectacular cove on the Carmel coast; this is Ansel's cove. He owns it. I'm not sure if that means he also owns the seal that pokes its head up out of the kelp and stares at us, but the sight of it makes John's dog, an Irish setter, go berserk. He dives in and swims out toward the seal, barking wildly.

When the dog gets within about ten feet of the seal, the little rubbery head disappears. It pops up moments later about thirty feet behind the dog, and gives a mocking bark of its own. So the dog turns and plows through the kelp toward his aquatic cousin. It's a losing game, repeated over and over. The seal is just toying with him.

As we watch these canine antics, I ask Martin about his oil company job. How could he do it, given what he knows, given the passion he used to have? "It's easy," he answers, shrugging. "I needed the money." He goes on to explain that this company isn't as bad as the others, and somebody would do the work anyway, but I have a hard time listening.

The dog has given up. Exhausted, it swims to the shore, turns and stares at the spot where the seal has finally disappeared for good. In the gathering dusk, the cove looks like one of Ansel's photographs, which it probably is. The dog issues one final, plaintive bark; the sound seems to hang there amid the reflections and shadows. By the time we get home, it is dark.

▲▼▲

Like most ideas that attain the status of myth, the notion that *growth equals progress* was founded on a considerable amount of truth. Most of the great technical and cultural advances of the past several millennia—from medicine to symphonies to satellite weather forecasting—were made possible by growth. Progress in the arts and sciences has always been fueled by economic surplus, and often by concentrations of wealth in the hands of a relatively enlightened nobility or merchant class.

It's a simple matter of arithmetic. If everyone must work all the time just to survive, there is no time left for scientific discovery or creative endeavor. Growth—of people, machines, and overall wealth—allows the World to allocate more time to activities that are not essential for survival. This scheme works at every level, from small scale to large. When you increase your personal income, for example, you can afford to allocate more time to leisure and personal interests. The larger and more profitable a company grows, the more time and money it has to invest in research and development. As a community or city grows, it can afford better amenities, such as libraries, theaters, and stadiums.

And in society at large, growth in the economic sphere permits investment in new technology, higher levels of education, even (hope springs eternal) better government. The fewer the number of people required to labor in the fields and factories, the greater the number who can pursue education, new ideas, public service, and personal passions.

It is a beautiful scheme, and it works—up to a point. That point is a wall comprised of the laws of physics, the principles of mathematics, and the limits of natural systems. Beyond that point, as the old maps used to say, "there be dragons."

▲▼▲

When *The Limits to Growth* hit the World, Dennis and Donella Meadows—then married, now amicably divorced—were still in their early thirties. They had spent the last two years working on the computer modeling project that would eventually make them modestly famous. The project was, at first, just something fascinating to do. "We didn't even think about trying to change the world," says Donella, who goes by the nickname "Dana." "We were just trying to make a good computer model."

After they had presented their preliminary technical results to a range of audiences, from fellow scientists to United Nations bureaucrats, and received mixed reviews, Dana had a realization. "There needed to be a little popular book that communicated the central idea in a way that the average reader could understand, without all the computerese and scientific jargon. And the central message was about growth and limits." She set to work on the "popular" book, and fought unsuccessfully with her colleagues and co-authors to keep the computer model totally out of it. In the end, it was the *inclusion* of the computer model that most captured the public imagination, and that—combined with the chilling message about the possible fate of humanity—propelled the book to the bestseller list.

The Meadowses foresaw none of this. Their ambitions for the book were modest and academic until they received a call from the soon-to-be U.S. publishers of *Limits*, a small outfit called Potomac

Associates, who said they were arranging to present a copy to every senator, representative, governor, and UN ambassador. They were also organizing a formal presentation and seminar at the Smithsonian Institution, which many of the most powerful people in Washington were expected to attend. "From that moment, everything changed," Dana remembers. "We realized that people were actually going to take notice." The leak of an early manuscript to *Time* magazine, which immediately published a grim, doomsday article about their research, underscored the fact that they had a tiger by the tail: "It was out of our hands at that point," she says. "It was something bigger than we could control. All we could do was show up and try to do a good job."

The event in Washington lived up to the publisher's advance billing. Attendees included chief justice of the Supreme Court Earl Warren; Dr. Philip Handler, president of the National Academy of Sciences; Dr. Wernher von Braun, known as the "father of the space age"; and a long list of ambassadors and leading intellectuals. Elliot Richardson, who was secretary of Health, Education and Welfare under President Richard Nixon, spoke somberly of the book's critical importance. And the press echoed the book's message—or a simplified version of it—in headlines all over the U.S. and the world.

MANKIND WARNED TO CURB GROWTH OR FACE CATASTROPHE, said the *Chicago Sun Times*. PANEL ON GROWTH STRIVES TO STAVE OFF WORLD RUIN, said Virginia's *Newport News*. WILL GROWTH KILL HUMANITY? asked the *Tampa Tribune*, adding IS 'HOW SOON' THE ISSUE? News reports were supplemented by opinion pieces in the *New York Times*, the *Washington Post*, and many other papers. To look back at these articles is to feel nostalgia for the days when newspapers took seriously their responsibility to educate the public.

The now-venerable *New York Times* columnist Anthony Lewis, for example, wrote four columns about *The Limits to Growth* in 1972, two before the book's publication (titled "To Grow and To Die," I and II) and two after ("Ecology and Economics," I and II). He declared that *Limits* was likely to become "one of the most important documents of our age," and he took great pains to explain the dangerous dynamics of exponential growth.

The crucial fact is that growth tends to be exponential. That is, it *multiplies*. Instead of adding a given amount every so often, say 1,000 tons or dollars a year, the factors *double* at fixed intervals. That tends to be true of population, or industrial production, of pollution, and of demand on natural resources—some of the main strains of planetary life. [Italics added.]

It is hard to imagine such an instructive paragraph showing up in *USA Today* at the turn of the millennium. After noting that 1972's population growth rate of 2.1% equated to a doubling of population in just thirty-three years, Lewis went on to explain why exponential growth is so hard to fathom:

Exponential growth is a tricky affair. It gives us the illusion for a long time that things are going slowly; then suddenly it speeds up. Suppose the demand for some raw material is two tons this year and doubles every year. Over the next fifteen years it will rise to only 32,768 tons, but *just five years later it will be 1,048,576* tons. [Italics added.]

That phenomenon is what makes it so hard for people to understand how rapidly we may be approaching the limits of growth.

Washington Post columnist Claire Sterling did a similar public service in explaining what the authors meant by collapse:

The crisis level comes when growth has gone too far: too many people taking up too much of the land that ought to be producing their food, demanding too many manufactured objects using up too many raw materials and polluting too much of our land, air, and water. When this happens, growth stops, either because people starve to death, or raw materials give out, or pollution surpasses livable limits, or the stresses of overcrowding provoke war. World population could then drop by as much as a fifth in a single generation, while the bottom drops out of life as we know it for the rest of us.

The computer, said Sterling, is primitive. "Nevertheless, it seems able to grasp more than we do."

On the critical issue of time, which was a topic misunderstood by most reviewers, *Village Voice* writer Ross Gelbspan did an excellent job of interpreting (and emphasizing) *Limits'* essential warning. He noted that the immutable mathematical laws of exponential growth meant that "*after about 1985 it will be too late to reverse the final stage of exponential growth which will cause the collapse of natural and social life-support systems. But the actual impact will not be totally felt until the mid-twenty first century. . . ."* [Italics in the original.]

In one of several articles concerning the book, *Time* magazine described it as written in "restrained, nonhysterical, at times almost apologetic language," and noted with sadness that "the study closes almost every escape hatch." Technology would solve the resources problem only to exacerbate the pollution problem. Efficiency could reduce pollution, but that wouldn't stop population growth from running rampant and using up all the land for growing food. "There is only one way out," says the report: "economic as well as population growth must be stopped cold some time between 1975 and 1990 by holding world investment in new plant and machinery equal to the rate at which physical capital wears out."

But as we all know, the human economy did not stop growing by 1990. Indeed, growth was just then hitting its stride. As a result, we have committed the World to global warming, a depleted ozone layer, water shortages, species extinctions, hormone-mimicking chemicals filtering through Nature for decades to come, and many other irreversible changes. *Time*'s summary proved prescient: Technology *did* solve the resources problem for the moment with ever-better extraction techniques—which in turn *has* worsened the pollution problem. Efficiency and clean-up technologies *did* make it possible to reduce emissions of various kinds—but growth in population and affluence erased many of those gains while increasing unforeseen forms of pollution such as greenhouse gases and ozone-layer destroyers. And in recent years, population growth—propelled by earlier advances in food production, medical care, and economic development—has begun to outpace the growth in food production, even as the amount of land available for growing food declines.

It is no wonder, then, that when the authors of *The Limits to Growth* updated their findings twenty years later in 1992, they called the new book *Beyond the Limits*.

▲▼▲

In retrospect, it seems foolhardy to hope that a book could turn the tide of civilization. But *Limits* was an international phenomenon. Dana and Dennis began to believe that the World could indeed be changed. "We were received politely wherever we went," recalls Dana. "It lasted about two weeks. Then the big guns came out."

The "big guns" were a small army of prominent economists, scientists, and political figures who took aim at *Limits* from all sides. They attacked the methodology, the computer, the conclusions, the rhetoric, and the people behind the project. The book's authors found themselves on an intellectual hotseat, like doctoral candidates defending their thesis before a hostile committee comprised of the World's loudest and most powerful voices.

Dennis Meadows, who served as the primary spokesman, accepted an invitation to debate Yale economist Henry C. Wallich before the American Society of Newspaper Editors. As soberly as he could, Dennis offered them his analysis that "the planet's population will double in thirty years if unchecked, creating intolerable problems of pollution, economic distress, and conflict over dwindling supplies of income and resources." He went on to say that "this growth cannot go on forever," and that "the decisions must be made soon" to slow down population growth and the increase in resource use and pollution that come along with it.

Wallich retorted that the World "could hardly make a more important—and, to my mind, more misguided—decision" than to follow Meadows' advice. Wallich agreed that present growth rates could not go on forever. But he said the World would simply stop growing naturally. "Even if the ceiling on growth were much lower than it appears," said Wallich, alluding to his belief that the Meadowses' hundred-year scenario was far too pessimistic, "the world, with a minimum of good management, could level off without the collapse he predicts."

By stopping growth too soon, Wallich warned, the World would be consigning billions to permanent poverty. Technology could solve all the problems Meadows was concerned about, but only if growth continued apace. "What I am proposing," said Wallich, "is a voluntary approach that will allow us as much growth as our resources and our environment can support, and that at some future time, probably in the very far future, will gently ease our descendants into a phase of slower and, eventually perhaps, zero growth."

Wallich's arguments—emphasized even more strongly by other economists such as Julian Simon—were polite in comparison with broadsides launched against *Limits* in the press. A typical blistering review came from economist Peter Passell and others, writing in the *New York Times Book Review*. They dismissed the book as "an empty and misleading work," "less a pseudoscience and little more than polemical fiction," and smelling of "technical chicanery." They also ridiculed the Meadowses' method of extrapolating current trends into the future: "as British editor Norman Macrae has observed, an extrapolation of the trends of the 1880s would show today's cities buried under horse manure." In fact, the authors of *Limits* had *not* simply extrapolated, but some reviewers did not let their ignorance of the model prevent them from attacking it.

These and other more technical critiques, including a devastating review in the journal *Science*, gave Dana, Dennis, and their colleagues a rude awakening. "It hurt most," says Dana, "to be dismissed by our scientific peers." But perhaps the most distressing and revealing rebuke came from Russell Baker, the widely read *New York Times* humorist and columnist. Baker had attended the Smithsonian affair, and he came away unmoved. "How typical, how depressing," he wrote in a piece called "The Machine, the Doom and the Fool," "that most of us, dependent upon a computer and a mathematical model for news of doomsday's imminence, don't even know what a mathematical model is, or what a computer does with it, or to it, or at it."

Elliot Richardson, another Smithsonian attendee and panelist, had listened to the presentation made by Dennis Meadows and commented that, faced with such information, "the mind boggles." But after reporting this, Russell Baker noted wryly that "the mind stops boggling very soon, absorbs the fact—'Yes, the world really is coming to an end this time'—and resumes functioning on the old ante-doomsday assumption that everything is going to come out all right in the end."

In the end, most of the World seemed to respond to *Limits* much as Russell Baker did. At the same Smithsonian event, the boggled Elliot Richardson offered a rationale for inaction that was at once insightful and self-serving. "The minds of the people," he declared, "are unprepared to accept the political leadership that these conclusions would compel."

▲▼▲

Seeking to understand how so many thoughtful people could have responded so strongly to *The Limits to Growth* only to have the book soon disappear from the public consciousness, I called up Anthony Lewis of the *New York Times*. His four columns did not exactly spring back to his mind. "If you expect me to remember something I wrote in 1972, I'm afraid you'll be gravely disappointed," said the congenial Lewis. But he did remember *The Limits to Growth*. "The book had a great impact on me," recalled Lewis, "because I was already sensitized to the issues of population and the environment." Asked what sensitized him, Lewis sang a little verse from Gilbert and Sullivan's *Iolanthe* to me over the phone, complete with instrumental fills. The song explained, with typical verve,

> how every boy and every gal
> born into this world alive
> is either a little liber-al
> or else a little conserva-tive. . . .

If Lewis's liberal leanings made him open to the message of *The Limits to Growth* when it was published in 1972, what did he think about the message now? Lewis professed a certain relief that "the criers of havoc turned out to be wrong. We're still here, and we didn't run out of resources." I pressed him gently: Were they completely wrong, or had they been misinterpreted, or perhaps premature in their predictions? "You mean, like premature anti-fascism?" he said chuckling, probably referring to the partisans of the Lincoln Brigade in the Spanish Civil War, who had been accused in America of fighting the rise of totalitarianism "prematurely." "Well, they were wrong in a certain respect. They greatly underestimated the adaptability of our technological society to substitute for materials—Julian Simon turned out to be right on that score. But I think that the psychological and economic effects of population growth and overcrowding are real. Take a look at Africa."

I wasn't sure I wanted to know what Lewis saw when he looked at Africa, so I changed the subject. What about an issue like global warming? "I believe in global warming," affirmed Lewis. "I understand there are uncertainties connected with normal variation in climate, but I also observe that this is the warmest winter Boston has had in my entire life." He recalled receiving materials in the mail from various fake grassroots groups, saying that measures to curb global warming would be very expensive and disrupt our lifestyle. "People don't understand that there will be far greater disruptions to our lifestyle, if we wait another fifty years."

So why, I asked, is it so hard to alert the body politic to global trouble? The answer, said Lewis, is depressingly simple: "People don't want to know. We are resistant to hearing things that could be devastating." He recounted a story about meeting a Catholic bishop in South Africa years ago, and asking how it was that the white people in his church could live alongside the horrible inequity and suffering of apartheid. "They suffer from existential blindness," said the bishop. "They blind themselves in order to go on living."

I offered the opinion that the press had a duty to alert the public to issues such as those raised by *Limits*, and Lewis agreed. "But these days," he lamented, "editors are leery of printing such alarms. It's been a bit like crying wolf." Lewis himself would no longer write about such topics, since there are now hordes of environmental journalists who specialize in them. He focuses, he said, on explaining the law. For most of the last year, Anthony Lewis had been writing about the impeachment of President Clinton.

▲▼▲

I had been planning to talk to many veterans from the era of *Limits*, but my interview with Anthony Lewis told me as much as I wanted to know. Ironically, *Limits* failed to convey the necessity that was at the foundation of its message: the critical need to understand global dynamics in terms of complex, interconnected systems. Lewis, for example, could acknowledge the problems of global warming or rising population in the poorer parts of the globe, but he could not recall the connection between those phenomena and the original argument of *The Limits to Growth*. Despite his sterling efforts to explain, in his own youthful columns, many of the underlying systems concepts, he remembered the book only in terms of the negative propaganda campaign launched against it. That campaign succeeded in distracting readers by focusing on a straw-dog argument: the computer model's apparent failure to predict when, exactly, the World would run out of oil and metals.

Indeed, *The Limits to Growth* is loaded with "errors," if you measure the results of World3 by how accurately it foretold real events. By the year 2000, for example, population was projected to reach 7 billion; instead, the turn of the millennium finds humanity crossing only the 6 billion mark. The authors underestimated the effect of soil erosion on cropland, but they also underestimated the power of fertilizers and pesticides to increase crop yields (errors that balanced each other out). They also underestimated some of the efficiency gains in industry (industrial output per unit of resource).

But the "errors" for which many critics condemned *Limits* largely resulted from the critics' own erroneous reading of the text. *Limits*, they claimed, failed because it predicted that oil, copper, and several other critical resources would soon run out; instead, most of these materials became cheaper and more widely available, thanks to advances in recovery technology and substitution by other sources. Copper, for example, was long thought to be a critical limiting factor for industrial development because of its growing use in telephone cabling. Now, most of those cables are fiber optic, meaning they are made of sand.

The authors of *Limits* were merely assessing trends based on data they got from the U.S. Bureau of Mines. They used that agency's numbers as the basis for analyzing the lifespans of various metals and materials, because they wanted to demonstrate what would happen *if* usage rates continued to climb exponentially. They also calculated estimates based on *five times* the known reserves for each substance, as a way of demonstrating what makes exponential growth tick (having five times the material does not mean it will last five times as long). They understood that new reserves could be identified and other materials substituted for those that became scarce. The authors of *Limits* were trying to alert people to something else entirely: the *dynamics* of the World system, its structural tendency to overshoot and collapse.

Dismissing *Limits* for "erroneous predictions"—as so many have done, and still do—is like faulting the seer Cassandra for her poor choice of metaphor on the eve of the Trojan War: it dangerously misses the point. The point is that the Earth has limits, and that human beings are exceeding them, far faster than they realize—and perhaps faster than they *can* realize. The authors of *Limits* were concerned not about the life span of various metals and fuels, but about the overall pattern revealed by their modeling exercise: a large population, growing exponentially, and becoming aware of the destructive impact of its growth too late to prevent disaster.

The joint authors of *The Limits to Growth* were not the first to raise such concerns, and they have certainly not been the last. Important books, sometimes even best-selling books, about humanity's uncertain future have appeared regularly over the years. Precursors to *Limits* included Harrison Brown's *The Challenge of Man's Future* (1956), Rachel Carson's *Silent Spring* (1962), and Paul Ehrlich's *The Population Bomb* (1968). The most notable documents to be published since 1972 include the sober *State of the World* reports issued by the Worldwatch Institute (produced annually since 1984); the internationally influential *Our Common Future*, published by the UN's World Commission on Environment and Development (1987); a literate and scientific lament entitled *The End of Nature*, by former *New Yorker* writer Bill McKibben (1989); and the passionate and intelligent *Earth in the Balance*, written by then-U.S. senator Al Gore (1992). The most recent addition to this pantheon is the compelling *Earth Odyssey*, by freelance journalist Mark Hertsgaard (1999), reporting on eight years of travel all over the globe to observe the demise of Nature and the degradation of the World. Other titles have sold fewer copies, but together they form a growing chorus of prophetic voices, documenting evidence that the World is growing dangerously and spinning out of control.

Along with the books have come the meetings, the conferences, and the huge global conclaves, topped by the so-called "Earth Summit" in Rio de Janeiro in 1992, the largest gathering of national leaders in history. Declarations of alarm and warning have come from scientists, doctors, artists, religious leaders, and children. Global Agendas, Earth Charters, and several international treaties have been written. All have done their best to inform the World of the growing danger and to create strategies for averting catastrophe. All have made some kind of beneficial impact. But in terms of arresting runaway growth, which could be leading to global overshoot and collapse, so far all have failed.

And the World careens on.

▲▼▲

Kuala Lumpur, Malaysia
January 1982

I am riding a battered and dubious bus back to the city of Ipoh, where I am working as a therapist for Malaysian heroin addicts. It's a holiday weekend, and every seat is taken; this bus appears to be an illegal gypsy, dragged into service to absorb the overload.

Outside the bus, the highway is bordered by dense jungle and geometrically ordered rubber plantations, in alternating swaths. The taxis are doing their usual daredevil passes, even around blind curves. I've heard that

Malaysian drivers have the lowest accident rate in Southeast Asia, but the highest fatal *accident rate: When accidents occur, they often involve a bus and a taxi in head-on collision.*

Night falls, and the driver turns on his headlights. Five minutes later they go out. He pulls over to the side of the road, miles from anywhere, and tries to fix them, to no avail. Then he does something I've never seen a bus driver do, before or since. He asks the passengers what they want him to do.

"Jalan! Jalan!" they say, almost with one voice. "Go on!" So he pulls back into traffic, going slower and steering by the oncoming headlights. Several taxis barely miss hitting us. Then it starts to rain. Hard.

Same thing: the wipers don't work. What to do? "Jalan! Jalan!" say the passengers. Unbelievably, he goes on, steering by the blurred glow refracted through the solid sheet of water running down his windshield. Twice we swerve off the road; twice he recovers. We can't see how many taxis miss hitting us.

A strange silence has settled over the bus. The passengers appear spellbound by the danger, almost ecstatic. As the lone orang puteh *(white person), I feel powerless to intervene. I have said my prayers and prepared to offer up my soul to the local Taoist gods, or Allah, or whoever's jurisdiction I happen to be in when the crash comes. I see the shine of oncoming headlights through the rain-drenched glass, and I close my eyes.*

▲▼▲

To understand that humanity is on a collision course with the laws of Nature is to be stuck in what I call Cassandra's Dilemma. You can see the most likely outcome of current trends. You can warn people about what is happening, and underscore the need for a change in course. Some people can understand you, and a few may even believe you and try to take action—but the vast majority can not, or will not, respond. Later, if catastrophe occurs, they may even blame you, as if your prediction set in motion the process that resulted in disaster (self-fulfilling prophets are the most reviled). If, however, the World manages to avoid the potential catastrophe, thanks in part to the work of those who were motivated to action by your warning, many will point to that escape from danger as evidence of your incompetence as a prophet.

The role of Cassandra, issuing unpopular warnings of avoidable danger, is a no-win situation. Failure to convey the message effectively results in catastrophe. Success in being understood means ultimately being proven wrong.

Being willing to be wrong is, by itself, not enough. Your timing, and your tone, must be perfect. You must be "wrong" at the right moment, because once proven "wrong"—and the World will use every possible means to label you mistaken, as soon as possible—your credibility will be destroyed, so that thereafter your effect on the World will be minimal. Moreover, your means of communication are severely limited: if your warnings are too shrill, you will be ridiculed; too sober, and you will be ignored.

Even the best-case scenario—predicting disaster at precisely the right moment, in the most strategically balanced tone of voice—does not guarantee the successful outcome: a failed prediction of disaster. Warnings are notoriously ineffective. People may believe you, and still do nothing.

The worst and most painful outcome for any Cassandra is to be proven right.

This book is about escaping from Cassandra's Dilemma, first by understanding what causes it, then by taking steps to ensure that the disastrous projections of the World's Cassandras will turn out to be wrong. This is not a book about the end of the World, nor about "saving" the World. The World is in a continuous process of transformative change. The task before us is to redirect that process toward an elegant set of solutions to the unprecedented problems facing humanity—and to do so quickly.

The pages that follow will give you a guided tour through the state of our World, explanations of how it came to be that way, and reflections on how to reckon on a personal and emotional level with the World's trajectory. The final four chapters offer ideas, case studies, and conceptual tools for tackling a creative challenge that is as urgent as it is rewarding: redesigning the flawed systems that are now speeding us in the wrong direction. The book is, above all, a call—not merely to action, but to the commitment of one's full energy and passion to the betterment of this World, and the preservation of what is precious and beautiful in Nature. Though the word is rarely mentioned, this book is fundamentally about *love*—the practical kind, the kind that undergirds visions, and ambitious initiatives, and hope itself.

▲▼▲

The central message of this book is that *Growth must cease*. If human beings do not stop their growth willingly, Nature will stop it force-fully. Paradoxically, however, for Growth to cease, *Development must accelerate*.

Through all of human history, these two concepts, *Growth* and *Development*, have been joined together like Siamese twins. They must now be separated, or human civilization inevitably will come to a screeching halt. For the genuine Development of humanity to con-tinue, our species' physical Growth must end. And for Growth to end, our understanding of Development must be reinvented.

It is important to be clear about definitions. By "Growth," I mean the increase in human population, resource use, and the emission of waste. "Development," in contrast, refers to improvements in human technology and advances in the human condition, including health, ed-ucation, intelligence, wisdom, freedom, and the capacity to love.

"Growth" and "development" both have alternate, informal defin-itions that are in some ways more common, but also more confusing. "Growth" often refers to "economic growth," as measured by the Gross Domestic Product, the value of the stock market, and other economic indicators. The term "growth" is misleading here, because in these mea-sures the only thing growing is the circulation of money, money that may or may not be linked to real products and services. Historically, eco-nomic growth, as measured in money, has been dependent on the pro-duction of ever-increasing amounts of actual goods. Increasingly, this is no longer true; the creation of economic value is more and more tied to the expansion of *knowledge* rather than the flow of physical materials. And of course, many monetary transactions involve only money itself.

Meanwhile, the word "development" is too often used to mean "Western-style industrial development"—also known as "growth"—which is tied to the propagation of free-market economies and ostensibly democratic governments. But this frame is far too limiting. Numerous writers, including India's Vandana Shiva and Germany's Wolfgang Sachs, have mounted vigorous intellectual attacks against the notion that this kind of development is inevitable or desirable (and even against the very concept of "development" or "progress").

My own view is that human beings have evolved to be ambitious, and are ambitious to evolve. We continually seek security, comfort, novelty, adventure, expression, understanding, and meaning. This search drives a continuous process of change in all cultures. Development is the never-ending quest for the true, the good, and the beautiful in human life. It can never be stopped, because the urge to develop is part of what makes us human. But Development can, and must, be guided in directions that do not equate to runaway Growth, do not undermine Nature, and do not cause the World to collapse.

In the simplest terms, then, Growth means increases in *quantity*, and Development means improvements in *quality*, and that is the critical distinction between these two words in the pages that follow.

The stories, ruminations, arguments, and prescriptions in this book rest on two fundamental assumptions:

1. *There are limits to Growth.* The Earth is a closed system, and it can support only a finite number of human beings. The limits to Growth include limitations in land and soil for food production; available water; renewable resources such as trees and fish; industrial resources such as oil; social stability; and the capacity of Nature to absorb our wastes. Unless Growth ceases, one or all of these limits will be crossed, resulting in a series of worsening "shocks to the system" and potentially a full-fledged collapse, as human beings struggle with each other and Nature to protect their lives and their livelihoods. Mountains of scientific evidence suggest that some limits have already been crossed. Given these conditions, Growth cannot continue much longer.

2. *There are no limits to Development.* The way we live can always be made better: more beautiful, more inventive, more creative, more efficient, more fulfilling. Technologies can be radically and

continuously improved. Humans can learn, change, adapt, and evolve, often with astonishing rapidity. We can repair most of the damage we have caused, restore some of what has been lost, reinvent the systems on which we depend for survival. We have transformed ourselves and our civilizations many times in the past, at both large scales and small; we are doing so now; and we will do so over and over again. Since there is no limit on humanity's capacity to evolve, Development can go on virtually forever.

Navigating this critical transition, away from "Growth equals Development" and toward "Development without Growth," is the great challenge of our generation, and must become humanity's fundamental project for the early twenty-first century.

▲▼▲

Obviously I survived my Malaysian bus ride. We had any number of harrowing escapes and near-misses, but the expected crash never happened. The bus arrived safely at the next town, and we all got out, stunned or jubilant, and hired separate taxis for the rest of our journey.

This all-too-real experience has long since become an allegory for me, with many layers of meaning. There, between the lines of my own tale, I have sometimes read human foolishness, denial, and bravado in the face of avoidable danger . . . or the momentum with which a bad situation can quickly, through cascading systemic effects, become much worse . . . or even, in my most lugubrious and overwrought moments, a metaphor for the global economy, careening out of control and steered by the market's invisible hands, driven to ever-faster speeds by a perversely erotic death-wish.

But these days, I see something else in that story: the simple, undramatic fact that we survived. I see evidence in that for the possible existence of grace. Call it chance, call it luck, call it whatever you like, but pray that we find a lot of it along the way. Our World can use all the help it can get.

CHAPTER 2

A Brief History of Cassandra's Dilemma

A civilization progresses from agriculture to paradox.
—E. M. CIORAN

Things that don't get better, get worse.
—ELLEN SUE STERN

THE IDEA THAT there might be limits to Growth is far from new. Plato, writing in 400 B.C., envisioned zero population growth for the "Republic," his imaginary perfect society. Plato also lamented the fate of Attica, a city that had stripped the surrounding hills barren of trees and silted up its rivers. The city of Ephesus, in western Turkey, was abandoned when silt from deforestation relocated the coastline to miles away, ruining the port and creating malarial swamps. The Roman Empire collapsed in part because it grew too big and could no longer maintain its supply lines, the value of its currency, or the loyalty of its far-flung armies—but also because it had poisoned its citizens with lead and turned once-lush parts of

Northern Africa into desert. The famously extinct civilization of Easter Island is a textbook example of human beings degrading their environment and battling their way to oblivion.

All these events have drawn rueful lamentations on the folly of humanity from commentators down through the ages. We do not know if these societies had their Cassandras—their Rachel Carsons and Worldwatch Institutes—who warned citizens and leaders of society's impending demise. But we can imagine that plenty of people understood what was happening, and where it would lead, yet believed they could do nothing to stop it. By taking a look at our own times, we can empathize.

Early in the modern era, the question of limits to Growth was framed by Thomas Malthus, a Scottish parson and writer of quasi-religious political tracts. Malthus gained both fame and scorn in 1798 for authoring the *Essay on the Principle of Population*, which declared that human beings were essentially lazy and lustful. For that reason, they would keep making as many babies as naturally possible, always staying just ahead of the ability to feed them.

Malthus noted that human numbers increased *geometrically*—that is, by doubling frequently, as in the sequence 2, 4, 8, 16, and so on. We now use the word "exponentially" to refer to this kind of growth, and we usually express it in terms of a percentage. An annual growth rate of 5%, for example, results in a doubling every twelve years.

According to Malthus, humans are so "inert, sluggish, and averse from labour, unless compelled by necessity" that they can only get food production to increase *arithmetically*: say, 10 tons of potatoes this year, 11 tons next year if we're lucky, 12 tons if we work very hard the year after that. Obviously there is a discrepancy here: exponential growth rockets upward faster and faster (32, 64, 128) while arithmetic growth plods along in a dull and incremental fashion (13, 14, 15). Very quickly there are too few potatoes to go around. Life, however, has an efficient way of taking care of this problem: death.

Malthus wanted to discourage the liberal idealists of his day, who believed that society would eventually achieve a state of perfection and equality, where everyone could live in comfort and happiness. Won't happen, argued Malthus. This conflict between fast baby-making and slow food-growing would always exist. Ergo, there would never be enough to go around, which gave the rich a good excuse to go on being rich and to stop worrying about starvation among the poor and other so-called problems. This was Malthus's real agenda; he was a conservative who opposed social programs. Feeding the poor, in his view, amounted to messing with Nature's laws; it got in the way of the efficient Mr. Death and his routine regulation of population size.

Five years later, Pastor Malthus had a change of heart, and apparently a change of politics as well. He revised his original *Essay* (which, according to one modern critic, was "hastily compiled, poorly documented, loosely argued"). In the newer version, Malthus adopted a much rosier view of human nature, which might be summarized as follows: "People can change. They can work hard, control their sexual urges, make sure there's enough to go around. We should educate the poor, be more democratic, etc." Malthus II was, in the words of Paul Robinson, "the first anti-Malthusian." Yet his more generous view of humanity's prospects is not what Pastor Malthus is remembered for. We remember the dour, conservative, Scottish stick-in-the-mud, the man who seemed to be saying (though ultimately he wasn't) that human beings were doomed to outstrip the Earth's capacity to feed them.

In a bizarre twist of historical fate, contemporary thinkers who worry that human beings might, indeed, outstrip the Earth's capacity to support them are casually dismissed as "Neo-Malthusians." It is a derogatory and scornful term, frequently used by conservative critics who might have been very comfortable with the motivation behind Malthus I and his original *Essay*. The association, and the implied criticism, is undeserved; the argument that there are limits to Growth is very different from the erroneous notion that humans always breed faster than they can grow food to support themselves. One of the great achievements of the twentieth century has been the (at least temporary) debunking of Malthus I on that score: thanks to the Green Revolution in agriculture and other technological advances, population growth has been matched by a corresponding exponential rise in food production—until recently.

Curiously, most professional worriers about the fate of the Earth *are* Neo-Malthusians, but more along the lines of Malthus II. They tend to believe that disaster can be avoided, and a better and more just World created, if only human beings will aspire to live as consciously, ethically, and equitably as possible. This conditional aspect of their message is as widely overlooked as Pastor Malthus's revision of his original grim prophesy.

▲▼▲

After Malthus, some one hundred and fifty years passed before a new wave of Cassandras emerged to question the outcome of humanity's Growth. Two books published in the 1940s warned of overshooting the limits: William Vogt's *Road to Survival* and Fairfield Osborn's *Our Plundered Planet*. Both were quickly forgotten, as was Harrison Brown's prescient 1954 treatise *The Challenge of Man's Future*. The public imagination was not seriously engaged by the notion that Growth might have to be moderated or regulated until 1962, when Rachel Carson published *Silent Spring*. In language both beautiful and wise, Carson documented the effects of DDT and other pesticides on people and wildlife, and warned that birds and fish and other animals would simply disappear if the problem were allowed to keep growing. She wrote so compellingly, and researched her topic so exhaustively, that the entire nation took notice and took action: North Americans have eagles and peregrine falcons in their midst today largely because her.

Rachel Carson did not relish being the bearer of bad news. She was an enormously popular writer of books about Nature. But she was also a meticulous investigator. A letter from a reader in Massachusetts, alerting her that DDT was killing birds, led her to confront a painful reality. "I may not like what I see," she confided to a dear friend, "but it does no good to ignore it." She could not pretend that she was unmoved by the evidence, nor could she avoid a sense of responsibility for reporting the emergency, given her skills as a writer and her access to publishers. Although she became concerned with the broader question of Growth in all its dimensions, she understood all too well the powerful forces she was contending with, so she focused her writing on pesticides—a specific, visible, solvable problem that was likely to engage the public's sentiment. The success of this strategy launched the modern environmental movement.

Carson's book was attacked not just by industry groups, but even by the American Medical Association. This was doubly ironic; she was privately suffering from breast cancer, quite possibly caused by the same pesticidal "sea of carcinogens" she had written about. She died two years after publication of *Silent Spring*, but her book has lived on, triggering a series of events that led to the first Earth Day in 1970 and to the tough laws to protect air, water, and endangered species that were installed in the next few years. While the World still suffers from pesticide and other chemical poisoning, Carson had demonstrated the power of one person's voice to make a difference. Her book saved the eagles and the falcons and many other birds, and as Vice President Al Gore wrote in the introduction to a 1994 re-release of *Silent Spring*, "It may be that the human species, too, or at least countless human lives, will be saved because of the words she wrote."

▲▼▲

The "Rachel Carson formula"—comprised of a powerful lament upon the likely fate of Nature and humanity, backed up by meticulous research—set a template for almost every book, organization, declaration, and public event that has represented the environmental movement ever since. There are variations in how stridently the alarm is rung, and how radically the call to action is phrased, but it was she who set the stage for all the Cassandras who have come after her.

When population biologist Paul Ehrlich, of Stanford University, published *The Population Bomb* in 1968, for example, he was following the same formula, while increasing the volume on the alarm. "While you are reading these words," said a banner on the front cover of the paperback edition, "four people will have died from starvation. Most of them children." The table of contents summed up his argument. "The Problem: Too Many People, Too Little Food, A Dying Planet."

Ehrlich is another Cassandra who is remembered for being

famously wrong. He lost a highly publicized bet with the economist Julian Simon on whether the price of certain metals would go up or down over ten years. Ehrlich thought scarcity would drive the prices up; instead, they went down. This did not prove that the metals were more abundant—they were undeniably scarcer, since the Earth is a closed system—but rather that *price* was an inaccurate measure of their availability. Alas, the subtlety of this point was lost on the media. In a 1970 essay called "Eco-Catastrophe!" Ehrlich also predicted the failure of the Green Revolution in food production, and he was extremely pessimistic about the power of technological innovation to keep up with population and its consumptive demands. He envisioned widespread starvation and social chaos by the end of the 1970s. The decade was not without its problems, but famine on the scale predicted by Ehrlich did not occur.

Yet to dismiss Ehrlich merely on the apparent inaccuracy of certain predictions is unfair. With his book, together with many appearances on television (including the *Tonight* show), Ehrlich single-handedly raised the World's awareness about population growth. As *Silent Spring* had led to controls on pesticides, *The Population Bomb* and its sequels helped create an international movement to address the population crisis with a combination of direct aid, economic development, education for women, and access to family planning. There is now an abiding awareness in the public mind about the importance of population, as well as a very large international bureaucracy focused on the issue, thanks in no small part to Ehrlich's wake-up call. It is even conceivable that we owe some fraction of our smaller-than-expected population at the year 2000—6 billion instead of the 7 billion projected thirty years ago—to Erlich's willingness to be loud, persistent, and proven wrong.

▲▼▲

The example of Paul Ehrlich falls into the positive side of Cassandra's Dilemma: A successful alert (that is, a warning that is heeded, if only partially in this case) ultimately provides confirmation of the prophet's fallibility as a predictor of the future; yet the stigmatized prophet can rest easier knowing he's made a difference. But the succession of books, campaigns, organizations, and personalities that we think of as the modern environmental movement has more generally fallen toward the opposite side of this Dilemma: a failure to communicate the warning persuasively enough, a failure to "get through" to people and avert disaster. True, there are victories: wolves are back in Yellowstone, some species of whale are rebounding. But too often we watch helplessly, as Cassandra did, while the soldiers emerge from the Trojan horse just as foreseen and wreak their predicted havoc.

Worse, Cassandra's Dilemma has seemed to grow more inescapable even as the chorus of Cassandras has grown larger. In the enormous impact of *Silent Spring*, the less acknowledged influence of *The Population Bomb*, and the controversy-followed-by-dismissal of *The Limits to Growth* one can detect a disturbing pattern: diminishing impact on the real World. It is almost as though the World is developing a resistance to warnings. Fast-forwarding twenty years—from *Limits* and the United Nations' Stockholm Conference on the Environment in 1972, through *Our Common Future* and years of Worldwatch *State of the World* reports, to Al Gore's *Earth in the Balance* and the Earth Summit in 1992—we see the pattern in full flower.

The Earth Summit was officially known as the United Nations Conference on Environment and Development (or UNCED, which, as critics loved to point out, is pronounced "unsaid"). This global conference, attended by thousands of people, produced weighty documents and a handful of very memorable quotes, such as President George Bush's remark that the American lifestyle was "non-negotiable." (What could be the connection between that assertion and the fact that Bush's Secret Service detail was housed in "two Rio motels better known for their hourly rates," complete with mirrors on the ceiling and X-rated movies?)

More than one hundred heads of state were assembled to consider *Agenda 21*, a complicated "blueprint for survival" that had been negotiated by environmental diplomats for months in advance. *Agenda 21* was an astonishingly comprehensive catalog of humanity's woes and what ought to be done about them. It covered everything from climate change to the loss of rain forests, from disappearing indigenous cultures to affordable housing for the urban poor. Each element was described in the inoffensive, least-common-denominator language that generally characterizes United Nations diplomacy. After much hemming and hawing, *Agenda 21* was adopted by the assembled delegates—not as a binding treaty, but as a voluntary set of agreements. In the years that followed, few nations have treated these agreements with much seriousness. Although the process did spawn important side agreements on issues such as biodiversity, the vast majority of American citizens today do not even know that the document exists. Europeans, by contrast, have "Local Agenda 21" committees in cities all over the continent.

Agenda 21, the Earth Summit that gave rise to it, and the international bureaucracy that has since grown up around it were all caught in an institutional version of Cassandra's Dilemma on a global scale. You could almost say that in this case, the World itself played Cassandra. A vast array of trends had been analyzed in detail by hordes of researchers. The likely future consequences of maintaining the status quo were clearly described, widely publicized, and passionately discussed. Heads of state nodded in somber agreement. But nothing—at least, nothing that can be described as globally transformative, direction-changing, or even very encouraging—really happened.

Of course, all over the World laudable initiatives have arisen in the name of *Agenda 21*, especially at the local level. A UN Commission, periodic global conventions, and national advisory councils meet, and some nations have made significant strides in environmental and economic policy. A list of projects launched by the Earth Summit and *Agenda 21* would fill the remainder of this book; but I contend they have all essentially been marginal. They have not resulted in a slowdown of carbon dioxide emissions, a significant reduction of toxic chemicals, radical technology advances or technology transfers to poorer nations, breakthroughs in energy and water conservation, or any change that can be characterized as making a measurable dent in the global sprint toward the threshold of overshoot and collapse. The problems have continued to intensify without so much as a hiccup.

All of these good-hearted efforts, even taken together, are stuck in Cassandra's Dilemma, because they have yet to result in genuine movement toward the imperative goal facing humanity, the only changes that really matter: the end of Growth and the reinvention of Development.

In a moment we will turn to an even more distressing, and instructive, contemporary version of Cassandra's Dilemma on the individual level: how it came to pass that a prominent political leader, with a truly prophetic vision of global problems and solutions, turned away from his own published declarations of radical commitment. We will examine that story in some depth.

▲▼▲

Seattle, Washington
Spring 1990

My mother has been cleaning out the old attic in Orlando, and she sends me a packet of drawings and art projects I made as a child. "They're just gathering dust here," her note says. "I thought you might enjoy having them."

I open the envelope and pore over the contents: two home-made alphabet books that I intended to sell to my first grade classmates for 5 cents each; a third grade drawing of Snoopy battling the Red Baron; assorted poems about animals ("Mice are nice, that's what I think / and when it rains, they get a drink . . .").

Then I come upon a fourth grade poster, colored in crayon. I have no memory of creating it, but it's consistent with my style. The poster depicts a large body of water, surrounded by sources of pollution. Untreated sewage, factory effluent, pesticide-laden farm run-off . . . it's all there. Dead fish, with X's for eyes, have washed up on the beach. Blotchy dark bits on the water serve as oil spills.

Across the top, in big bold letters, I'd written this headline: "Mommy, why can't I go swimming?"

▲▼▲

Among the attendees at the Earth Summit in Rio de Janeiro was a young, ambitious U.S. senator with an avowed desire to save the World.

Primed in youth by his mother's interest in *Silent Spring*, and shaken at mid-life by a failed presidential bid and the near-death of his young son in an automobile accident, Al Gore had experienced an epiphany. "I was, in a sense, vulnerable," he writes in his best-selling book *Earth in the Balance*, "to the change that sought me out in the middle of my life and gave me a new sense of urgency about those things I value the most" (p. 14).

Because of that vulnerability, and the political courage that grew from it, I fell in love with Al Gore in early 1992. (Note to Tipper: Not to worry. Nothing happened.) It was my first, and only, political love affair. Reading *Earth in the Balance* moved me so deeply that I attended my Seattle, Washington, political caucus (the equivalent of the presidential primary for that state) as a Gore supporter, even though he wasn't running.

Gore was the first prominent American politician to understand the global environmental crisis in its fullest measure. His book was bold, literate, extremely well-informed, and deeply inspirational. As an editor for a journal on global sustainability, I had read many books about the increasingly dangerous relationship between humanity and Nature. Gore's was the best. On finishing it, I literally jumped out of my chair and shouted, "Yes!" Finally I saw a realistic ray of hope. Finally someone with a real chance to alter the political landscape was calling for massive, transformational, politically practical change to avert catastrophe. Had Gore run for president that year, I would have followed him to the ends of the earth; my love, and my naiveté, were that strong.

I met Gore in Seattle, while he was on his book tour, and rode around with him for a couple of hours between television and radio appearances. He disarmed my nervousness, and we chatted along the way, much of our conversation captured on tape for an interview with our magazine, *In Context*. At the time, Bill Clinton's presidential primary campaign was in tatters, and *New York Times* columnist William Safire had floated the idea that only a Cuomo-Gore ticket could save the Democratic party from going down in flames. Both men would have to be drafted, since neither was running for office.

On the way back to Gore's hotel, while stuck in Seattle's rush hour traffic, I asked Gore what he thought of this idea. He offered me a chocolate from a box someone had given him, and said, "Is that tape recorder still running?" I turned it off, and showed him that the red light was extinguished. "Would *you* want to be vice president under Cuomo?" he asked wryly. "Well, it's not really an option for me," I replied. "But it seems that it might be an option for you."

Then he sort of grumbled, and said something like, "If I wanted to be vice president, I'd be running for president." Though Gore had removed himself from the 1992 race to be with his family and young son (who was still recovering from the accident), I sensed some regret in his voice. But he clearly wasn't interested in pursuing the topic further.

From my conversations with him, and from reports I heard from friends in the environmental and religious communities, I knew that Gore's passion for these issues was sincere. As a former journalist, his book was his own; he had written it by getting up at 4:00 every morning for months. His speeches on this book tour had nothing of the "wooden" or "stiff" quality that journalists so often criticize him for. Gore was electrifying, a politician with a mission, a crusader attempting to awaken people to the truth in order to take bold action.

His book remains a remarkable summary of our situation. Gore surveys the history of climate and civilization, analyzes the full range of current global environmental issues with concision and depth, and reports on his travels to see thinning ice caps and disappearing seas with his own eyes. He proposes an incredibly daring scheme to make the rescue of the global environment the "central organizing principle" of civilization, and to approach it with the kind of political and financial commitment we gave to the Marshall Plan, which rebuilt Europe in the wake of World War II.

This excerpt from his introduction conveys something of the ardor with which Gore wrote:

> The global environmental crisis is, as we say in Tennessee, real as rain, and I cannot stand the thought of leaving my children with a degraded earth and a diminished future.

> That's the basic reason why I have searched so intensively
> for ways to understand this crisis and help solve it; it is also
> why I am trying to convince you to be a part of the enor-
> mous change our civilization must now undergo. I am
> struggling to be a part of that same change myself, and my
> hope is that you will open your heart and mind to the
> words and ideas that follow. (P. 16)

But then Bill Clinton's candidacy was revived, and Al Gore accepted the
nomination for the vice presidency. I was shocked so deeply by this turn
of events that I actually dreamt about it.

In my dream, I was strolling with Gore down a city street, and I
said, "So, Al, you said you didn't *want* to be vice president!" He just
looked at me and smiled. "I said I didn't want to be vice president under *Cuomo*."

And in fact, Clinton's choice had been brilliant. He promised a
full working partnership with Gore, and there has been a remarkable
level of cooperation between the two men: Gore has been the most em-
powered vice president in recent history, and possibly in the history of
the office. His influence on environmental policy was felt immediately
in Clinton's choices for senior positions. Many in the environmental
movement breathed a sigh of relief; the Earth had a friend in the White
House.

But as I write, the appraisal is gloomy. Nearly two terms of a Clinton-Gore administration have produced nothing in the form of decisive
proposals to "rescue the global environment." Our race toward the catastrophes Gore wrote about so eloquently has only accelerated; indeed,
a Gore-led negotiating team argued for *lower* greenhouse gas emission
targets for the U.S. at the climate-change negotiations in Kyoto in 1996.
Along the way, Gore, planning for a Year 2000 presidential run, has
repositioned himself as a friend to business—as usual—by promoting
the virtues of global trade and the Internet. My most memorable image
from his two terms in office is of Gore in Mexico City, standing in front
of seventy cash registers and check-out stations, celebrating the grand
opening of Mexico's first Wal-Mart.

When he took on the role of vice president, the passionate and courageous Senator Al Gore, political prophet for the Earth, who had called for "a bold effort to change the very foundation of our civilization" (p. 14), for all practical purposes ceased to exist. The loss to the environmental movement was significant, not just because a strong ally had fallen relatively silent, but because the movement itself experienced widespread disillusionment and loss of hope.

It's important to make clear that I do not fault Al Gore personally for this apparent reversal. Nor do I believe that he has lost either his profound understanding of the dangers posed by climate change and chemical pollution, or his hope for making a significant difference. I imagine that he experiences private sorrow, and feels that his hands are tied by political realities. Interviewed by Bill McKibben early in his first term, he observed the following: "We are in an unusual predicament as a global civilization. The maximum that is politically feasible, even the maximum that is politically *imaginable* right now, still falls short of the minimum that is scientifically and ecologically necessary." And that was *before* 1994, when self-declared anti-environment Republicans took control of Congress.

Gore, in echoing Elliot Richardson from 1972 ("The minds of the people are unprepared to accept the political leadership that these conclusions would compel"), has undoubtedly made a political calculation: as vice president, he can safeguard and promote environmental issues more effectively than in the Senate (and more aggressively than another vice president might have done), help hold the line against a conservative political insurgency, and position himself for the presidency. As president he could then, if the political winds were right and Congress more progressive, advocate more far-reaching proposals in the spirit (if not the letter) of *Earth in the Balance.*

But the cost of this quasi-Faustian bargain is exceedingly high: a loss of integration. The loss stems from the growing distance between Gore's political behavior and his published declarations, such as this one from *Earth in the Balance*: "The integrity of the environment is not just another issue to be used in political games for popularity, votes, or attention. And the time has long since come to take more po-litical risks—and endure much more political criticism—by proposing tougher, more effective solutions and fighting hard for their enactment" (p. 15).

Regardless of how Gore calculated the political costs and benefits of his new identity, the result was the defection of many of his support-ers in the environmental movement. Some of its most prominent lead-ers privately confess a sense of betrayal, bordering on disgust. Absurdly, the man who wrote *Earth in the Balance*, one of the most visionary and widely read environmental books of our time, is now the target of oc-casional demonstrations by environmental activists.

▲▼▲

It is possible to view the new Al Gore in at least three less-than-charita-ble ways: (1) as a sell-out, (2) as a savvy political operator whose previ-ous "epiphany" was little more than shrewd self-marketing, or (3) as a young sixties-style idealist who finally woke up from his mid-life crisis and accepted the realities of the World. I know people who hold each of those views.

But I prefer to see Al Gore as the predictable product of the U.S. political system, and as this century's most prominent and tragic victim of Cassandra's Dilemma. Not only does civilization have a hard time heeding warnings about likely and dangerous futures; even politically powerful people, who issue warnings and advocate dramatic plans to avert catastrophe, find it extremely hard not to contribute to that disas-ter's eventual realization. As Gore explains in *Earth in the Balance*, "civ-ilization now rushes ahead with enormous momentum, and even the individual who believes we are on a collision course with the global en-vironment will find it difficult to separate his or her course from that of civilization as a whole" (p. 12). Larger, impersonal, systemic forces are at work that can overwhelm individual action. Al Gore is by no means alone in falling prey to both the seductions of power and the apparent benefits of compromise.

After a period of personal disillusionment, I discovered the easiest way to forgive Al Gore and to understand his supposed failures: by looking in the mirror. Most of us who carry some awareness of global trends find ourselves making painful, even hypocritical compromises every day—driving cars, flying in planes, all the routine activities of modern life that involve an increase in carbon emissions or the release of a toxic compound. We are all, those of us who try to be conscious of such things, making the same kinds of calculations I imagine Al Gore to have made. We are all weighing the costs and the benefits, the long-term possibilities, the political and economic realities. We are all waiting for the right opening, the right moment to be principled and visionary.

But in some ways, that moment may have already come and gone. Here is another excerpt from *Earth in the Balance*, in which Gore likens the increasing possibility of global environmental and civilizational collapse to a kind of "black hole." If we do not change course, we will fall more and more quickly into its powerful well of gravity:

> The potential for true catastrophe lies in the future, but the downslope that pulls us toward it is becoming recognizably steeper with each passing year. What lies ahead is a race against time. Sooner or later the steepness of the slope and our momentum down its curve will take us beyond a point of no return. But as the curve becomes steeper and catastrophe's pull becomes stronger, our ability to recognize the pattern of its pull is greatly enhanced. The odds that we will discern the nature of our plight improve dramatically as we get closer to the edge of history. . . . (pp. 49–50)

It is impossible to say what might have become of the environmental movement had Al Gore stayed in the Senate and pursued the role of prophetic visionary. Rachel Carson, an inspiration to Gore, demonstrated the force one person can have if she is willing to hold fast to principle and stand up to power. An Al Gore who had chosen to remain an unshakable voice of conviction, rather than an Al Gore who compromised principle in exchange for political position, might have had more impact on the course of history. We will never know.

▲▼▲

The core of Cassandra's Dilemma is the awareness of our global predicament, and as time marches on, more and more of humanity is beginning to share the burden of that awareness. In the previous two chapters, I have alluded to critical global issues such as population growth, climate change, and pollution under the assumption that most readers are generally familiar with them. Many may have read reports (such as those from World Resources Institute or Worldwatch Institute) that catalog global trends and back them up with reams of data. Most have heard mention of some of these trends in the news, and young people are increasingly exposed to them in the course of their studies. But the statistics can be mind-numbing, and the facts emotionally overwhelming. It is hard to see the big picture, and even harder to sustain one's gaze.

So in the chapter that follows, I would like to reintroduce you to a few of these trends, and invite you to consider the big picture from a different, and I hope fresh, perspective. Our journey will be grounded in data, but not burdened by it. I would like take you on a brisk guided tour through the Gallery of Global Trends.

CHAPTER 3

In the Gallery of Global Trends

Quick are the mouths of earth, and quick the teeth that feed upon this loveliness.

—THOMAS WOLFE

The sign of a truly educated man is to be deeply moved by statistics.

—GEORGE BERNARD SHAW

CONSIDER SEX.

Human life begins with it. Most people desire it, and its consequence, children, more than anything else in the world. The allure of sex is unstoppable. Orgasm is the most extreme pleasure the mammalian brain is naturally capable of producing. Rats with electrodes plugged into their sexual pleasure centers have been known to starve themselves to death, choosing multiple orgasms over food.

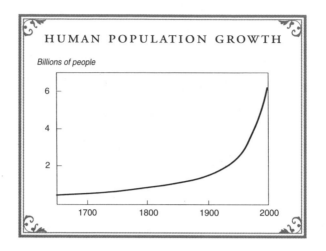

When you look at a graph labeled "Human Population Growth," think first about sex. Every individual human being represented on that graph began with at least one orgasm (a man's; female orgasm can aid conception by speeding the sperm to their destination, but unfortunately this is not a requirement). The steep rise in the curve representing population growth reflects increasing numbers of men and women, coupling and pleasuring each other—a kind of planetary orgy. For some, these are moments of maximum emotional ecstasy, a wild celebration of love that brims over into mystical experience. For others, sex is purely a physical thrill, the ultimate biological roller-coaster ride. But remember too that for many women, all over the World, there is no pleasure in sex save the satisfaction of duty; and for too many women, this graph reflects a moment of considerable suffering, with the unequivocal love of the resulting child their only consolation.

When you consider this graph, see the human desire for children. For reasons that can be emotional, economic, cultural, political, purely biological, or more often, a combination of these, people want daughters and sons and families. More often than not, this wanting is felt as an ache, a kind of desperate longing. People want the joy of seeing the world through a child's eyes again. They want company. They want help gathering firewood or fetching water. They want more people like themselves around, people loyal to themselves, in order to feel secure about the future.

This wanting is primeval. It connects us to the time before the World's history began, when our ancestors were few and barely aware of themselves. Nature was both vast and dangerous. "Strength in numbers" was the only road to survival.

As Nobel laureate Elias Canetti wrote in his masterpiece, *Crowds and Power*,

> Early man, roaming about in small bands through large and often empty spaces, was confronted by a preponderance of animals. Not all of these were necessarily hostile; most, in fact, were not dangerous to man. But many of them existed in enormous numbers. Whether it was herds of buffaloes or springboks, shoals of fish, or swarms of locusts, bees or ants, their numbers rendered those of man insignificant.
>
> For the progeny of man is sparse, coming singly and taking a long time to arrive. The desire to be MORE, for the number of the people to whom one belongs to be larger, must always have been profound and urgent, and must, moreover, have been growing stronger all the time.

The desire to be MORE grew strong enough that Leontina Albina, a living resident of Chile, bore fifty-five children over thirty-eight years, including five sets of triplets. It grew strong enough that today, 326 cities on Planet Earth have more than one million people in them, and the equivalent of another city of one million is added to the Earth's population every four and a half days.

But numbers like this are hard to grasp. Annie Dillard, in an essay called "The Wreck of Time," quotes a Hartford newspaper headline: HEAD-SPINNING NUMBERS CAUSE MIND TO GO SLACK. "But our minds must not go slack," writes Dillard. "How can we think straight if our minds go slack? We agree that we want to think straight."

To think straight about population, we must think in curves. Consider the graph again: This curve is the signature of exponential growth, a puzzling and dangerous phenomenon. Every point on the curve represents a moment in time, and the number of people who were alive on Earth at that time. If you selected any one point on that curve, and talked with all the people it abstractly stands for, few of them—few of the millions, or the hundred millions, or the billions, depending on which point in time you selected—would express the slightest worry about population growth. Few would mourn the Nature replaced by human structures, or fear the tendency of humanity to grow ever larger in number. For almost every point in time on the graph, there would appear to be plenty of space for more people. Whatever size humanity was at that moment, that size would be "normal." Growth would appear to be slow, methodical, manageable. It is only now, suddenly, in our lifetime, that it is possible for a person to be born into a World of two billion, and die when the population has more than tripled in size, to six billion and more.

Continued population growth is an inevitable fact for the near future. Nothing short of a comet striking the Earth's surface could curtail this growth anytime soon. Even if everyone, everywhere, were firmly committed (or forcefully limited) to having no more than two children starting *tomorrow*, humanity's presence on the Earth would continue to grow for decades. Why? Because as of today, there are one billion girls under the age of fifteen. The vast majority of them will grow up, become sexually active, take lovers and husbands, and bear children over the next thirty years. Fewer people will die than are born to those young mothers, and the new arrivals will live increasingly longer lives. Human beings born today can expect to live, on average, nearly *twenty years* longer than those born in the 1950s.

The human crowd is certain to get much bigger. The only question is by how much. Will it level off at eight billion, or ten? Or will it swell to twelve billion, and then crash? As Joel Cohen points out, projecting population is notoriously difficult, and "examples of the failures of past population forecasts abound. Reciting them seems to be one of demographers' favorite forms of self-flagellation." Of course, it is always possible that a comet *will* strike the Earth, as Hollywood movies like to remind us, or that rapid breakthroughs in technology will permit us to let off steam by colonizing Mars. But it would be far more prudent to plan for several billion additional people at the dinner party of humanity.

There are strategies for slowing down population growth, for gently turning the rocket at the top of that graph—driven by the desire for sex and descendants, and fueled by rapid advances in agriculture and medicine—into a more stable, sideways trajectory. These include increasing the economic and educational opportunities for women, as well as fostering changes in culture worldwide to support broader use of birth control. Where applied, these strategies have worked: population growth rates have even turned negative in a few wealthy European countries, and access to contraceptives and small loans for women has dramatically reduced growth rates in Bangladesh.

But up to now, these strategies have traditionally required more of the one factor we can no longer afford: Growth. Our swelling World has run up against a wall of limits when it comes to cropland, soil, fish, fresh water, fragile ecosystems, the atmosphere, and the social stresses of hunger, poverty, and profound inequality. In order to live within that non-negotiable wall of limits—which is buttressed by the laws of physics—we will have to find some rather ingenious ways to feed, educate, employ, and provide fulfillment for the increasing masses of humanity, without a matching expansion in what we extract from and dump into the Earth. Otherwise, the "teeth that feed upon this loveliness" will gnaw it to the bone.

▲▼▲

Cape Cod, Massachusetts
February 1999

I've been trying to read this new Worldwatch Institute paper, "Sixteen Dimensions of the Population Problem," but it's too depressing. The number of human beings has become a swarm, stripping the planet like a plague of locusts, and eighty million more are added every year. "Stated otherwise," say the earnest and somber authors at Worldwatch, "there has been more growth in population since 1950 than during the 4 million years since our early ancestors first stood upright." Water, fish, forests, climate, all going haywire. It's more than I can take on a bleak day in February.

So I've come out to Betsy's Diner for a hamburger, and I'm reading Douglas Adams's comic novel, The Long Dark Tea-Time of the Soul. *Two young women, both peroxide blondes, are cleaning the tables. "You want to come out to this reggae party on Saturday?" says one. "Nah," says the other. "I'd probably get plastered and end up getting another tattoo."*

When the tattoo-girl comes by my table, she sees the Worldwatch paper. "So, you're another one that believes in the population problem." I look at her warily, as though she's about to attack me for being a kook. "What do you think?*" I ask.*

"Well, it's pretty obvious," she says. "There's too many of us, and we're just using everything up. Eventually we're going to start running out of stuff—land, water, food, something." I shake my head and try to look sardonic and melancholy, which I am. "What do you think we should do?" I ask her. "Personally, I'm not going to have any children," she says matter-of-factly. "I'm just twenty years old. I'm probably going to live a long time, and I know I'm going to see a lot of bad craziness. There's just too many forces already set in motion. I don't see any way to stop it.

"And I definitely don't want to bring a child into any of that."

▲▼▲

Flowing through the lives of each of the six billion people alive on Earth today is a stream of stuff. Some of the stuff flows through their bodies, some of it merely passes through their hands. Some stuff they keep for a while, some they discard immediately, and some they are simply moving from one place to another. A huge amount of stuff just gets used to make other stuff. Most of it people never actually see, but it does something for them, like making the aluminum for their can of Coke, or cleaning the circuit board in what will someday be their Gameboy. Some stuff is razed, blown up, or cut down, because it's in the way of something else they want. And some unwanted stuff (say, for instance, a little tonguefish off the coast of North Carolina) becomes stuff by accident, because it happens to be in the vicinity of some other very desirable stuff (say, shrimp).

This enormous flow of stuff—out of field, forest, ocean, and mine, through the factories and processing plants and transportation systems of the global economy, into a brief lifespan of use by human beings, and back out into the world as junk, sewage, poison, or waste—is called *throughput.*

People are like dams in the river of throughput. Their lives are like reservoirs where stuff accumulates for a while, before it finally flows past the dam to join the waste stream. The wealthier and more acquisitive people are, the bigger the dam they form, and so the bigger their reservoir of stuff becomes, whether they fill it with blue jeans or Caribbean vacations, Buddhas or basketballs.

Of the stuff that departs the reservoir of a person's life, very little ever becomes stuff again. Most throughput ends up as something else: pollution. In industrial nations, for example, somewhere between one third and one half (by weight) of the stuff people use is fossil fuel, which when it gets burned becomes heat, smoke, water, and gasses including ozone, carbon monoxide, and carbon dioxide—most of which is useless, worthless, or just plain poisonous.

As humanity increases, in terms of both our cumulative numbers and our aggregate desires, the river of throughput grows. More throughput equals more pollution and less Nature, for throughput starts with the conversion of Nature into stuff. How much more pollution, and how much less Nature, depends on how many people there are, how rich those people are, how materialistic they are, and what kind of technology they are using. Rich, materialistic people (owners of Sports Utility Vehicles), using very inefficient technologies, call forth and dam up very large rivers of stuff. Poor, nonmaterialistic, efficient people (Tibetan monks) sit by very tiny streams and use very little stuff at all.

The process of moving stuff around on Planet Earth—mining it, growing it, assembling it, packaging it, shipping it, buying it, throwing it away—is called "the global economy." To measure and regulate and facilitate transactions in the global economy, we use money. Wherever stuff goes, money flows in the opposite direction: people pay money for stuff. Find out how much money is flowing through the global economy, and you have some idea of how much stuff is flowing as well.

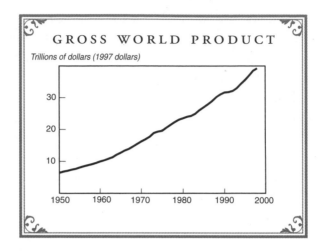

Enter, stage right, the Gross World Product.

The "GWP," or "GDP" if you're talking about an individual country ("W" is for "World," "D" is for "Domestic"), is a measure of all the money that changes hands in the market economy in one year. This is what economists use to measure economic activity. A rising GWP is called "economic growth," and a downturn in the curve is called a "recession" or, at its worst, a "depression." A rise in the GWP is generally equated by most economists with a rising standard of living. Higher GWP is supposed to mean more jobs, more machines, more houses, more products moving across the laser beams at the checkout stands of the World.

It is important to bear in mind that the "Gross World Product" does *not* actually measure the World's products and services; it measures the flow of money. Although much of the money moving through the economy is not directly attached to anything physical (for example, the royalty paid to a songwriter for the right to broadcast a song), there is always an indirect link to the consumption of stuff in the material world (the new CD player at the radio station, the electricity it used, and so forth). Although materials recycling and energy efficiency are beginning to reduce the amount of stuff required to generate a dollar of economic activity, "economic growth" still requires the use of increasing amounts of Planet Earth. Therefore, the growth in the GWP gives us reasonably accurate insights into physical Growth as well.

When the flow of money grows, the river of stuff also swells, together with the size of humanity's collective dam in that river. The reservoir of stuff that results is the entirety of what we extract, manufacture, build, use, and eventually discard. It takes the form of ore heaps, cities, suburbs, farms, factories, billions of consumer products, and enormous piles of garbage. It doesn't matter to the GWP whether the things we make out of that river of stuff are beautiful or ugly, enduring or disposable, nourishing or poisonous. The GWP simply tracks every dollar spent along the way, for whatever reason, and subtracts nothing; "G" is for "Gross."

When you look at a graph of the GWP or of your nation's GDP (again, Gross Domestic Product), which is the number your newscaster is referring to when she says something like "the economy grew at an astonishing 5.6% annual rate last quarter" (as I just heard my newscaster say), think about all that *stuff*. Think about accelerating, exponential growth in the number of open-pit mines, clear-cut forests, oil rigs and sweatshops and landfills, Dilbert-style office cubicles filled with sentimental knick-knacks, imitation Beany Babies made by Chinese prisoners, fast food restaurants in Ulaanbaatar. If you are an American, think about the fact that every $100 of economic activity in the U.S. is linked to the consumption of 660 pounds of stuff. Whoever you are, think of aboriginal tribes in Borneo forced into resettlement camps, struggling to resist while their forests are decimated by logging companies and their children watch TV commercials for the Gap.

I invite you to think about these impacts, distressing though the thoughts may be, because the economic newscasters almost certainly never will. Starbucks will never explain to you that a cup of coffee, on its journey to your mug, (1) displaces tropical rainforest and the creatures who live there, (2) gets sprayed with pesticides that leach into the soil and water and accumulate in the bodies of animals, poisoning or killing these animals (including some humans), and (3) contributes to global warming while being transported halfway around the world and heated to the boiling point. If Starbucks printed a warning to this effect on their paper cups, you might hesitate to buy their product, and even a slight hesitation might add up to a reduction in the company's annual revenues (and a reduction in your nation's GDP).

When examining a graph of the GWP or GDP, imagine what the curve would look like if the negative costs associated with the flow of all that stuff were subtracted from it, instead of added into the total, as they are now. That's right: oil spills, car wrecks, gunshot wounds, and disasters of all kinds currently *add* to the GWP, because they create additional "economic activity."

People in some countries don't need to imagine these revisions to the GDP; real figures are readily available. Not surprisingly, they paint a very different picture of those nation's economies. In the United States, for example, a policy institute called Redefining Progress periodically releases the "Genuine Progress Indicator," or GPI. This alternative index takes some of the same basic data as the GDP, but subtracts the activities and effects that it believes should be counted as negatives (including crime or environmental damage), while adding the positives we don't count (such as the value of volunteer work). The difference is dramatic. In terms of the flow of stuff and money, our economy is indeed growing. But in terms of genuine quality of life, by the GPI we appear to be losing ground.

▲▼▲

Morehead City, North Carolina
February 1997

*I'm at K-Mart, and I'm experiencing a flashback: Hang Ten shirts, poly-ester pants, the purchase of my first record album with saved-up allowance money (*Close to You, *by the Carpenters). Many of my formative shopping experiences took place in a south Orlando K-Mart that looks just like this one.*

Lenore and Scott have brought me here for a photo shoot. Scott's doing the cover for my new CD, Whole Lotta Shoppin' Goin' On, *and Lenore is the art director. Her nine-year-old daughter Sara is my Assistant Shopper.*

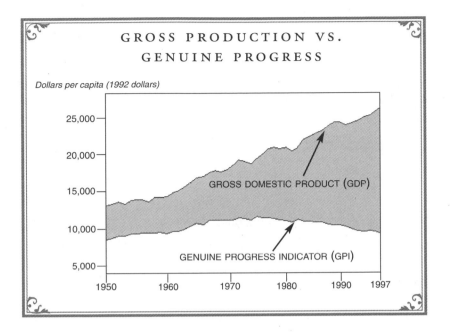

We take a shopping cart and zip through the aisles, picking up one of everything: a hula hoop, a hockey stick, a talking Teddy bear, a plaid vest, fishing poles and footballs and a pool cue and a huge pile of really tacky clothes. What I can't wear or hang on my body is spilling out of the cart. Even more stuff is pouring out of my handbasket. I'm wearing two hats and a pair of sunglasses with the tag dangling on my nose. I look ridiculous, which is the whole point.

Scott hurriedly snaps photos of me. What we're doing feels slightly illegal, so we keep looking around for the manager, or a sales clerk, or a crowd of curious on-lookers to interfere with our tomfoolery.

But no one even notices. They walk right by without looking.

Puzzled, we finish the photos, and carefully return each item to its place on the shelves. On the way out, we see long lines of people waiting to pay for their purchases, and we realize why we were being ignored: I looked no different from any other K-Mart shopper in the store.

▲▼▲

Most Americans don't know that they are damming up bigger rivers of throughput than the rest of the World. When they do hear about that truth, they find it difficult to care. Statistics such as this—*Americans each consume an average of 260 pounds of meat a year, while in Bangladesh, the average is 6½ pounds*—are provocative, but there's not much one can do except feel guilty. After all, the average in America is "normal" for Americans, and the average for Bangladeshis is "normal" for them, too. Cultures, economies, dietary habits are all different. You can't really compare them.

The problem is that people all over the World do, indeed, compare them. Americans are the global "Joneses," the family with whom everyone on the block is trying to keep up. We are beaming pictures of our lifestyle all over the World via movies, television shows, and advertisements. Our corporations are constantly strategizing how to convince people that they should consume more hamburgers, more cola drinks, and more blue jeans. Most people in the World, given a choice, would choose the American lifestyle (in terms of stuff). They seem practically helpless to choose otherwise.

Helena Norberg-Hodge, who documented the introduction of Western-style industrialization to the remote central Asian region of Ladakh, tells of meeting a young man who was very proud of his country. "We Ladakhis are all wealthy," he said with pride. "We have nice clothes, and cows, and plenty of food." Less than two years later, she met the same young man again. He had since been exposed to television, blue jeans, and cars. "We Ladakhis are so poor," he said. "You must help us."

Studies have shown that people's sense of satisfaction with their material wealth is determined not by how much they actually have, but by how much they have *compared to everybody else.* Rich or poor, if your neighbors have more than you do, you are likely to feel inferior. You will struggle to improve your status. Translate this to the global village, where everyone is your virtual neighbor, and it is easy to understand why consumerism is running rampant.

Yet a World where everyone tried to live as Americans do—eating tremendous amounts of meat, driving large cars, buying dozens of little kitchen doodads—would be an ecological nightmare. Countries that are trying to achieve that standard rapidly, for instance China, are allowing such nightmares to come true. In researching his excellent but harrowing book *Earth Odyssey*, Mark Hertsgaard learned that "the Chinese people wanted to join the global middle class, with all that entailed—cars, air conditioners, closets full of clothes, jet travel." But in their quest to attain the Asian version of the American Dream, the Chinese are sprawling across precious farmland, endangering their ability to feed themselves, and killing two million people each year with air and water pollution. Hertsgaard writes that he and his translator, Zhenbing, "had walked amid air so thick with coal dust and car fumes that even sunny days looked overcast and foggy." Zhenbing was from a poor family, and was "quite willing to put up with filthy air and dirty water if it meant better pay, more jobs, a chance to get ahead." But after they narrowly escaped being engulfed in chlorine fumes exploding from a Chongqing paper factory, Zhenbing was reduced to murmuring, "My poor country. My poor country."

Watching the nightmare happen is the painful essence of Cassandra's Dilemma. It actually takes little prophetic ability to know that the combination of population growth, materialistic aspirations, and highly inefficient technologies is a deadly one. But the World keeps pursuing that dream anyway.

So when you are reading statistics about economic growth, side-by-side with statistics confirming the growing disparity between the haves and the have-nots, consider the American dream. It was once described by former U.S. president Ronald Reagan this way: "What I want to see above all is that this country remains a country where someone can always get rich." Globalized and universalized, this translates to everyone in every country eventually getting rich—which is precisely the vision held by many economists and futurists, and perhaps, unconsciously, by most of the World, even if the cost of "sharing the wealth" in this scale would be rapid exhaustion of the planet's resources. The British writer Martin Amis, in a recent science-fiction story, imagined a future age of "Total Wealth." Unfortunately, the totally wealthy citizens of the planet in question—Martians, in this case—got bored with being rich and turned to thermonuclear war just for the fun of it.

Whatever your views on total wealth, we are far from attaining equitability at any reasonable level of prosperity. The United Nations' *Human Development Report* brings us up to date every year on the growing disparities in the World economic system. We can compare how much Americans and Europeans spend on pet food ($17 billion in 1997) to how much money would be needed to insure basic health and nutrition for everyone in the world ($13 billion). We can reflect on the basic indicator of inequity: the world's richest 20% (about 1.2 billion people, mostly concentrated in North America, Australia, New Zealand, Europe, and Japan, and in rich pockets all over the World) consumes *86% of all the stuff and all the services produced by the global economy.* Meanwhile, the poorest 20%—another 1.2 billion, concentrated in Africa, Asia, and slums everywhere—consumes just *1.3 percent.*

Consider this champagne glass. Its shape is lovely, but its message is grim. In the shallow basin on top are the rich and all their riches. They have attained the American dream, whatever country they live in. But everyone else is in the stem, which gets longer and narrower every year. To

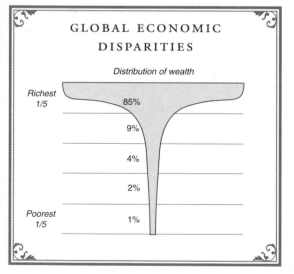

GLOBAL ECONOMIC
DISPARITIES

Distribution of wealth

Richest
1/5   85%

                    9%

                    4%

                    2%

Poorest
1/5   1%

put it bluntly, the rich have close to everything, while the poor have next to nothing. The rich are getting still richer, and the poor are staying poor. (You can't keep getting poorer if you start from zero.)

Not surprisingly, the poor also bear a disproportionate share of the negative impacts of the fortunate rich. For example, 70% of all the stuff that gets dug up, chopped down, polluted, and otherwise turned into waste in order to drive the economy of the Netherlands *never touches Dutch soil.* People in far-flung places who are poisoned by mines or displaced by logging companies probably don't even know that their suffering makes possible the creature comforts of Amsterdam.

Knowing such facts does not change the World: no one is likely to advocate sacrificing all pets, confiscating everyone's pet food budget, and giving the money to starving children. That might alleviate symptoms in the short term, but it will not solve the structural problem of poverty. Neither, however, will Growth. Growth tends to concentrate the accumulation of wealth in the hands of the already wealthy. Growth is making the problem worse.

▲▼▲

Shanghai, China
June 1982

I'm striding around, blonde-head-and-shoulders above a sea of black hair in this crowded city, which strikes me as having a combination of Communist squalor and colonial splendor. I have my journal, my tape recorder, and two cameras—one for color slides, one for black and white prints. China, closed to outside visitors for my entire childhood, presents a once-in-a-lifetime opportunity. I'm determined to record everything in detail.

Everywhere I go, I'm noticed. At first I think it's my looks, then I think it's the various technologies I'm carrying around. But neither properly explains the reactions I'm getting from every quarter: people either laugh and give me the thumbs-up sign, or they spit in my general direction.

Finally I rejoin my group and question my tour guide. What could possibly explain people's response?

"It's your T-shirt," he says laughing, and points to my chest. I had bought it in Malaysia. It has a big Chinese character on the front, and I suddenly realize I have no idea what that character means. The tour guide tells me: "You're an American walking around Shanghai in a shirt that says, 'Wealth!'"

▲▼▲

Recently I was in a diner, paging through a discarded issue of *Business-Week* magazine. I marveled at the trends in mag-lev train systems and ever-more-powerful computer chips. The cover story concerned the Mexican economy, and its ability to provide the global market with

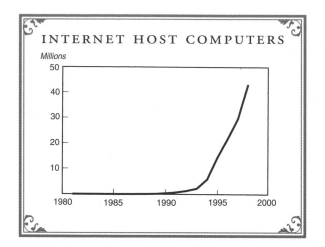

INTERNET HOST COMPUTERS

highly trained workers at a fraction of American salaries. HOW DO THEY DO IT? said the headline. I was pondering that question too, and others: How does the *World* do it? Where is it all headed? Then I noticed the date on the top of the page: 1993. My mind had been boggled by a six-year-old magazine.

The growth in people, stuff, and the flow of money is of course not merely a question of increasing size and disparity. It is also about speed, shape, and direction. The World is metamorphosing faster than we can comprehend, faster than our minds can keep up with, driven by exponential growth in trade and technology. International agreements, development aid, private investment, and most global diplomacy are focused on accelerating these changes even further. We are linking together everything and everyone in the World in a network of asphalt, airports, satellites, fiber optic cables, computers, telephones, televisions, and money. The process is known as "globalization."

To understand this trend, it is important to understand the vision behind it. The architects of what George Bush called "the new world order" were not, in their minds, simply trying to get rich and take advantage of poor people's cheap labor. The most enlightened among them were motivated by a vision of universal prosperity and peace. They remembered, with horror, the two World Wars, the atomic bomb, and countless smaller conflicts of the twentieth century. They wanted to win the Cold War without firing a single nuclear shot. And they wanted to design a World where future global conflicts would be impossible. "A world community can exist only with world communication," wrote Robert Maynard Hutchins in 1945, in "The Atomic Bomb versus Civilization." This means more, he wrote, than just a lot of shortwave radios (or cell phones) scattered around the planet. It means "common understanding, a common tradition, common ideas, and common ideals. . . . The task is overwhelming, and the chance of success is slight. We must take the chance or die."

Hutchins was not exaggerating the risk. Mao Tse-tung, the founder of Communist China, once boasted that the atomic bomb was nothing to be afraid of, and that he was willing for China to sustain the loss of 300 million people. But today's China depends for its wealth and economic stability on the U.S. market, and U.S. companies depend on Chinese workers and cola-drinkers. Neither country is in a hurry to fire missiles at the other, despite the tensions raised by the NATO bombing of China's Belgrade embassy, or China's alleged nuclear espionage in the United States. Globalization is based on the principle that peace is profitable. *An economically interdependent and prosperous World is less likely to go to war.*

The strategy of globalization seems to be succeeding, with amazing benefits and dismaying costs. For both good and ill, the diverse babble of languages spoken by the World's 6 billion people is slowly diminishing. Some 850 million people, 14% of all human beings, now speak English fluently, and nobody knows how many more can already get by in this complex dialect, once confined to a smallish rainy island in the North Atlantic. (Elementary English texts are now about as popular with the Chinese as Mao's *Little Red Book* used to be, and British TV sitcoms are very popular.) Add to these trends the steady rise in adult literacy, especially female literacy and education, together with the spread of CNN and MTV, and you get a World that is slowly becoming mutually comprehensible at a level not seen since the fall of the

Tower of Babel. The level of interconnectedness—real, not theoretical—is unprecedented. As Lewis Thomas notes in *The Lives of a Cell*,

> Any word you speak this afternoon will radiate out in all directions, around town before tomorrow, out and around the world before Tuesday, accelerating to the speed of light, modulating as it does, shaping new and unexpected messages, emerging at the end as an enormously funny Hungarian joke, a fluctuation in the money market, a poem, or simply a long pause in someone's conversation in Brazil.

Not only can an Inuit and a South African talk to each other more easily; they can find common topics to talk about. The World has a growing number of matters to discuss—ranging from global climate change to the future of the world's most famous man, basketball player Michael Jordan—that span distances, cultures, and generations. With each passing day this sense of global commonality grows stronger, as young people grow up watching the same shows on TV, wearing the same clothes, and struggling with the same rite-of-passage decisions, including when to get their first tattoo, and on which body part.

It is fashionable, and justifiable, to worry about these trends. We are losing the richness of diversity in culture, as in biology. Languages, cultures, and entire mental libraries of experience are going extinct at least as fast as the ecosystems, animals, and plants they once interpreted. The loss is both tragic and catastrophic.

But who can deny the trade-off? Globalization has brought into regular and frequent contact people who, not so long ago, viewed each other as distant mortal enemies, creating new businesses, new relationships, and new mutual understanding. The risk of global nuclear war, which would be the ultimate environmental and cultural disaster, has been greatly reduced (the situation is still ominously dangerous). In the 1950s, a single telephone call between heads of state in Russia and the United States was difficult to arrange; now, people on the streets of Moscow and New York jabber to each other on their cellular phones. This is a World where it's possible to meet your future spouse in an intercontinental Internet chat session, or to run your small business as a virtual corporation with a Web site in Winnipeg and nonexistent offices on five continents. These days, the Net will also translate (rather badly) your e-mail letter into a dozen different languages—a sort of gibbering prototype for the "Universal Translator" portrayed on *Star Trek*. Such are the strange building blocks of peace.

All of these trends together—rising literacy, telephonic connectedness, shared media and cultural experience, linguistic simplification, and the multiple and lightning-quick communication possibilities of the Net—are a new thing under the Sun. Their combined systemic effects are so widespread, complex, and transformative that we can barely begin to imagine where they might take us over the next fifty years. Phrases such as "the Information Age" are woefully inadequate; something more like "the Global Brain," a phrase popularized by futurist Peter Russel, comes closer to the mark. Nathaniel Hawthorne, writing in *House of the Seven Gables*, had a prophetic vision of this era, 150 years ago:

> Is it a fact that, by means of electricity, the world of matter has become a great nerve, vibrating thousands of miles in a breathless point of time? Rather, the round globe is a vast head, a brain, instinct with intelligence! Or, shall we say, it is itself a thought, nothing but thought, and no longer the substance which we deemed it!

If the World is indeed awakening to a kind of self-consciousness, it is an oddly timed awakening, for it comes just as the World threatens to completely displace Nature. Development-by-Growth has reached the point where we have the capacity to monitor what's happening everywhere on this planet. We have attained this capacity at precisely the moment when it allows us to observe that our Growth has gotten out of control, when the chain of destruction may prove unstoppable. The irony of this coinciding is breathtaking. The first truly global thought to rise to the level of conscious awareness is Cassandra's Dilemma.

▲▼▲

Swansboro, North Carolina
Summer 1998

Struggling with a recalcitrant poem, I go into the local office supply store to buy a new pen. Maybe that will get the words flowing, I think. Behind the counter, posted on the bulletin board, is an arresting photograph. It shows a black bear, standing on the North Carolina beach, surrounded by sun-bathers and condominiums. The bear is a smallish blur in the center of the photo, but it is still possible to read puzzlement in its stance. It does not belong there, and it does not know where to go.

I ask the shop owner about it. It's genuine; he took the photo himself. "I was just out there on the beach one day, and there was this bear. I asked around, and I learned that a demolition crew had just bulldozed the woods on the other side of the highway, to make way for a new condominium and retail complex. I don't know what ever happened to the bear. I hope it found a new home."

▲▼▲

In the last 50,000 years, human beings have eaten their way through a lot of animals. The evidence begins with the fossils of huge Australian flightless birds, passes through the woolly mammoth 10,000 years ago, and continues, relatively recently, with the passenger pigeon. Along the way we gulped down the Steller's sea cow, the great auk, the dodo, and many more. All these animals became extinct because they had two traits in common: they were very tasty, and they were easy to kill. The giant Steller's sea cow, a manatee of the Bering Sea measuring some thirty feet in length, was eaten to extinction by European sea-otter hunters a mere twenty-seven years after it was first documented by English explorers in 1741. The great auk, which had the poor judgement to live in the North Atlantic within easy reach of the sailing routes, was similarly exterminated in sixty years, for feathers as well as for food. Sailors would just walk up to an auk (a flightless swimmer reminiscent of a large penguin), conk it on the head, and carry it back to their ship for roasting. Live auks were captured and cooped up in the hold, like chickens.

The less sentimental among us might say that such vulnerable animals would have fallen to evolution's merciless ax eventually. Unfortunately, we haven't stopped with the easy prey; and although eating endangered species is not our only means of dispatching them, it remains grotesquely popular in some circles.

One of the less-publicized impacts of the Indonesian economic crisis of the late 1990s was an all-out attack on the nation's endangered species. "Nature is being pillaged," reported the *Wall Street Journal* in a front-page story in 1998, "as a nation hit by economic calamity falls back on land and sea to survive." Specifically, desperate Indonesians were capturing rare creatures in the jungle, and either eating them or selling them as delicacies to rich foreigners. Certain wealthy Taiwanese, for example, have a taste for raw baby monkey brains, eaten directly from a freshly opened skull.

Species routinely go extinct. That's normal. But the current level of human-caused extinction is not normal. We are killing off our brother and sister creatures at a rate *one hundred to one thousand times* faster than they would die off on their own. Our weapons have included habitat destruction, habitat fragmentation, chemical poisoning, and of course guns, nets, and the ancient custom of hand-to-hand combat. (Fighting animals to the death was particularly popular with the armies of Genghis Khan, who would conduct trainings by sweeping across the land on horseback, circling up around the wild animals they flushed, and proceeding to practice their bowmanship, swordplay, and beheading techniques.)

Let's start with the birds. Somewhere around 10,000 different kinds of birds exist in the world. Over 400 of them are in "immediate danger of extinction." Over 700 more are "vulnerable to extinction," meaning their numbers and habitat are under attack. And nearly 900 more are "nearing threatened status." That makes 2,000 birds—20% of all the different kinds of birds surveyed by the International Union for the Conservation of Nature, one out of every five—in danger of disappearing forever.

The next to go may be a whole lot of fish. In a 1998 issue of *Science*, buried at the end of an article that would be impenetrable to the average reader, was the following all-too-clear sentence: "It is likely that a continuation of present trends will lead to widespread fisheries collapses. . . ." The United Nations reported that as many one hundred violent international clashes occurred in 1997 over rights to dwindling fisheries.

Reptiles and amphibians are not faring much better (the sudden worldwide decline of frogs is well-documented), and we haven't even begun to discuss the desperate situation of the tiger, the rhinoceros, the chimpanzee, and others among the much-photographed rare animals that some call the "charismatic megafauna." By the mid-twenty-first century, those animals—and these are the creatures most of us *think* about when we think about animals—are not likely to be seen outside of zoos or the open-air zoos we call "wilderness parks." At the far opposite end of the charisma spectrum, every tiny parcel of rain forest contains unique species that are found nowhere else on Earth, most of them insects. When their corner of the forest goes, they go. While it may be "A Bug's Life" in the fantasy world of Disney cartoons, countless thousands of real insect species have gone to their deaths, and will continue to do so, without even getting cataloged by a human being. It is as though Eden had begun to die before Adam and Eve finished naming the animals.

Not all the animal news is bad, thankfully. *Life* magazine recently ran a photo spread on the North American species that had gone to the brink of extinction and recovered, thanks to massive human intervention. These include the gray wolf, the brown pelican, the bald eagle, the peregrine falcon, and the ever-popular heliotrope milk-vetch. Meanwhile, the ubiquitous bumper sticker SAVE THE WHALES! apparently worked; whales of nearly all species have made astonishing recoveries in recent decades, thanks to international legal protections.

When human beings set their minds to protecting Nature, they do a reasonably good job. Unfortunately, it is not a job that has attracted enough applicants for us to be able to get the work done; and now one rather enormous problem may render even our best efforts at conservation moot.

▲▼▲

In the 1950s, scientists on top of Hawaii's big volcano, Mauna Loa, began measuring the concentrations of carbon dioxide (CO_2) on a regular basis. We have very complete, very accurate records since that time, as well as very credible data from ice cores for 160,000 years preceding that. We know *with certainty* that CO_2 levels have increased over 30% since the Declaration of Independence was signed, and that the rate of increase is itself increasing. We also know *with certainty* that CO_2 in the atmosphere acts like the glazing on a greenhouse to increase the Earth's retention of heat. Moreover, measurements over the last hundred years show the temperature of the Earth slowly climbing.

Therefore, we know *with certainty* that we are heating up the Earth. We know this regardless of what scientists, whether they are paid by oil companies or simply exercising due professional caution, might say about uncertainty in global temperature measurements. As oceanographer Richard Barber, one of the first scientists to describe El Niño, told me in 1998, "Global warming is a misnomer. The problem is not really surface temperature; it's the build-up of heat in the global system."

Carbon dioxide, exhaled from our cars and our power plants like a long, collective sigh, traps heat. To steal a line from an old commercial for Roach Motels, "Photons get in, but they can't get out." Once trapped inside the Earth's thin layer of atmosphere, these jittery little bundles of heat energy from the Sun have to go somewhere. Many of them are going into the ocean, creating more frequent and more intense occurrences of El Niño, the huge pool of warm water that forms in the Eastern Pacific ocean and plays havoc with the planet's weather. (No prominent scientist will declare that El Niño is intensified by global warming, because it's impossible to prove, but most are worrying about the link "off the record.") In addition to raising ocean temperatures, other photons are going into the hydrological cycle, accelerating the massive pump that pulls water up from the Earth's surface, moves it somewhere, and deposits it again as rain or snow: hence the increase in floods and blizzards in recent years. Since heat tends to dissipate, flowing in the direction of areas that are colder, the especially warm water vapor hanging over the tropics gets tugged more strongly toward the poles, resulting in stronger typhoons and hurricanes (including the one in 1998 that destroyed 70% of Honduran roads, flattened entire villages, and killed 20,000 people). The extra photons also contribute to record heat waves and unpredictable ice storms. They make spring come early and summer stay late—which are shifts that most people don't seem to mind—and they drive temperature-sensitive species to migrate. Meanwhile, the unmistakable signs of this photon-surplus have convinced the Dutch to start planning to raise their dikes, at the cost of billions of dollars, and prodded German insurance magnates to consider declaring some hurricane-prone coastal areas uninsurable. And all this is just the beginning of what "global climate change" really means.

As Browning-Ferris CEO William Ruckleshaus put it, "Nature seems to be running a fever. We are the flu." By the time all the feverish heat has been distributed around the planet, glaciers have receded a bit, ice caps have melted a bit, and the ocean has warmed up a bit (which also causes it to expand and take up more space). All those bits together add up, over time, to a lot. There is already evidence that the Antarctic ice shelf is in danger of breaking up—maybe soon, maybe in two hundred years. Tourists have been swimming in the fjords of Alaska for the first time in memory. Costa Rican researchers have linked the extinction of twenty species of frogs to global climate change and its impact on that nation's famous cloud forests. If trends such as these continue (note the "If"), much of what is now the Florida coast could make for fascinating scuba dives by the year 2050.

When looking at a graph of global CO_2 levels, think first not about the calamity-in-progress known as global warming. Think instead about the enormity of humanity's accomplishment that changing the composition of the atmosphere represents. Ten thousand years ago, our ancestors were nomadic hunters and gatherers struggling to survive at the margins of an ice age. The ice came and went and dragged us and our history along behind it. Today, after just four hundred generations, we have grown and developed to the point where we can collectively al-

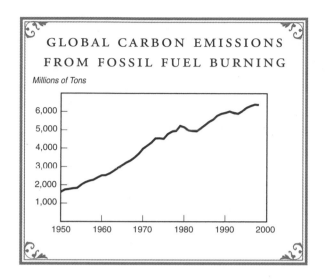

GLOBAL CARBON EMISSIONS
FROM FOSSIL FUEL BURNING

Millions of Tons

ter the planetary thermostat, simply by going about our daily lives: driving, working, watching TV. We are no longer passive victims of the climate system's slow oscillations; we are now, as a collective, atmospheric engineers.

Secondly, begin to contemplate the degree to which human beings are adaptable—extremely so. Try to make peace with the notion that your grandchildren may be growing kiwis in Siberia. On the other hand, they may be wearing fur hats in Oslo in August, because if Greenland melts, that could halt the North Atlantic current, sending much of Europe into a perverse, global-warming-fueled ice age. This is not to say that we six billion atmospheric engineers should not be readjusting our management plan, and trying to learn how to control the planetary thermostat instead of just cranking it up to "high." Nor does it mean that we should just keep expanding our messy, inefficient, nineteenth-century, fossil-fuel-energy systems as fast as possible, instead of replacing them with viable, clean hydrogen and solar power. Still, whatever we do, some amount of climate change, like population growth, is already inevitable and already in progress. Global warming is certain to disrupt "the best laid plans of both mice and men." But given our extreme adaptability, it is unlikely to kill us all.

Finally, think about the whole World, the big *enchilada*, the relationships among sex, human desire, population growth, economic expansion, inequity, globalization, technological innovation, interconnectedness, the decline of nature, and climate change. Let global CO_2 emissions, humanity's most astonishing collective achievement, stand as a kind of abstract symbol for all of that. Consider it the way you might consider horrific paintings such as Picasso's *Guernica*, or Goya's *Saturn Devouring His Son*. What do you see? I see an act of daring creativity, what we're doing with the Earth and ourselves, in the same way that all acts of creation involve destruction.

The question is, is it Art?

▲▼▲

This concludes our tour through the Gallery of Global Trends. Feel free to wander back in and explore in more detail the "exhibits" that particularly interest or puzzle you. The Worldwatch Institute's annual *Vital Signs* series and the World Resources Institute's biannual *World Resources* report have many more exhibits to consider as well. Try to look at them from different angles. Sit with them for a while, as you would a provocative painting, and notice what feelings come up. As George Bernard Shaw was reported to say (albeit ironically), "The sign of truly educated person is to be deeply moved by statistics."

In the following chapters, we will consider what to do about these trends: how to understand them more deeply, how to reckon with the powerful emotions they engender, what strategies to pursue to redirect them. Knowing about these trends has plunged us deeper into Cassandra's Dilemma. For the remainder of the book, we will begin to look for a way out.

CHAPTER 4

It's the System

The major problems in the world are the result of the differences between the way nature works and the way people think.
—GREGORY BATESON

Anyone who isn't confused doesn't understand what's going on.
—DIMITRI SIMES

THIS CHAPTER IS designed to release you from the feeling that you are personally to blame for what is happening to Nature and the World, and to explain what is actually to blame.

Unless you are a wildlife poacher who formerly worked for Greenpeace, a corporate executive who has personally enslaved child laborers, or a black-marketeer in the CFC business with a Ph.D. in atmospheric chemistry, what's happening to the planet is not your fault. Even those whose intentions are genuinely evil cannot be blamed for the overall trajectory of history. Immense and impersonal forces are at work that are bigger than any individual actor could possibly command, whatever their motivation. The problem is not you, or "them," or any one of us. The problem is, the World is literally out of control.

In the 1960s in America, a common way to complain about what was "goin' down" with Vietnam, Mother Earth, or the urban ghetto was to say, "It's the system, man." As a child of the 1970s, who grew up in the disco years, I can't say this authentically, but I will say it anyway: "Right on." ("Right on" is making a big comeback.)

Sixties slang-slingers didn't know exactly what they meant by that phrase, "It's the system"—for them "system" meant something like "the establishment," the power structure—but they were more right than they knew, even when they were stoned. "It's the system" is an accurate identification of the source of our contemporary global problems. A more accurate way to say it would be, "It's the systems, plural."

The power structure is certainly a partial explanation—"Economics and politics are the governors today, and that's why everything is screwy," said Joseph Campbell—but that's not even close to being the main problem. By looking at two much larger systems and at the way they currently relate to each other, we can find the source of so much of our trouble. These two systems are Nature and the World. Please allow me to explain.

First, let me provide a very brief introduction to the structure of systems—worth reading, because understanding systems will alleviate that nagging feeling of global guilt.

A *system* is a collection of separate elements that are connected together to form a coherent whole. Your body is a system, and it is comprised of many smaller systems, all working together: the circulatory system, the digestive system, and so on. The connections between the elements of a system come in two forms: stuff and information. For example, you eat food (stuff), and when your belly gets full it sends a signal (information) to your brain telling you to stop eating.

The science of system dynamics uses a lingo, and it is easy to learn. In the example above, the food moving through your gullet would be called a *flow*. Your belly, filling up from the flow of food, would be called a *stock*. And the signal sent to your brain, indicating whether the stock of food in your belly has reached that comforting level known as "full," is called *feedback*.

The feedback from your belly has an impact on your eating behavior, which in turn causes more feedback from the belly. All that circling around of stuff and information, which controls (or should control) how much you eat, is called a *feedback loop*. This feedback loop, like most others, operates in two directions: it tells you to stop eating when you are full, and it starts your search for food again when your belly is not full. Feedback loops essentially give one of two messages to the system: "do more" or "do less."

Systems can be described in terms of their stocks, flows, and feedback loops. In the World3 computer model described in chapter 1, population is a stock, birth and death are flows, and signals about what is happening in that system travel around many different kinds of feedback loops. For instance, when people notice that more of their babies are surviving, and their parents are living longer, they eventually start having fewer babies. You can project the level of population twenty years from now by looking at how big it is at the moment (the current stock), how fast it's growing (the flow of babies in, minus the flow of dead people out), what else is changing in the system (including infant mortality and life expectancy), and how long it takes before people adjust their breeding behavior in response to the feedback.

A critical point to remember: *Delays in feedback slow down response.* You can't react to changes you don't know about. And when you *do* know about the changes, you may not have enough time to respond. We will return to this point, because it is the crux of the problem.

Here are two more important systems concepts: *sources* and *sinks*. Sources are where stuff comes from; sinks are where stuff ends up. Farmlands and oceans are the *source* of the food you eat. In certain more enlightened societies, farmland is also the *sink* where the compostable residue ends up; for most of us, though, the sink is some local body of water connected with a sewage treatment plant. Mines are a source of materials; landfills are often their sink, or final resting place. When garbage is burned or incinerated, the atmosphere acts as a sink. Sometimes even the human body acts as a sink, as when lead builds up in the tissues. The impact of that lead is not felt directly for years, and this is another example of a delay in feedback. By the time you notice the symptoms of lead poisoning, it's too late: you're poisoned, and there is no way to get the poison out fast enough to prevent further damage.

The critical thing to know about sources is that they can run out. As for sinks, they can fill up and spill over, just like the sink in your bathroom. A disappearing source creates a shortage; an overfilled sink creates a mess.

Obviously, the issue of how quickly we get feedback about what's happening in the sources and sinks is extremely important to understanding and managing systems. In the 1972 version of the World3 computer model, the attention of the press and the critics was on *sources*, for instance metals and fossil fuels. Given that era's knowledge about current stocks and the growth rates of various flows, certain materials seemed likely to run out, with challenging consequences. But it turns out that the real danger was in the *sinks*. Fueled by runaway growth, they've been filling up and overflowing. "Overloaded sinks" is one way to describe the cause of global warming, chemical pollution, and the rising rates of cancer and genetic abnormalities. Had we been watching the atmospheric sink carefully, had we understood the dynamics of what was happening, and had we gotten more compelling feedback sooner and responded to that feedback in time, we might have turned off the faucet of CO_2 and prevented the climate system from going out of balance.

But we didn't. So it went.

Climate is but a single story in a long series of stories about what happens when an exponentially growing World begins to hit up against slow-to-respond Nature. The problem is inherent in the structure of both. Nature and the human World are both comprised of a tremendous number of systems and subsystems, ranging from the very small (say, a gnat, or your personal checking account) to the extremely large (the global climate, or the global economy). These systems interact with each other in ways that are mind-boggling in their complexity. No one person could thoroughly understand even the smallest fraction of it. But buried deep inside that tangled web of sources, sinks, stocks, flows, and feedback loops, both human and natural, lies the answer to a Sphynxian riddle of life-or-death importance: What, exactly, is the problem here on Planet Earth?

The precise location of the problem that is driving the World to the brink of collapse, and pushing Nature dangerously out of balance, can be found at those critical points where the World and Nature are intimately communicating with each other.

The problem is, they *aren't*.

Nature and the World affect each other mightily—but they don't dance very well. It's a matter of feedback loops. They're not hooked up right. Stuff flows out of Nature into the World, depleting critical sources (such as forests and fish). Or stuff flows from the World into Nature, filling the sinks with things it doesn't need and can't get rid of (such as chemicals that mimic the hormone estrogen). The feedback signals coming back from Nature to the World—telling us that sources are falling, or sinks filling—arrive too slowly, or not at all, or get ignored on arrival. The World's responses to the signals it *does* get from Nature generally come too late, or only partially, or not all. Instead of a complex and elegant marriage of the human World with the systems of Nature, joined in the matrimonial bonds of highly integrated feedback loops, there is a dangerous estrangement. What we've got here is a pair of dance partners who don't do the same steps, don't feel the same rhythm, don't listen to each other, and have a growing number of bruised and bloody toes.

Add it all up, and you get a World that is out of control, and virtually uncontrollable—at least, as currently designed.

The relentless depletion of our fisheries, including for example the North Atlantic cod, provides a tragic illustration. After the cod have already started to disappear, scientists study the cod and determine that they are disappearing (feedback delayed). Fishermen retort that they are still catching plenty of fish, from what they perceive as big schools (feedback discounted). Scientists explain that they only *look* like big schools, because the remaining cod have all banded together; it's as though the fishermen were shooting ducks in an ever-shrinking barrel. Fishermen scoff, and complain loudly to the regulatory authorities that they will have trouble feeding their families if they cannot fish (feedback diluted). (And the fishermen are right: the U.S. economy provides almost no transition assistance for fishermen, or loggers, or anyone eventually forced out of a job because they have been encouraged to exhaust a natural resource.) This delayed, discounted, and diluted feedback results in an even more delayed and diluted response, including regulations for slightly reduced fishing, but hardly enough reduction to save the fish. Goodbye cod.

Although it might be therapeutic to blame Nature for not responding adequately to humanity's growing, changing needs—by, say, learning to grow fish faster—it's hardly helpful. We're the ones with consciousness, after all. Nature is going to do the rhumba, no matter what we do. So it is incumbent upon us to learn the music, the rhythm, the steps. In dance-floor terms, Nature leads. We have to learn to anticipate her next move.

Take, for example, the aforementioned CFCs. The story of this human-created gas and its near-devastation of the ozone layer is an indispensable case study in the systemic clash between World and Nature. It is also the encouraging story of an escape from Cassandra's Dilemma.

CFCs were created because ammonia, the chemical in refrigerators and air conditioners that CFCs replaced, was killing people. Ammonia gas is poison, and smelly, and it has a nasty tendency to blow up and start your kitchen on fire. The fires were feedback to the World that something was wrong, and the World, through the agency of the DuPont corporation, took action.

Chlorofluorocarbons, or CFCs, were a beautiful solution to the ammonia problem. CFCs didn't burn, they didn't poison anyone, and they were cheap to make. Since they also didn't combine with other chemicals, they had many other uses as well. Some people reading this will be too young to remember, but virtually every spray can in the World made before the mid-1970s, from antiperspirant to furniture polish, was charged with CFC propellants such as freon. (I myself, as an American teenager very concerned about body odor, shot a great deal of freon into the atmosphere.) The atmosphere seemed a perfectly safe, almost unlimited sink in which to release these harmless chemicals after we were done with them.

Then a couple of chemists by the name of F. Sherwood Rowland and Mario Molina discovered that CFCs had the potential to destroy the ozone layer, a thin band of concentrated molecules high in the stratosphere. At the Earth's surface, ozone is a poisonous component of smog; but at high altitudes ozone is a protector of life, a shield, a blessing. Ozone deftly blocks out excess ultraviolet radiation from the Sun, which, if it were to shine full-strength through an ozone-free atmosphere, would kill, mutate, or otherwise inconvenience most living things.

When CFC molecules drifted up to the stratosphere, as they tend to do, a terrible thing happened: they lost their chlorine atoms. Chlorine eats ozone. Worse, chlorine can keep eating ozone—converting it to simple oxygen—through many thousands of chemical reactions, like a molecular Pac-man. Worse still, CFCs took about fifteen years just to get to the stratosphere. That meant that even if humanity stopped releasing the stuff into the atmosphere yesterday, it would be fifteen years before the ozone-eaters in the stratosphere began to decline. Further complicating the matter, CFC production had been growing exponentially for years, which meant that any delay in ceasing production resulted in ever-increasing threats to Earth's protective ozone shield.

According to Bill McKibben, whose book *The End of Nature* contains an excellent summary of this and other harrowing stories, Rowland came home one day and told his wife, "The work is going very well, but it looks like the end of the world." He and Molina began the slow and thankless process of alerting people to their findings. Governments were slow to take the warning seriously, and chemical companies were adamantly resistant. An international agreement, known as the "Vienna Convention," was reached in 1985, but it was toothless. Two months later, the World got lucky: a massive hole in the ozone layer over Antarctica was detected—five years late, because the computers had been programmed to ignore weird phenomena such as that—but the sudden flurry of publicity caused a rapid scramble to strengthen the Vienna agreement. The negotiation of the 1987 "Montreal Protocol" led to an eventual worldwide ban on CFCs, and a 1995 Nobel Prize in Chemistry for Rowland, Molina, and their Dutch colleague, Paul Crutzen. This was one team of Cassandras who made good.

▲▼▲

Rowland and Molina were, you might say, the point of contact between Nature and the World. They were the critical link in the feedback loop—a very, very tenuous feedback loop, since it rested on the shoulders of two scientists. What if they had turned their attention elsewhere? Or had been purely academic researchers, too isolated or too shy to present their information to a resistant Congress? We would certainly have found out about the ozone problem eventually, but it might have been far too late to prevent terrible damage to every form of life under the Sun. As it is, ozone depletion in the stratosphere is still growing (remember that delay in the system) and is expected to reach its worst around 2001, then slowly get better as natural processes replenish the ozone layer. Without Rowland and Molina's curiosity about CFCs and their effect on the stratosphere, it might have taken a much stronger feedback signal—say, dying crops, or skyrocketing rates of skin cancer—to alert us to the danger.

The chief culprit in the story of CFCs, as in so many stories about destructive global trends, is not human evil; it is a delay in feedback. The structure of the combined World-Nature system is currently rigged to cause enormous problems, because we humans often do not get the feedback telling us that we're doing something wrong until we've already done a great deal of harm. Or the signal comes in (as it did to Rowland and Molina), but it takes too long to get to the right place. Or it gets to the right place, but it has little or no effect (as in the first Vienna Convention). Or it gets noticed but actively resisted, even suppressed (as chemical companies resisted the news about ozone depletion for many years, until the scientific evidence became irrefutable).

Without timely feedback, there can be no timely response. Even when the feedback does get where it's supposed to go, and has the desired impact—as in the case of CFCs, where chemical companies actually acknowledged the problem relatively quickly, and cooperated to find a solution—humanity then confronts another property of large-scale systems that causes them to experience dangerous delays: momentum. Think of the infamous ship Titanic. The iceberg was spotted, the rudders were instantly turned, but it was too late. The momentum of the huge, heavy ship carried it into the ice (and on into the Hollywood record books). You can't argue with the laws of physics.

The example of global climate change provides another excellent illustration. Human beings have been emitting atmosphere-changing levels of CO_2 for about two hundred years, in exponentially growing amounts. A brilliant Swedish chemist, one Svante Arrhenius, spent nearly all of 1895 figuring out that this would cause global warming. Arrhenius's calculations about the level of warming caused by a doubling of CO_2—4 to 5 degrees Celsius—were practically identical to what today's best computer models now estimate. He published his results in 1896, and was promptly ignored. In the 1930s, a British physicist mumbled a few words of concern about global temperature increases. He was ignored. Actual measurements of CO_2 began in the 1950s; these were of interest only to scientists. More serious concerns were raised publicly by a number of scientists in the 1970s; they, too, were ignored. The U.S. Congress first heard scientific testimony on the mounting data and noticeably hotter temperatures—the first feedback to be felt by the average person—in 1989. The testimony was duly noted, headlines blazed briefly, and then the evidence was both ignored and suppressed by the oil industry (though countries such as the Netherlands, to their credit, had started to respond by then). Temperatures continued to rise, becoming increasingly hard to deny, until a global agreement to try to slow the process down was reached in Kyoto in 1996. But this agreement is exceedingly weak, and it has yet to make a dent in actual emissions. Even if fully implemented, the Kyoto agreement would merely slow CO_2 emissions, not stop them. One can only hope that the toothless Kyoto accord, like the first Montreal Protocol, will ultimately lead to far stronger measures; but it is likely to take a few undeniable shocks to the system, like the Antarctic ozone hole, to make that happen.

What a different World it would be if our ancestors had paused to consider the findings of Svante Arrhenius. Instead, that hundred-year delay in feedback has allowed a tremendous amount of momentum to build up, in Nature's systems as well as the World's. Humans cannot stop using fossil fuels now without shutting down their electrical systems, agricultural production, transportation networks, manufacturing sectors . . . in other words, without going out of business and condemning billions to starvation. It will take a generation, *if we start now*, to completely replace our energy sources with greenhouse-friendly alternatives. The Earth, meanwhile, will not stop heating up any time soon, any more than your wood stove will get cool the instant you stop putting logs on the fire. A small stove will take hours to reach room temperature, but delays in the Earth's enormous and complex climate system are much, much longer. Stabilization of climate will not come for decades *after* we stop adding carbon dioxide and other heat-trapping gases. We have committed ourselves to living in an ever-warmer world.

▲▼▲

Consider virtually any major global problem, and you will see the telltale signature of systemic feedback delays, together with runaway momentum, powered by exponential growth. Remember endocrine disruptors, those common chemicals that act dangerously like hormones in the body, probably a chief culprit in many forms of cancer? Hardly noticed until wildlife had begun turning up with malformed penises, and human sperm counts had dropped by 50% in some countries. Europe and Japan are moving to ban endocrine disruptors, which are found in everyday products such as plastic wrap, but the United States still pretends officially that these chemicals are no big deal. Or remember population. Birth rates generally take a generation to fall in the best of circumstances, and population keeps growing for another fifty years after that. Meanwhile, the Pope still preaches against contraception.

Human beings have a hard time getting Nature's messages. Nature has to turn the volume up very loud. The problem is structural, but it's also partly biological. Human brains have evolved to respond to immediate, obvious threats—such as leopards—rather than abstract signals like graphs of atmospheric CO_2, which simply do not *look* very threatening. Our brains are also very good at filtering out unpleasant and inconvenient information. As my hairdresser said about global warming, "If it brings us more 65-degree days in February, I'm not going to complain."

Douglas Adams, in his famous *Hitchhiker's Guide to the Galaxy* series, explains how large spaceships could land in the middle of London and not get noticed. They put out, he writes, a sort of a force-field called a "Somebody Else's Problem Field," which causes anyone who looks at the spaceship to dismiss it by thinking, "Whatever that is, it's not my problem." Then they go on about their business.

The list of environmental, social, and economic problems that seem to be similarly equipped is long indeed.

▲▼▲

Another impersonal, systemic, and rather annoying factor working against the marriage of World and Nature is a phenomenon called "The Tragedy of the Commons," described in an essay by Garrett Hardin in 1968. Hardin used the word *tragedy* very precisely, taking his definition from the American philosopher Alfred North Whitehead. "The essence of dramatic tragedy," wrote Whitehead, ". . . resides in the solemnity of the remorseless working of things." One could hardly pen a more elegant phrase to describe the current status of human and natural affairs.

A tragedy is a chain of calamitous events that, once set in motion, cannot be stopped. The essence of this particular tragedy, wrote Hardin, has to do with how rational, individual acts add up to collective catastrophes. The "commons" in his title was a public pasture for sheep. Each shepherd, Hardin explained, is rationally motivated to put as many sheep out to graze as possible, because it clearly benefits the shepherd, and nothing prevents him from doing so. If the sheep degrade the commons in the process, the degradation is a cost spread among all other shepherds. No individual shepherd will immediately feel the negative impacts of his supposedly rational decision. But when all shepherds make the same rational decision, all those sheep (most irrational animals) soon destroy the commons altogether.

Let's update the example. It makes sense for me to burn the gasoline in my car, even when I know it contributes to global warming, because:

1. I get lots of benefits but experience few immediate environmental costs, and;
2. whatever costs there are get shared by everybody else in the World (including, say, citizens of the Maldive Islands, whose homes will get drowned under rising seas much sooner than mine will).

Since everybody is making the same rational calculation—benefits to me, costs to everyone else—and can act with absolute freedom in this matter, the atmosphere gets trashed.

Hardin's essay was very widely read, and "The Tragedy of the Commons" is now part of the basic canon of social science, used to explain everything from littering to the exhaustion of fisheries. Hardin even used his theorem to explain humanity's propensity for ignoring difficult facts, claiming that "natural selection favors the forces of psychological denial." In other words, denial gives you a sexual advantage. How could this be so? Because genetically speaking, individuals benefit from denial. Both nature and society can be crashing down around our heads, but if we can make ourselves believe, like Scarlet O'Hara in *Gone with the Wind*, that "Tomorrow is another day," then we will go on to live and reproduce. As Hardin put it, "The individual benefits as an individual from his ability to deny the truth even though society as a whole, of which he is a part, suffers."

Hardin himself was using "the tragedy of the commons" to explain population growth, and why people had very little incentive to limit their family size, because they received the benefits of big families, while society and Nature bore most of the costs. His essay was, in effect, an argument for voluntary-yet-mandatory birth control: "mutual coercion, mutually agreed upon." As he wrote in his seminal essay, "The only way we can preserve and nurture other and more precious freedoms, is by relinquishing the freedom to breed, and that very soon."

Needless to say, his advice was not taken by anyone but the Chinese (and by them not voluntarily). Hardin, a prominent biologist and geneticist, developed a classic case of Cassandra's Dilemma. His reasoning was sound. His foresight was prophetic. He was heard, acknowledged, applauded, then ignored. I have rarely seen a better short description of the resulting feeling than this paragraph, which he wrote in 1971:

> My essay had a curious reception: much notice, but only guarded comment. It has, to date, been reprinted in some two dozen anthologies in the fields of biology, ecology, political science, sociology, law, and economics. I am sure people are aware of it; but few grapple directly with the issues raised therein. I sometimes feel as if I were living in the eye of a hurricane, waiting. . . .

"The Tragedy of the Commons" helps us to understand why so much feedback from Nature gets ignored by the World: because it seems "rational" to ignore unpleasant or inconvenient information. Worse, the system *rewards* us for ignoring such signals at least in the short term. Built into the structure of our economy is a set of carrots and sticks known as "perverse incentives." We get rewarded for doing the destructive thing (like hunting down the last few fish) and punished for doing the right thing (like refraining from the use of gasoline for transportation). Donella Meadows describes our quandary this way: "It's as if we had a banking system that charged you for making a deposit, and paid you to rob the bank."

Combine these structural challenges with the glacial slowness with which Nature begins to send its distress signals; the relatively limited listening posts set up by humanity to receive those signals; and our jittery "fight-or-flight" nervous system, which is more geared to survival on the savannah than planetary management, and it is all too easy to understand why we are in a predicament.

Of course, systemic effects get compounded by common human character flaws such as arrogance, stubbornness, selfishness, and greed. Add it all up, and it's a wonder we've made it this far.

▲▼▲

Beaufort, North Carolina
Summer 1976

My father and I have been driving this U-Haul truck, filled with my grandmother's old furniture, for two very long days. We've detoured off to see our friends on the coast. I'm barely sixteen, and I'm thrilled to be driving a truck.

My Dad tells me to pull our very big truck into our friends' very narrow driveway. I'm a little worried about it, but he's insistent. "Keep going, keep going," he says. "Are you sure?" I say. "That gable over the porch looks too low." He just gives me a dangerous look that means, "Don't talk back to me," and says, "I can see just fine, you've got plenty of room." I know we're going to hit it, but for obvious reasons, I keep going. My ears get that hot feeling that comes whenever I have to hold my tongue to avoid my father's wrath.

Suddenly we hear this terrible crunching and splintering sound.

Sure enough, the truck has torn off the corner of the gable over the porch. Our friends come rushing out, shocked. I'm mortified, and angry. My Dad is, too, but he tries not to show it. It's me he's angry with, because I was right.

"Oh well," they say graciously, whisking us into the house. "That wood was rotten. It was going to have to be replaced anyway." Something else needs to be replaced, too: fear of my father with trust in my own perceptions.

▲▼▲

People in Cassandra's Dilemma, whether they know it or not, are people who see a missing feedback loop and want to correct it. They are monitoring a stock (for instance CO_2 in the atmosphere), they see the change caused by a flow (exhaust from increasing numbers of oil-driven engines), and they try to send a feedback signal to the rest of the World that will be heard and acted upon. As the foregoing makes clear, it is a daunting task, because the World generally doesn't want to know.

Bringing news of ozone depletion, species extinction, climate change, and other comparable catastrophes involves trying to change the World system. Trying to change the direction of the World is like being a third-class passenger on the Titanic, and attempting to get a message to the Captain about a prophetic vision you had concerning icebergs. The Captain is not likely to pay much attention. Even if you, yourself, are the Captain, you will have been rigorously trained to ignore "prophetic visions"—to the point where you might even increase your speed and become *less* watchful of icebergs, just to prove how rational you are. And most critically, you would be economically motivated to keep going as fast as possible. Consideration of vague warnings—even the scientifically well-grounded warnings of a first-class passenger with a background in Arctic glaciology—would cost too much money.

Money is the single greatest obstacle to the effective reception of feedback from Nature. Money is not a thing; it is a collective idea. Unlike water, or sunlight, or carbon dioxide, the monetary system has no reality outside the minds of human beings. It is the lifeblood of the World, but it is fundamentally not Natural. The monetary system registers occurrences in Nature only if we engineer a mechanism—economically and politically, with taxes, subsidies, penalties, and trading permits.

Even conscientious climate scientists and environmentalists, who know exceedingly well what gas-burning cars do to the atmosphere, are still discouraged by money from making the best choice for the Earth (like perhaps driving an expensive, early-prototype electric vehicle), and strongly encouraged by money to make destructive choices (like buying a larger house, because of the mortgage interest deduction and a low interest rate). It's hardly their fault that they fly around in jets attending global-warming conferences; it's the system, man.

And people are people. They want food, sex, children, mobility, freedom, comfort, entertainment, and control over their lives. They want light, heat, and power. They choose from what is available to satisfy those wants—and they have very limited choices. They make decisions based on what they are told by advertisers and what's available in the market, and most especially, based on the strong signals of price. Getting virtually every one of their basic needs met, not to mention achieving their aspirations, requires money. So they sell their time for as much money as they can get (that's called "a job"), and they shop for the best quality at the lowest price ("bargain-hunting"). It takes an extraordinary expenditure of conscious awareness for the average individual, or even the very concerned and aware individual, to think about anything more than that in daily life.

Yet it is not inherent in the nature of money that it should so constrain us from doing the right thing. The money system was created at a time when the World was relatively small and Nature was incomprehensibly huge. There was no real need to incorporate feedbacks from Nature into the money system by putting a price on the services Nature provided. Nature could absorb seemingly everything we threw at it, and provide us with everything we needed, seemingly for free.

But times have changed. The money system—the most powerful transmission channel for feedback in the World—will have to change as well.

▲▼▲

Penang, Malaysia
February 1997

For the first time in fifteen years, I'm back in Malaysia. Penang, a wildly diverse island city, was always one of my favorite places, especially because of the food. In addition to giving a speech and performing a concert here,

I'm planning to eat my way through a list of my favorite dishes, from the tangy fish stew called assam laksa *to the rich variety of curries and satays.*

My hosts, Salma and Lubis, are giving me a tour, and I can't believe how much has changed. Penang, once just a colorful market town, is now home to some of the largest microchip-manufacturing plants in the world. The city has grown like crazy.

They take me to see the new mall. It is a huge, windowless monolith, blocking the beach. It reminds me of the featureless obelisk in 2001: A Space Odyssey, only a million times bigger. There are a hundred stores inside.

"How could they build such a thing here?" I ask. "Aren't there zoning regulations? Open-space requirements? Rules for public access?" "Oh yes," says Salma, "but money talks, you know, so they found a nice little loop-hole."

"You see, on the roof of the building, there is a very large aquatic park, one of those places with waterslides and such. That was declared open space, accessible to the public."

▲▼▲

If the properties of systems can excuse humanity's indifference to global environmental trends, why not excuse everything else? Why not the Holocaust, slavery, *apartheid*?

The difference lies in the development of morality. There were, indeed, systemic forces at work in the Holocaust, slavery, and *apartheid*, including inadequate feedback to the World system, and delays in both feedback and response caused by all the same troubling features outlined above. Such forces are still at work today, in situations such as the West's tragically delayed response to the crisis in Kosovo (after years of nonviolent resistance led to their being overlooked at the Dayton peace accords, Kosovo Albanians switched to violence to get the World's attention), or the growing problem of slavery in the Sudan (it took a group of Denver schoolchildren, spending their own money to buy people back out of slavery, to bring the issue to broader notice in the U.S.).

But in circumstances of genocide or gross oppression, virtually all the World's societies have moral and ethical codes that identify what is happening as immoral, evil, and wrong. Ignoring the earliest credible signal is a moral lapse of the highest order. Unavoidable delays may still occur, but no avoidable delay is excusable.

In contrast, most industrialized societies have developed no such clarity of moral code with regard to Nature, resource use, wild animals, or the size of their populations. Indeed, many of our moral codes encourage us to do *more* of whatever is causing the problem—bear more children, kill more animals, make more profits by any means legal and possible. Morality thereby becomes yet another systemic impediment to arresting the dangers of growth. Cassandra's Dilemma deepens all the more.

▲▼▲

On the first page of *The Limits to Growth* appears an epigraph, a quotation attributed to UN secretary-general U Thant and dated 1969:

> I do not wish to seem overdramatic, but I can only conclude from the information that is available to me as Secretary-General, that members of the United Nations have perhaps ten years left in which to subordinate their ancient quarrels and launch a global partnership to curb the arms race, to improve the human environment, to defuse the population explosion, and to supply the required momentum to development efforts. If such a global partnership is not forged within the next decade, then I very much fear that the problems I have mentioned will have reached such staggering proportions that they will be beyond our capacity to control.

After that, it became something of a tradition among professional Cassandras to declare that humanity had no more than ten years to turn things around. The cry of "ten years left" has been repeated periodically ever since, particularly at the turn of each decade. In retrospect, the prediction has always been true.

Had the World listened to U Thant in 1969, for example, there might have been no Chernobyl, no Bhopal, no Love Canal. A ban on

CFCs might have come fifteen years earlier. There would still be global warming, but there would be less of it—fewer heat-stroke days in Texas, fewer concerns about warm waters and resulting tiny salmon off the coast of Alaska, fewer worries about ski slopes going out of business and coastal property going under water. There might have been a billion fewer people, and a better life for the billions alive today.

At any point in the last thirty years, we could theoretically have taken more dramatic action, which would have allowed us to reduce our worries for the future and mourn a bit less for the past. But it would have taken either an extraordinary act of collective consciousness or a great stroke of luck. The impersonal, systemic properties of the World-Nature system I have been describing—exponential growth, delays in feedback, delays in response, tremendous momentum, limitations of human biology, the Tragedy of the Commons, perverse incentives, the disconnection of money from Nature, and the lacunae in our moral codes—amount to a long list of very persuasive excuses for why, as a species, we didn't choose a more noble and enlightened path. Understanding the system releases us from the obligation to feel guilty or the temptation to blame someone else.

But this kind of understanding does not release us from Cassandra's Dilemma, from the imperative to take action, or from the emotions that come with consciousness. And frequently, knowing about systemic forces increases the emotional intensity. We can see what's already happened, we can predict what's coming, and we can understand why nobody's doing much in response. This position is a painful one, and the pain is a result of an irreversible condition: awareness. We stand, like Garrett Hardin, in the eye of the hurricane, and we know that from now on, we will never have more than ten years to turn things around, and we will always be ten years too late.

CHAPTER 5

Cassandra's Laughter, Cassandra's Tears

More than at any time in history mankind faces a crossroads. One path leads to despair and utter hopelessness, the other to total extinction. Let us pray that we have the wisdom to choose correctly.
—WOODY ALLEN

We sang the loudest when we were losing.
—ERNEST HEMINGWAY

I WAS BORN A MODERATE Republican—fiscal conservative, social liberal. In 1968 I campaigned for Richard Nixon (eight years old at the time, I was enamored with the "X" in the middle of his name). Then as a college student in 1980, I became a bleeding heart. I saw the World around me in New Orleans, and grew incensed by the obliviousness of my fellow students to the racism, poverty, and ecological destruction happening in plain view. That delicious sense of righteous indignation launched me into an extremely varied and passion-driven career that led, in a roundabout way, to the basement of a suburban house on Bainbridge Island, Washington, thirty-five minutes by ferry from Seattle.

It was there in 1988 that I first met Robert and Diane Gilman, cofounders of a little magazine called *In Context*. Robert was (and still is, though Diane has passed away) a visionary. Concerned about global trends, and fully able to appreciate the mathematics of exponential growth, he had left his promising career as an astrophysicist to try to do something about the state of the World. "The stars could wait," he told me at our first meeting, "but the planet couldn't." The Gilmans had gone back to the land in Washington's Olympic Peninsula, building an inexpensive solar house and growing their own food. They wanted to demonstrate a globally responsible lifestyle. They started a network of back-to-the-landers called the "North Olympic Living Lightly Association." Its newsletter covered everything from how to card your own wool to how to give birth at home, and ultimately the newsletter itself gave birth to the more ambitious and philosophical journal *In Context*, which Robert awkwardly subtitled "A Quarterly of Humane Sustainable Culture."

It was thanks to Robert and *In Context* (or *IC*, as we called it) that I came to meet a great many of Planet Earth's living Cassandras—people such as Donella and Dennis Meadows, energy analyst Amory Lovins, Indian grassroots leader Sunderlal Bahuguna, citizen diplomat Danaan Parry, experiential workshop leader Joanna Macy, and dozens more. It was a comprehensive education, for which I am eternally grateful. This also intensified my experience of the condition I have called Cassandra's Dilemma. *IC*'s mission was to promote solutions to the panoply of environmental, economic, and social problems, and to provide readers with a "whole-systems perspective." In other words, our job was to know everything, and to save the World.

I loved my years at *In Context*, even though the work often made me depressed. The issues we covered (including population, global warming, the decline in the public schools) were not exactly lighthearted. Good news, our stock in trade, was difficult to find. Hidden away in our little subterranean think-tank in the rainy Northwest, it was hard to believe we could make a difference, even though we could see other flickering candles out there in what looked, to us, like darkness.

Then in 1990, I attended a sparkling conference in Los Angeles called the "Globescope Pacific Assembly." It was sponsored by a now-defunct organization called the Global Tomorrow Coalition, and it featured a host of luminaries; CNN-founder Ted Turner and former U.S. president Jimmy Carter were among the speakers. Around a thousand people gathered at the famous Biltmore Hotel to consider how to end poverty, slow population growth, and rescue the global environment. I was thrilled to see evidence that we were not alone in our crusade, but I was also greatly disturbed by the experience, in a very useful way.

Globescope marked a turning point for me. At that conference, with its All-American ice sculptures and celebrities and *hors d'oeuvres*, situated two blocks away from a less-fortunate street lined with Mexican *taquerias*, homeless persons, and stores selling cheap images of the Virgin Mary, I had an epiphany. I listened to the speeches about global warming and ozone depletion and the scourge of poverty, delivered by well-to-do people who had arrived in large kerosene-burning jets to enjoy the CFC–air-conditioned luxuries of the Biltmore and its low-wage immigrant serving staff, and I thought, "We're done for."

Any civilization, my epiphany went on to say, whose most well-informed and influential leaders could experience the discrepancy between what they declared to be absolutely necessary for planetary survival on the one hand, and how they personally conducted their lives on the other, without collapsing into sobs of repentance or hoots of self-mocking and ironic laughter—such a civilization probably faced long odds.

Call it denial, call it rationalization, call it very bad taste, but the phenomenon appeared to be almost universal, and I was hardly exempt from it. At the Globescope Pacific Assembly, most people's idea of globally responsible living was to make sure their recycling bin was placed by the curb on Tuesday night. There were, I knew, a great number of people in the industrialized parts of the World who had struggled to extricate themselves from the onrush of technology and consumerism, to "live lightly on the Earth," but I was not one of them. I liked technology. Living without its comforts in contemporary North America seemed to me like camping out in the backyard: it's fun for a night, but it's a relief to have a hot shower in the morning.

By the time I met them, the Gilmans had retreated back to a simple but comfortable suburban life, driven by stress and illness. The hard work of self-reliance, the challenge of running a magazine, and an increasing allergy to the wood in his own house had left Robert chronically ill. But some of these retrograde pioneers had succeeded, leading exemplary, even saintly lives of simplicity and integrity. (Scott and Helen Nearing, radical back-to-the-landers extraordinaire and authors of *Living the Good Life*, come to mind.) They could go to their graves content with the knowledge that their contribution to flattened rain forests, oppressed child labor, and rising seas had been virtually nil. For the record, I considered myself to be in a middle ground of virtue, somewhere between the humble saints and the hypocritical Pharisees, because I rode my bicycle to work and composted my kitchen waste in a worm bin.

But saints are rare. It was frankly ridiculous to believe that billions of people might follow their example and aspire to a low-consumption life. At the same time, it was hardly possible for the World to simply stop producing dangerous substances like fossil fuels, given that the entire agricultural sector depended on them. And nothing was going to stop the planet's growing numbers of people from wanting sneakers, screen-savers, high-quality dental work, and rather nifty cars.

Based on the evidence at hand, symbolized by the strange ironies of Globescope, it seemed likely that the disconnection between global imperatives and societal responses was somehow built into the structure the World, rather than issuing from any lack of data or correctable moral lapse on the part of humanity.

The situation, I realized, was fundamentally absurd.

▲▼▲

Absurdity is an enormously liberating idea. I would take absurdity over original sin, the wheel of karma, or the Buddha's "Four Noble Truths" any day of the week. (I'm especially not fond of Noble Truth Number

One, which is the idea that "life is suffering." "Life is absurd" has a much better ring.) Absurdity is particularly helpful at times of planetary crisis, because by embracing absurdity, you open the door to that great *Reader's Digest* medical prescription, laughter.

So it came to pass that after years of moral outrage, somber reflection, and earnest lament for our predicament here on Earth, punctuated by episodes of dark mourning and even darker cynicism, I began learning how to laugh.

It started awkwardly, even furtively, in a café at the back of the Biltmore Hotel, during a break in the Globescope conference. I was sitting with my friends Vicki Robin (who, inspired by the ironies of Globescope, went on to write the bestseller *Your Money or Your Life*), Duane Elgin (author of *Voluntary Simplicity*, who was soon to complete his magnum opus on the evolution of consciousness, *Awakening Earth*), and the irrepressible Diane Gilman, an artist who loved to dance. The four of us were in a booth, shaking our heads ruefully at the proceedings inside the hotel. Had we been Parisian, we would have been dragging smoke off our *gaulois*, sipping tiny cups of thick black coffee, and quoting Sartre's *Nausea* to each other. Instead, we started telling "Dead Planet Jokes."

These were similar to a popular form of tasteless, offensive, juvenile humor known in America as "Dead Baby Jokes," but our jokes were far less funny. They do not bear repeating. They did, however, get me started on something.

By the end of the conference, I had begun to hum a little melody. By the end of the next week, it had become a song. The song was the "Dead Planet Blues," and it was sung (and growled) from the perspective of the Creator, nursing a beer in some cosmic bar-room equivalent of "Cheers."

> Pull up a star and hear my tale of woe
> I built a planet just a few billion years ago
> It was a lovely little blue-green ball . . .
> One of my life-forms became self-aware
> They started messin' with my recipe for air

And now that planet's got no life at all! Yeah, it's a . . .
Dead Planet
(Yeah, I'm just gettin' back from the funeral . . .)
Dead Planet
(Don'tcha hate it when they leave the casket open?)
I got them old Dead Planet Blues . . .

After a hard day of editing, which generally involved poring over the ever-more-harrowing news about the relentless unfolding of Growth-fueled global disaster, it was an enormous comfort to sing the "Dead Planet Blues" to myself as I biked or walked to the ferry. Apparently I wasn't alone in my need to laugh in the teeth of a slow-motion tragedy that most people didn't even know was happening. When I began, tentatively at first, to sing it in public, the response was surprising. "Dead Planet Blues" became my most-requested song. College radio stations in the Pacific Northwest played my homemade cassette recording of it. After ten years of songwriting and performing, "Dead Planet Blues" was the closest thing I had ever experienced to a hit single.

So I wrote more songs, with titles like "Whole Lotta Shoppin' Goin' On" and "The Extinction Blues" ("The dodo bird's gone bye-bye / The great auk squawked its last . . ."). Perversely, they put a spring in my step, and a smile on my face. Neither the songs nor the laughter changed the fact that certain aspects of the World were going to hell in a handbasket, but they made the work of putting fingers in the dike less depressing. And ultimately, this linkage of music and song to the intellectual work of seeking solutions to global problems began opening doors, and hearts, in ways I did not expect.

▲▼▲

Csopak, Hungary
August 1994

It's midnight. I've come by myself to the shore of Lake Balaton for my ritual swim. There's a storm across the lake, and the water's freezing, but I take off all my clothes and wade in anyway.

It still amazes me that I'm here. This is my second time attending the annual meeting of the Balaton Group, an international network of leading thinkers in the field of global systems. The group was founded by Dana and Dennis Meadows. It's strange: years ago I was deeply moved by their little book, The Limits to Growth. *Now the authors have become friends.*

Although I've been invited both times to give professional presentations, it seems that my real contribution to the proceedings is music. This group of highly accomplished scientists, government officials, foundation executives, and activist-researchers likes to sing and be sung to. My guitar seems more important than my overhead transparencies.

The group loves the eco-satire songs like "Dead Planet," but they also need to be uplifted. Dana has several times "commissioned" me to write something more inspirational, but somehow, that's harder.

My mind is racing. We call it the "Balaton Buzz." Urban planning in India gives you new ideas about civic activism in Seattle. A media campaign in Thailand inspires a brainstorm on initiatives for Central America. You don't have to keep politely quiet, as you often do with people back home, about what's happening to the planet. Everybody here knows all too well.

I should probably get out of the lake. The storm is still distant, but it's moving this way, throwing off lightning. Peals of thunder are rippling over the water.

But something is keeping me here. I'm not a church-going man anymore, but the feeling at this moment reminds me of those days, as a child, when I would go into the empty church alone, after Sunday services, and pray. I was drawn there by a mixture of fear and awe, joy and trepidation. I'm feeling similarly now. It's as though there's a prayer that needs to be said, here in this place.

I start to speak the prayer out loud, and it comes out as a song.

▲▽▲

To speak about profound emotion is difficult. Words do not suffice. Yet they must be pressed into service. Words are the way we signal to each other, across space and time, about the content of our intimate experience: the truth as we see it and feel it. And when the words are carried on the breath by melody and rhythm, so much the better, for songs unearth the words from a deeper place in the singer, and deliver them more powerfully to the listener.

Through music, I've learned to expand the range of what I can say to other people about what I know about these times, and what I feel about them. Just as many people write in order to find out what they think, I sing in order to know what I think *and* feel. As a 1940s-era Broadway songwriter known as the "Lemon-Drop Kid" explained it once, "Music helps you feel your feelings, and words help you think your thoughts, but a song helps you feel a thought."

That is why making music, for me and for so many people, is such an essential companion in times like these. Music, poetry, painting, dance . . . many people I know who wrestle with Cassandra's Dilemma find solace—as well as hope, and vision, and inspiration—in the arts. The arts permit the expansion of the sphere of intimacy. They are a refuge of humanness in a universe that is essentially nonhuman and mute. Simply by existing, the arts defy the impersonal forces of Nature, the mechanical and digital systems of the World, the ignominy of one's fellow human beings. They persist even when oppression, fear, and ignorance are rampant on every side. Somehow, when direct words of warning, or fear, or anger about the troubles in the World cannot be said, or will not be acknowledged by the culture, a song can still find an audience. A poem can still find a reader. We can still feel heard, even if only by an audience of one, or two: oneself, one's partner. That is a beginning.

▲▼▲

Washington, D.C.
11 January 1999

The Potomac is frozen, and the capital city of the World's most powerful nation is slick with ice. Everyone is distracted and titillated by a presidential sex scandal that most of the World views as ridiculous. I hear a cryptic news report on the radio: "Scientists reported today that 1998 was the warmest year on record, with global surface temperature setting new highs by a wide margin. And on the New York Stock Exchange, prices rose slightly higher in heavy trading . . . "

At dinner, my friend Peter, a well-connected environmental leader, is incensed about the ineffectiveness of the nation's largest and most powerful environmental groups. "Their only reason for existence is to raise money," he complains. "The three largest groups could all disappear tomorrow, and the only impact would be the sudden availability of their combined budget of $100 million, money that could then be better spent on real work."

Peter's got inside information that Vice-President Gore—author of Earth in the Balance—*signed an internal memo urging the nation's top environmental official not to implement new restrictions on pesticides in food. Peter is disgusted, and he's getting tired of trying to work the political process. He wants to work on promoting cultural change instead. "The system's just too corrupt," he says bitterly. "We're never going to get anywhere."*

That night, on e-mail, I read a newspaper column by Donella Meadows. Despite being as knowledgeable as anyone in the world about global trends, Dana is usually cheerful. She holds fast to the belief that we can turn the tide, just in time, with a combination of ingenuity, wisdom, and love. Her scientific analyses suggest that if we wanted to, we could eliminate poverty and heal Nature. I admire her optimism; on my best days, I share it.

But this week's column is about despair. She'd spent a day learning about the state of shrimp fisheries, the spread of AIDS in Africa, the butchering of endangered species caused by the financial crisis in Indonesia. "I gave up," she writes, explaining why she had to put her head down on her desk and weep. "Too much is going wrong too fast. I'm powerless over any of it. Maybe I should just quit writing, researching, farming, teaching, get a job that pays real money, eat shrimp while they last, and zonk out on television.

"Of course I won't do any of that. But there are days when I wonder why not."

▲▼▲

Consciousness of our predicament is an extremely difficult burden. Knowing that the World (or any piece of it that you love) is hurtling toward disaster, and feeling like there's nothing you can do to stop it, nothing you can do to be heard, can be painfully frustrating, not to mention depressing, terrifying, and downright annoying. It is essential to find ways to express those feelings. They are legitimate. They are real. If denied, they can freeze you in cynicism and bitterness. When expressed, they can fuel you to action. And when received and understood by others, these feelings can catalyze the process of escape from Cassandra's Dilemma.

Joanna Macy, a gifted teacher who describes herself as a "Buddhist scholar," has been helping people work with such complex feelings for many years. She creates environments for people to express their emotions about what is happening to the World and to Nature, in creative and ritualistic ways. For some people, this can be an essential help; society at large does not provide many safe situations for expressing strong emotion of any kind, much less grief for lost species, or despair about the difficulties bequeathed to future generations. Many people are afraid even to acknowledge such feelings. Joanna's workshops show them that it is possible to feel strong emotion and survive, even to be strengthened.

Joanna Macy and Australian rain forest activist John Seed created a ritual that has been popular with people from many different backgrounds and religious traditions. Called "The Council of All Beings," it involves making masks of various creatures on planet Earth—people, animals, and plants of all kinds—including the Beings of the past and the future. Participants choose a mask based on what they are drawn to, and then, in a council setting, each gets the opportunity to speak the imagined hope, fear, grief, anger, or vision of that Being. For some people, especially those who have previously had difficulty expressing their feelings about what they know to be happening, the experience can be transformative.

Innovations for helping people contend with the strong feelings associated with Cassandra's Dilemma are multiplying and taking many different forms. Joanna Macy and John Seed are part of a philosophical movement that is also very experiential, a movement called "deep ecology." An entire new branch of psychology, "ecopsychology," has been growing in recent years, as people search for reasons why humans are so estranged from Nature, and sometimes for therapeutic help with the powerful emotions they feel. Mainstream religions are also, increasingly, waking up to the gravity of this moment, and providing people of faith with an opportunity to mourn, to hope, and to pray for the Earth. Many traditional religious leaders, from the Dalai Lama, to the Pope, to the Patriarch of Eastern Orthodoxy have declared humanity responsible for the well-being of Nature, and environmental initiatives are growing ever-deeper roots in Christianity, Judaism, Buddhism, and Islam.

If you are new to Cassandra's Dilemma, be assured that there are many ways to find solace and inspiration. It doesn't matter whether you are more comfortable following a path that is philosophical or artistic, psychological or religious. It doesn't matter whether the forms of expression you use are contemporary, or ancient, or a mixture of both. My own reckoning with Cassandra's Dilemma has taken different forms at different times, from helping to start a mainstream Christian environmental organization, to visiting with Native American spiritual leaders, to participating in the innovative expressions of deep ecology. In each of these contexts, I have often found the greatest consolation, and the greatest revival of my sense of hope, in the intimacy of ritual.

▲▼▲

Whidbey Island, Washington
July 1995

The fire is like a dancer. I have been watching it all night. Mostly we sit in silence, but every so often one of us will start a song, or say a prayer.

The vigil was convened by Elias Amidon, a writer on nature and spirituality. It began at dusk, when the first sticks were ignited, and it will end when the Sun warms this part of the Earth again with its own resplendent fire. Psychologist Robert Greenway has been keeping a soft drum going all night, like a heartbeat.

We are mourning the animals and the cultures that have disappeared.

We are keeping watch over this patch of ground, this encampment. We are safeguarding its passage through the night.

We are watching for signs of morning, waiting to see what the future will be like. We are preparing ourselves to meet that future.

When dawn comes, we stand up and look around. The world is still there. Sand is shoveled on the fire. The dew, as we walk down toward breakfast, is like cold silver on our feet.

▲▼▲

Being in Cassandra's Dilemma forces us to live with fears and uncertainties about the future. But we must also bear our knowledge of the past, and our awareness of what has already been sacrificed to Growth. The World most of us were born into is gone, and gone with it are a great many things that were precious—or that would have been precious, had we known them.

When I was a child growing up in Florida, my family was adopted by a manatee. It spent its summers in the marina where we kept our sailboat, at the south end of Merritt Island. Most summer days it would swim up to our slip and wait, and my sister and I would paddle out in our lifeboat to say hello.

The manatee was eight feet long, weighed a thousand pounds, and was as docile as a house cat. It had the usual scars across its back from encounters with boat propellers. We had a ritual game we played: the manatee would push us in our little rowboat for a few yards, and then she would roll her belly up in the air to be scratched. (We knew it was a "she," because one year she arrived with a calf.) Gobs of gray manatee skin would get stuck under our finger nails.

So when, twenty years later, I learned the story of the gigantic arctic manatee known as Steller's sea cow—extinct since 1768, wiped out by human hunters in the span of twenty-seven years—I wept like a child. It was as though I were eleven years old again and had lost an animal companion.

Perhaps the hardest thing about this grief was the loneliness that came with it, the knowledge that very few human beings were sharing it. None of us alive would ever know the awkward beauty and simple kindliness of those great creatures. No television or film crews existed to record their quiet lives in the Bering Sea, no *National Geographic* expeditions went to observe them in their habitats. These extraordinary manatees simply vanished. They were transformed into food for our ancestors, and forgotten.

"For one species to mourn the death of another," wrote Aldo Leopold of the passenger pigeon's extinction, "is a new thing under the sun. The Cro-Magnon who slew the last mammoth thought only of steaks. The sportsman who shot the last pigeon thought only of his prowess. The sailor who clubbed the last auk thought of nothing at all. But we, who have lost our pigeons, mourn the loss."

Our capacity to mourn for an animal that has disappeared into the distant past is evidence that we are evolving—evidence that has been produced at a terrible price. As Aldo Leopold went on to say, "Had the funeral been ours, the pigeons would hardly have mourned us." Ours is both an essential grief, and an absurd one.

▲▼▲

Hermannsdorf, Germany
September 1997

Today, I am a wandering minstrel. I have come with Dana Meadows and our friend Joan Davis, a prominent aquatic chemist, to visit the extraordinary organic farm created by Karl Ludwig von Schweisfurth. I have been instructed to bring my guitar.

Karl Ludwig is an enormously rich man of enormous vision. After an ecological epiphany, he sold his enormous company—the largest meat-packing company in Germany—and created the enormous farm called Hermannsdorf, where the enormous pigs get plenty of sunshine and the enormous cheeses practically vibrate in your mouth. "It's alive," Karl Ludwig likes to say about the cheese. "You won't taste anything like it, anywhere else."

As farms go, Hermannsdorf is luxurious. There is light, and art, everywhere. Karl Ludwig has commissioned many artists to create unique works for the place, many with ecological themes. Some of these pieces are outdoors and gigantic, on the scale of earthworks.

He and his wife, Dorothee (do-ro-TAY), are touring us around the place, and here's where the minstrel bit comes in. At each artistic installation, he asks me to choose an appropriate song of mine, and perform it. It's hard to say no to a man like Karl Ludwig. I feel like I'm reliving some past life where I wandered around Europe, entertaining the Lords and Ladies on their estates.

One typical installation looks like a miniature Stonehenge: huge, upright stones, set in an ellipse. You walk in, and engraved on the stones are the names of every animal species to go extinct by the hands of humanity. It's emotionally overwhelming, much like a Holocaust memorial. I sing "Extinction Blues," but the song seems to lose its already tenuous humor.

Scenes like this get repeated over the course of the day. I'm moved by the monumental nature of Hermannsdorf, but an awkward feeling of sadness and absurdity shadows me all day. Then we come to the cows.

Our tour ends at a nondescript cow pasture, and I'm not sure why. "You must sing to the cows," says Karl Ludwig. Apparently I look puzzled, because Dorothee closes her eyes and nods as if to say, "Yes, you must." Oh, what the heck, I say to myself. Who will ever know.

The cows seem a little skittish, so I choose a quiet love song, based on a poem by Rainier Maria Rilke. I try to croon it to them, making my voice velvety and seductive, as though coaxing them to approach the fence. They look increasingly concerned. Finally, as I'm about to finish the song, a couple of cows turn, lift their tails, and begin emitting bountiful volumes of urine.

It's hard to give my closing notes their usual emotional resonance. But then Dorothee is there at my side, patting my arm in a motherly way, soothing my distress. "That's good," she says. "That means they liked it. It's the way they do applause."

▲▼▲

I have, on occasion, been chastised by a few of my professional colleagues for singing songs such as "Dead Planet Blues." "Too ironic," they say. "People walk away feeling distressed about having been encouraged to laugh at something so painful." The possible End of the World, in their view, is serious business. Levity is inappropriate.

But in my experience, human beings have a limitless emotional capacity. We can take it all—the grief, the absurdity, and even the laughter. Like Patch Adams, the real-life jester and medical doctor portrayed by Robin Williams in a 1998 Hollywood movie, I believe we *need* the laughter. The laughter reminds us that at the most fundamental level, we don't really understand what's happening, or what's going to happen.

We know something about what has transpired on Planet Earth over the past millennia, and we can make some good guesses, with the aid of science and computer models, about what is likely to happen during the next hundred. But we have no idea what it all means. Nor can we ever know. We are stuck in not knowing. Such a situation is the precise definition of absurdity, the message of the great absurdist plays like Beckett's *Waiting for Godot*. "Well? Shall we go?" asks Vladimir at the play's end. "Yes, let's go," replies Estragon. *They do not move*, says Beckett's stage direction. *Curtain*.

In dealing with Cassandra's Dilemma, it helps to keep this absurdity at the forefront of one's mind, where it can rightfully be the object of laughter, tears, or a quizzical shake of the head, depending on one's mood. There is no "right way to feel" about the possibility of global collapse. All emotions are appropriate. In my own wrestling with grief, fear, and uncertainty about the future, I take inspiration from the Italian writer Umberto Eco. In his classic novel *The Name of the Rose*, Eco wrote:

> Perhaps the mission of those who love mankind is to make people laugh at the truth, TO MAKE TRUTH LAUGH, because the only truth lies in learning to free ourselves from this insane passion for the truth.

No matter how clear our foresight, no matter how accurate our computer models, a belief about the future should never be mistaken for the truth. The future, as such, never occurs. It becomes the present. And no matter how well we prepare ourselves, when the imagined future becomes the very real present, it never fails to surprise.

CHAPTER 6

Armageddon, Utopia, or Both?

*The major advances in civilization are processes that all but wreck
the societies in which they occur.*
                    —ALFRED NORTH WHITEHEAD

The worst way to improve the world is to condemn it.
                    —PHILIP JAMES BAILEY

P ROPHECY MAY NOT BE THE
oldest profession, but it is certainly one of the most venerable. The
Bible's Old Testament, known to Jews as the Torah, is full of the accounts of prophets, most of whom were well-versed in the agonies of
Cassandra's Dilemma. In story after story, people are warned to
change their ways, but few pay heed. Many are consequently destroyed, or at least "smitten," by God. Disgusted by the wickedness
of His human creations, God first drowns the entire World in a great
flood without so much as a "last chance to mend your ways" message. Noah, the ark-builder, starts the World over again, and pre-

sumably God expects that this time around, human beings will have a keener sensitivity to the rules and regulations. Alas, they don't, and so a string of prophets (Moses, Daniel, Jeremiah, et al.) must labor on with the business of warning. The slave-holding Egyptians are warned to let the Israelites go, but they ignore Moses and end up losing their first-born sons in a divine massacre. The immoral inhabitants of Sodom and Gomorrah are warned of their impending doom, but they orgy on toward destruction nonetheless. And of course, out of Judaism grew another religion—Christianity—which introduced the greatest prophecy of doom in Western history: the vision of the apocalypse in the Revelations of St. John, with its horrific imagery of an evil Beast, four deadly Horsemen, and general fiery unpleasantness for those unfortunate enough to be alive at the end of time.

Apocalyptic visions of the end of the World are not limited to the Judeo-Christian tradition. Many ancient belief systems, from Hindu to Hopi, include the provision that things are likely to get worse—much, much worse—before they fall apart completely. Beliefs vary widely on when these competing versions of Armageddon might occur. A few contemporary Mayans who are popular on the New Age circuit preach that collapse will happen relatively soon (the year 2012), while Hindu texts suggest we are in the midst of a several-hundred-thousand-year-long slide known as the Kali Yuga.

Whether or not you are a believer in religious prophecies, some of them have shaped global civilization and its relationship to the future in important ways. For one example, a deeply ingrained belief in Western culture, at the subconscious level, is that societies and peoples who sin get punished, usually by divine catastrophe. For another example, many of these age-old stories suggest that global apocalypse, followed by the dawning of a new era, might be a good thing—*après le déluge*, the rainbow. The attitudes that arise from such beliefs show up in surprising places, far from the Jewish temple, the Christian church, or the New Age Mayan workshop. Confronting the subtle influence of these attitudes is an important step in breaking out of Cassandra's Dilemma.

No matter how much most people would deny this response, the idea of welcoming or even encouraging the advent of catastrophe can have a certain grotesque appeal. To start, the catastrophe may bring vindication to the marginalized prophet. (Imagine the feeling of relief experienced by Moses when the plague of frogs arrived in Egypt, right on schedule.) Notice that some religious prophets do not seem regretful when their warnings go unheeded; they almost seem to prefer the destruction of their depraved audience over a last-minute conversion and reprieve. Especially for the prophet who has been scoffed at, to be proven right about the wages of wickedness might seem a sweet revenge. A hearty "There, I told you so!" brings with it the pleasure of self-righteous satisfaction. But this feeling is not to be confused with success. Success for a prophet, let us not forget, is *repentance*, a "turning back," a change in behavior that results in the *avoidance* of doomsday.

If it seems unnecessary to remind the reader of so basic a truth, I must regretfully inform you that a number of contemporary prophets seem all too ready to welcome the advent of Armageddon. In addition to those of an apocalyptic religious bent—whose obsessions are never more evident than at the turn of a millennium—one strain of the environmental movement would be profoundly disappointed if the World sped down its present course, giving only perfunctory nods to warnings about global warming, species extinction, and the like, and did not ultimately face disastrous consequences. It would undermine environmentalism's core belief in the fragility of Nature and, more critically, the growing conviction that the only way to solve global problems is to proselytize consumer self-denial.

The fact that human beings are contentedly engaged in making and selling this World on the one hand, and buying it on the other, is a great disappointment to some people. Indeed, there are some who so dislike the World that is being created through the forces of consumer capitalism that a collapse is actually seen as the preferred outcome. Nothing else, in some people's minds, can reduce population and the impact of technology to a level that will save Nature from near-complete destruction. Nothing else can wake up humanity to the spiritual horror of lusting after ever-bigger cars and shopping malls. According to this line of reasoning, given our greed and ignorance and lack of concern, we probably deserve obliteration.

Cassandras like these, prophets in the Old Testament tradition, are the people I describe as "longing for the end of the World," or at least for an end to this version of the World, with its mindless consumer fads and greed-driven free-market race for riches. I do not deny that most consumer fads are mindless, or that much of what passes for commerce in this World is essentially a con game where the most cunning and merciless get rewarded with cash. But I am making the case for expunging, as a first step out of Cassandra's Dilemma, any subtle attachment you might have to the medicinal benefits of global collapse. As long as part of you, especially an unacknowledged part, secretly hopes for the end to come, it will undermine your ability to prevent that catastrophe.

For the environmentalist, the challenge is to be pro-Nature without being anti-World. For the champion of ending poverty and injustice, the challenge is to love the poor and oppressed without hating the rich and powerful. It is possible to develop Gandhian compassion for people as they are, including people who seem to oppose your values, without indulging in self-righteousness.

If you want to change the World, you must first accept the fact that some aspects of human nature are fundamentally unchangeable— or at least, not changeable in time to create a massive cultural transformation that results in quasi-monastic, Nature-friendly, loving-kindness lifestyles worldwide. For now, we humans are restless, acquisitive, fearful, greedy, and easily manipulated by promises of love and power and sex. We are desirous of comfort and luxury and prestige, and we occasionally kill each other. We have many more noble qualities besides, of course, and individuals vary widely in their level of depravity, from Mother Theresa to _____ (fill in the name of the person you think of as most symbolic of our least saintly qualities). But even the saints have shadows.

Here's the bottom line: bemoaning humanity's faults, or prophetically condemning our species to extinction because we are not picking up on Nature's warning signs, will not save the World, or Nature, or you. Cheering on the apocalypse can only result in one of two very undesirable outcomes: apocalypse, or profound alienation from the rest of your fellow human beings.

In Oregon some years ago, a satirical group whose name encapsulated the anti-World point of view succinctly preached not just zero population growth, but zero population, achieved by the cessation of human breeding. They called themselves the Voluntary Human Extinction Movement, which somehow got shortened to "VHEMNT" (pronounced "vehement"). "Leave Nature to the animals" was their fictional philosophy. "Humanity is a failed experiment. Let's just call it quits." But like the Shakers before them—an eighteenth century Christian sect who abstained completely from sex, in order to bring themselves closer to the divine—actual adherents to the VHEMNT philosophy would probably nonbreed themselves to oblivion before their views could have much of an impact.

Less extreme but more serious versions of that point of view can be found in many circles, from deep woods encampments of "Earth First!" to the offices of well-known scientists. But promoting such views can be dangerous. Though most critics of humanity's excessive presence on the Earth are quick to distance themselves from extremists, all share something in common with the Unabomber, an American back-to-the-land hermit who took a variant of this view to a far extreme. Ted Kaczynski committed murder by letter-bomb in order to slow the march of technological progress and to call attention to his anti-technology, pro-Nature philosophy. He managed to get his "manifesto" published in the *New York Times* and the *Washington Post*, but neither his argument nor his prose were compelling enough to do more than raise eyebrows and lead the FBI to his hideaway. The violence of his protests may have set the work of his more responsible nonviolent counterparts back ten years.

The Unabomber demonstrated a very inappropriate way to relieve the anxiety of Cassandra's Dilemma: instead of waiting around for the end of the World, attempt to engineer it. This is not a path to be recommended—and not just because of the moral and legal imperatives against murder, which this author heartily endorses. A sudden, engineered collapse of industrial civilization would likely cause even greater havoc, human suffering, and ecological ruin than a "natural" one of the kind modeled in World3. A mad, slow scramble for food and resources spread over a generation would be horrible enough. A sudden cessation of the systems keeping humanity fed and sheltered and occupied would add the element of mass panic; it would be like setting fire to a theater with over six billion people in it.

This nightmare scenario is similar to the one imagined by Y2K extremists: global computer shutdown plunges humanity into chaos and destruction from which we never fully recover. A collapse of this kind has also been imagined by scores of science fiction writers. The French author René Barjavel, in his 1943 classic *Ravage*, imagined a world where electricity simply ceases to work. The result he envisioned was mass mayhem, the emptying of cities, and a speedy return to near Stone Age conditions ("Ah, back to the land . . . with polygamy," sighed one contemporary French reviewer on a Web page). Many writers and filmmakers have reminded us that global nuclear war, followed by a nuclear winter, would surely create a comparable chaos and collapse, and that possibility remains with us as long as nuclear weapons do.

So we can picture many ways to that a global collapse might occur. But among true believers—those who suffer most profoundly from Cassandra's Dilemma, and live with a feeling of certainty that the end is approaching—one future scenario may be the most terrifying of all. This scenario is difficult for them to consider intellectually, and even more challenging to take in on an emotional level. For some, merely mentioning this scenario brings up staunch denial, because it undermines their very sense of identity. Yet it must be considered.

By now the reader is, perhaps, prepared for the worst.

There is always the possibility that everything will turn out fine.

▲▼▲

Playa del Carmen, Mexico
6 January 1999

The day is perfection. A light breeze pushes tiny waves up a beach of white sand. The sun is warm and delicate. Cold beers are close by.

My friend Rick—an expatriate developer of hotels on Mexico's fast-growing Caribbean coast—is explaining his views on global environmental trends, human destiny, and the grand sweep of history.

"The way I look at it, life is getting better for most people," he says cheerily, "and it will keep getting better. Population growth is already slowing down, and besides, people don't take up that much space. And there are lots of very positive things happening in the world. For instance, for the first time in history, most people can read. That's an astonishing development, considering that books were hoarded away by monks only a few hundred years ago. People are healthier. They're living longer. And they're more prosperous than at any other time in history. Of course a lot of people are poor; a lot of people have always *been poor. That doesn't change the fact that the overall trend, for the past several hundred years, is up."*

I start to protest. "But what about species extinction, what about . . ." But Rick is irrepressible in his pragmatic optimism, and interrupts me.

"Sure," he says, "we've lost some species, and we'll probably lose a lot more. But whenever we put our minds to it, we're almost always able to bring them back before they go extinct. Look at the great whales, or the wolves of Yellowstone. People thought they were gone, and now they're back. Maybe someday we'll even be able to bring back extinct species using genetic engineering."

It's hard to argue with this line of reasoning when you're sitting on the beach, sipping a beer, watching a parade of nearly nude people walk by. Still, I protest. "What about global . . ."

"Of course I'm worried about the global environment," Rick cuts in. "There are two really big problems: chemical pollution and climate change. We've spread toxic compounds all over the Earth, and a lot of people will suffer as a result. But I'm convinced that someday we'll develop a really

smart technology that will basically go out and find every unwanted poisonous molecule and clean it up.

"And yes, my hotel may eventually have to be rebuilt a little farther inland, thanks to rising sea levels and hurricanes. But human beings adapt. They suffer, but they adapt. There has always been suffering. And suffering is not Armageddon."

▲▼▲

What if, in the decades ahead, things get bad, but they don't really get *so* bad? What if the school of thought that believes that "human beings always find a way to muddle through" turns out to be the correct one? Or what if even the most wild-eyed techno-optimists turn out to have *under*estimated humanity's capacity to innovate, and we find safe and easy ways to fix global warming, bring back the dodo, restore huge tracts of wilderness by floating castles in the air, preserve indigenous cultures and languages by giving them huge endowments and sovereign nation-states, and provide everyone in the World their own matter transformer and flying Hypercar by the year 2050? What then?

If any of the above scenarios should occur, from "not so bad after all" to "peace, prosperity, and ecological restoration beyond your wildest dreams," a dedicated Cassandra should either take public credit for having helped to save the World, or privately breathe a huge sigh of relief.

There is, for example, a small-but-legitimate chance that the ninety-five-percent-plus majority of the world's climate scientists—and their computer climate models, and sophisticated climate projections—will turn out to be wrong. Or even just partly wrong. Yes, we have enormous amounts of data indicating that glaciers are melting, heat-loving species are migrating a little closer to the poles, El Niños are coming every four years instead of every seven, and so on. But the possibility that both Nature and the World will take all this more or less in stride, without much in the way of calamity or collapse, certainly deserves consideration (and that may even be the view that you hold). It's not absolutely impossible. And indeed, many well-informed and perfectly reasonable people believe this rosy scenario to be true, and a predominant optimism of this sort continues to be the foundation of the World system. So it behooves us to understand this perspective.

In fact, a Netherlands team has developed a computer-based global model—a direct descendant of World3—that helps us to do precisely that. The model is called TARGETS, and it does something no other global model has ever attempted. It incorporates differences in the ways human beings perceive the World.

TARGETS stands for "Tools to Assess Regional and Global Environmental and health Targets for Sustainability." It was developed by Jan Rotmans and Bert de Vries, together with a team of researchers at the Dutch government's National Institute for Public Health and the Environment, and documented in their 1997 book, *Perspectives on Global Change: The TARGETS Approach*. What TARGETS does is allow people to consider several major trends in global history—what has already happened since 1900, together with what is likely to happen up to the year 2100—from a number of different possible perspectives. The model does this by running its calculations on population, water, energy, land and food, and "biogeochemical cycles" (for example CO_2 in the atmosphere) through an additional analytical lens: culture.

Culture, or more accurately *cultural perspective*, has so far been missing from most quantitative analyses of global trends. TARGETS borrows from the work of cultural theorists including Michael Thompson, who categorizes people and societies in five main groupings: Individualists, Egalitarians, Hierarchists, Fatalists, and Hermits. (Thompson considers himself to be in the Hermit category, on the fringes of society, which gives him license to chuckle at the other four.) TARGETS considers what the past and the future of both Nature and the World look like from those different perspectives, and it puts credible numbers on the results.

Actually, TARGETS leaves out the Fatalists and Hermits, because they tend not to be active players in the system. They just go along for the ride. For Fatalists, "everything is a lottery," according to Rotmans and De Vries, and reality is "capricious." ("Life is like a box of chocolates," says the movie character Forrest Gump in a Fatalist moment. "You never know what you're gonna get.") And Hermits are, well, Hermits.

That leaves three kinds of active players in the game called the World: Individualists, Egalitarians, and Hierarchists. Let's consider them each in turn.

Individualists are believers in the ingenuity of human beings and the resilience of Nature. Nature is there for us to use, there's plenty of it to go around, we can't do much to hurt it, and if we do, technology will fix the problem. Any risk to Nature is worthwhile, because the rewards—freedom and prosperity for all—are too great to pass up. Human creativity, hard work, and the free market will carry us over any hurdles and up to unimagined heights. Think Newt Gingrich and Bill Gates.

Egalitarians hold quite the opposite view. Nature is already buckling under the pressure of humanity, and must be protected. No further risks should be taken or we will lose our planetary life-support system. We should guide people toward a more equitable, less environmentally damaging lifestyle. As the authors of *Beyond the Limits* write, in an exemplary Egalitarian phrase, "The future, to be viable at all, must be one of drawing back, easing down, healing." Think the Greens.

Hierarchists occupy a kind of middle ground, but with a twist. They believe in partnership and control. Stability is their core value. They will accept a certain amount of risk to Nature in pursuit of broader social goals. But they also think human nature is basically problematic, and only by a solid system of clear rules, regulations, and financial incentives can you prevent people from pushing Nature—or the World—too far. Think European bureaucrat.

To give you a fuller flavor of the differences between these types, consider the following sentence, written by Paul Robinson in his 1992 book, *The Third Revolution: Environment, Population, and a Sustainable World*:

> Human history is the history of increasing numbers, increasing consumption, and increasingly invasive and disruptive technology.

This is clearly an Egalitarian speaking. What if the sentence had been written by an Individualist like, say, the economist Julian Simon? It might go like this:

> Human history is the story of triumph over the terrors of nature, increasing mastery over the earth and its resources, and increasingly brilliant technological achievement.

And finally, here's a version that might have been penned by a Hierarchist—let's say a deputy minister for economic planning in Brussels:

> Human history is the record of a steadily rising population, meeting its needs through careful stewardship of both people and resources, and pursuing least-cost technological solutions to the inevitable problems encountered along the way, with the help of effective government and justly administered laws.

Notice that the Individualist seems to write the most sparkling, ad-ready prose. Most of commercial culture in the industrialized world is profoundly Individualist in nature. The Individualist holds out the promise of freedom, expresses pride in human progress, and celebrates opportunity ("Come to Marlboro country . . ."). Egalitarians, by comparison, tend to sound upset, earnest, and pessimistic ("We must save the Earth"). Hierarchist prose is very responsible and balanced, but boring. It's no wonder the Individualists currently run the World.

▲▼▲

When you program a computer to be a model of the World, and you instruct it to consider the progress of history from various cultural perspectives, a fascinating set of pictures begins to emerge. The designers of TARGETS called some of these pictures of the future "Utopias" and "Dystopias" (represented in their book by the usual charts and graphs, but we're using our imaginations here). For example, if you're an Egalitarian, and it turns out that you're right about the imminent danger to Nature and humanity, *and*, by stroke of political luck, you also get to decide what would happen in the World over the next hundred years—well then, you would create an Egalitarian Utopia. (Being an Egalitarian, you wouldn't do it alone; you'd convene a large and participatory consensus process.) This is not to say that the World would then be perfect, but it would be as Green as you could make it, given what you had to start with in the Year 2000. You'd slow down economic growth, put a very high tariff on oil, and tax the rich to feed the poor. You'd probably consider "voluntarily mandatory" controls on population as well. Nature would be saved (in part), and people would have enough to eat—but there might be less happening downtown on a Friday night.

By contrast, if the Individualists ran the World, and if their assumptions about the World and Nature turned out to be right, the resulting future Utopia would be a wildly successful economic party that slows down of its own accord, just in time to save Nature, and after everyone in the World has gotten a nice house, a sports utility vehicle, and a fat stock portfolio.

Finally, the Hierarchist's Utopia would be a not-too-bad, just-a-few-huge-problems, we've-set-up-departments-to-study-the-options sort of World. It's not much to write home about.

But what happens if you're an Egalitarian, and you're in charge of the World, but you're totally wrong about the way Nature and the World work? What if it turns out the Individualists were right all along? You slow down growth and increase taxes . . . and thereby create the Individualist's *Dys*topia, the worst of all possible worlds from the Individualist's perspective. People who could have been saved from poverty by economic growth are still struggling along without indoor plumbing. All the lost profits, all the lost technological innovation . . . it wouldn't be Armageddon, but there would be needless suffering and a severe shortage of golf courses.

As annoying as that might be, the reverse scenario—the Egalitarian Dystopia—is far more frightening: The Individualists are in charge, but the Egalitarians are correct in their ominous prophecies. The results would be rather like a popular story that has floated around the Internet for years, about a man who strapped a couple of surplus rocket engines to his car, and lit the fuse. He had a fast, exciting ride, which ended rather suddenly when he smashed into a cliff eight miles away, crushing his car to the thickness of a pancake. (Rockets have no brakes.) The Egalitarian Dystopia is what people in Cassandra's Dilemma fear most: explosive Growth, followed by overshoot and collapse.

Obviously, it matters quite a lot whose assumptions are right. It also matters a great deal who's in charge. As the designers of the TARGETS model put it, in their restrained academic prose:

> If the world is a place of abundance . . . [and] emerging problems are tackled with pioneering ingenuity, humankind will follow a path that is sometimes dangerous but never catastrophic. If, on the other hand, life is an intricate and vulnerable web of connections easily destroyed or impoverished, it would be foolish and irresponsible to continue unconstrained growth.

That "If" is one of the largest "Ifs" in the history of human civilization. Humanity's choices for the future amount to a tremendous gamble. The choices have been the same since the Egalitarian authors of *The Limits to Growth* first tried to suggest that humanity should slow down Growth in favor of Development, only to be met by scoffing Individualist and Hierarchist retorts that even faster Growth was, instead, the wisest course. It is clear which way the dice have been cast over the past three decades.

Yet it is possible, and helpful, to imagine the roles reversed. If the voices in favor of more rapid economic expansion to solve the World's problems—Individualists all—had been nudged aside in 1972, and had watched in horror as a Green-obsessed humanity gently stifled the economic goose that could have continued laying golden eggs, they might feel trapped and frustrated and fearful of the future. They might be issuing dark predictions, and feeling ignored. They would be the ones who needed songs of solace and quotations of Brecht's poetry ("In the dark time, will there be singing? / Yes, there will be singing about the dark time"). And it is entirely possible, though not very probable, that they would be right.

But that is not the World we live in. Growth, Individualist-style, is the name of the game. Egalitarians huddle together in think-tanks, universities, and activist groups, looking for ways to pull the emergency brake. Hierarchists in government and the United Nations try to keep the peace and fashion compromise solutions. (There are exceptions to this summary, as in Germany, where the Greens are currently sharing authority in the central government.) Meanwhile, the scientific data seems to favor the notion that Nature is a rather delicate flower whose petals are being plucked off. Only the Egalitarians, not surprisingly, seem to give such data the attention it probably deserves. From their perspective, we are rushing headlong into the rough waters of Dystopia. Meanwhile, the Egalitarians continue to enjoy certain benefits of business-as-usual (including foundation grants and university tenure), while only the Individualists and Hierarchists seem to understand (and control) the World-as-it-is well enough to change the status quo.

Voilà, Cassandra's Dilemma, with all its absurdity, its complexity, its demand for a more creative strategy for changing the World.

▲▼▲

Somewhere over North Dakota
Summer 1996

From my window seat in this Boeing 737, I have the illusion of being poised motionless over a near-empty landscape of breathtaking beauty. But in my mental landscape, it feels as though I am poised between two different worlds.

I love flying. To be honest, I love the whole technological infrastructure of Western civilization, from the airports to the car rental agencies to the highways that carry me with such ease wherever I want to go, together with the stores that supply me with food, the comfortable hotel rooms with Internet hookups for my laptop, the coffee shops and movie houses and bookstores where I spend my leisure time. I know all too well the ecological damage this civilization is causing, the crazy economics on which it's built. But this knowledge doesn't change the fact that I enjoy, immensely, this amazing and comfortable way of life.

I've also lived in a one-room cottage in Malaysia, showered with a bucket, scrubbed my clothes by hand—and I enjoyed that too. But when I realized that, like me, most people seem to prefer the cities-and-planes-and-e-mail lifestyle, I became more interested in understanding how to redesign the World so that people could do what they liked without destroying the planet. Hence my double life.

For the past few days, I've been facilitating a national training for senior executives in a very large telecommunications company. The company had decided that its leaders needed to learn about political campaigning, and they hired the biggest names in the business, from both sides of the political aisle. These household-name experts taught the group how to do political strategy, image-making, polling, advertising, even how to create a phony grassroots group.

My job as a consultant was to help design and moderate this complex series of lectures, workshops, and planning sessions. I found myself having lunch with the creators of Democratic Party TV ads, and dinner with the Republican architects of Ronald Reagan's presidency (a fact that would appall some friends, but please my departed grandmother). I learned a lot, but I also felt like a spy with a secret identity.

When I land in Seattle, I will drive immediately to an island retreat center in the heart of the rain forest, where I will teach at a summer school on deep ecology. There will be songs and prayers and rituals. There will be small-group conversations on the intricacies of Nature, the tragedy of what is happening to peoples and environments everywhere, and the evils of the corporate system. I appreciate these gatherings because they allow such freedom of self-expression far more than is permitted in the world of business. But again I will feel like a spy with a secret identity.

Among the deep ecologists, I don't say much about my corporate consulting work. But I don't hide the fact that I live in a group house in Berkeley, California, that was formerly a Zen monastery. If I mentioned my current living situation to my clients, some of them would cease to be clients. If I explained my consulting work in detail to the deep ecologists, I probably wouldn't be invited back.

How to reconcile these two lives, these two perspectives on the World? There is truth, and merit, in both of them. The ecologists understand what's happening to the planet. The business people understand what it really takes to create economic value, and also how to sell new ideas. Increasingly, I will be searching for something many people in both business and the environmental movement are searching for: synthesis.

▲▼▲

Obviously, the real World is not neatly broken into categories like "Individualist" and "Egalitarian." But familiarity with these differences in perspective can help in understanding why some people are grieving over the fate of the Earth, while others are singing "Don't Worry, Be Happy." Some look at global warming and see ecological catastrophe; others see longer summers in Siberia. It takes all kinds, as they say, to make a World.

But at some point, people of all persuasions must face up to certain facts. Differences in perspective have very little effect on verifiable data, and enough data points together suggest a trend. If a trend continues long enough in a dangerous direction, prudence demands prediction. And if the predictions of catastrophe are credible, they warrant serious reflection and preventive action. *What* to do may be a matter of debate between people of varying backgrounds and mutual goodwill; but after a certain threshold is crossed, *whether* to take action ceases to be a reasonable question.

If you have read this far, and it still seems ridiculous to you to entertain any serious global collapse scenario, consider the following. On May 8, 1998, the very-mainstream journal *Science* (the same publication that harshly critiqued *The Limits to Growth* in 1972) published a two-page article by the esteemed British scientist James Lovelock, calling for a special effort to "encapsulate the essential information that is the basis of our civilization to preserve it through a dark age." Lovelock, a world-renowned atmospheric chemist, recommended doing this on old-fashioned, durable paper, rather than any supposedly more advanced technology, because the latter would be more vulnerable to the ravages of time. Paper has been proven to last through the centuries; computers have no such track record.

Why did Lovelock make this ominous prescription? Because civilizations, which generally last for no more than a few hundred years, "are ephemeral compared with species." Civilizations invariably collapse, and Lovelock is worried that ours might come due.

In reporting and commenting on Lovelock's essay, biologist David Ehrenfeld noted that Lovelock's remarks are not themselves the most remarkable thing to notice. "What commands our attention first," writes Ehrenfeld in the pages of the liberal journal *Tikkun*, "is that *Science* magazine was willing to print two precious pages based on the premise that our scientific-technological civilization is in real danger of collapse." Ehrenfeld, founding editor of the journal *Conservation Biology*, goes on to make the case that such a collapse is indeed imminent, and that it is more likely to be of the swift (five to twenty-five years) than the slower, one to two generation variety, because of our top-heavy technological and economic systems. "Techno-economic globalization is nearing its apogee," he claims; "the system is self-destructing. There is only a short but very damaging period of expansion left."

Ehrenfeld's interpretation of the evidence is clearly in the Egalitarian mode, as are the warnings of most Cassandras. But the scientific data on which he bases that interpretation is undeniable. Moreover, the warnings have been echoed by enormous numbers of individual scientists, as well as such conservative institutions as the U.S. National Academy of Sciences and the United Kingdom's Royal Society. Under these conditions, the Individualists and Hierarchists of the World must at least consider the data, even if their response is to do something other than initiate the development of an Egalitarian Utopia.

When serious scientists in serious journals are writing serious articles about the possibility of civilizational collapse, it behooves people of all cultural perspectives to reflect on what the scientists have to say. But it also behooves us to do everything in our power to demonstrate, as the future unfolds, that doom is avoidable. *We must ultimately prove*

Cassandra wrong. Why? Because some of the deadly dangers facing our civilization depend, for their avoidance, on continued technological stability and advance, not to mention cultural vigilance over the next several millennia. If our civilization does collapse, it could loose horrors upon the planet that would permanently alter all life and probably threaten the existence of humanity itself.

▲▼▲

Cannon Beach, Oregon
September 1992

I'm sitting in front of a lavish breakfast at a small seaside inn, watching the mist roll up the beach. My companion and I strike up a conversation with the woman next to us, the only other guest. For some reason, she decides to confide in us about something that's really bothering her.

She works for the U.S. Department of Defense, and her job involves assessing issues of risk and safety. She had recently attended a meeting in Idaho about the future of nuclear waste. Many of the military's top engineering minds had been assembled, she says, and the meeting was classified. Armed guards were posted outside the door.

The meeting involved a report to the top brass on the current state of the art with regard to managing nuclear waste, some of which will continue to be dangerous for up to 240,000 years. "It was a very unusual meeting," she says, "because these engineers basically admitted that they didn't have a clue what to do about it. In fact, they were personally overwhelmed by the enormity of the problem. A couple of them actually broke down and sobbed."

"I shouldn't be telling you this," she adds quickly, trying to hold back her own tears. "But I had to tell somebody." I have no way of knowing if she's for real, or if she's just making it up. She doesn't tell us her name. But there's something about what she's saying that makes me think, it doesn't matter whether this story is real. At a deeper level, she's telling the truth.

▲▼▲

For most of my adult life, I have worried deeply about nuclear waste. Whenever anyone argued that there were no fundamentally unsolvable problems on the one hand, or that a technological collapse was potentially a fine thing on the other, I had a snappy one-word retort: "Plutonium." Plutonium is the most toxic compound on Earth. Inhaling a single molecule can kill you. Its primary use is in the production of tremendously destructive weapons, and it remains extremely radioactive for tens of thousands of years. We know its danger, and we know that we *don't* know how to guarantee that it won't eventually kill us, or our descendants. And yet humanity continues to produce it, stockpile it, explode it, send it up in rockets, and sometimes even misplace it.

If humanity were to suffer a techno-economic collapse of the kind Lovelock and Ehrenfeld are worried about, of the kind some hard-line Greens and old-time religious fundamentalists long for, or of the kind the Unabomber was eager to trigger, it would probably ensure that the World's stockpile of plutonium would be loosed upon the Earth like a plague of demons. The released plutonium would be accompanied by far greater quantities of only slightly less dangerous materials, such as concentrated uranium, strontium, and cesium.

The threat is not theoretical. In 1987, a piece of hospital equipment abandoned in the city of Goiana, Brazil, was picked up by scavenger, who sold it to a junk dealer, who discovered a strange, glowing substance inside. The junk dealer showed it to his friends and neighbors, and the neighborhood children proceeded to smear the glowing blue dust on their faces. Only when dozens of people exposed to the material began to get sick and die did it come to the attention of informed people, who could identify the substance as highly radioactive. In fact, it was a block of cesium-137, left over from a machine used for the radiation treatment of cancer patients.

Imagine a similar scene repeated over and over in a World where technological collapse has left unguarded, even unrecognized, many tons of even more dangerous materials. Allowing poisons such as plutonium to be spread upon the Earth would create an even greater ecological calamity than climate change, because this would, through genetic mutation, poison evolution itself.

When it comes to radioactive elements—and a host of other toxic compounds, as well as genetically engineered life forms—we have opened Pandora's Box. We cannot close it again. We cannot restore the Earth to some pristine and inherently safe condition before the advent of human technology and its byproducts, including nuclear waste and other long-lasting dangers. We cannot restore the World to innocence about such matters, either, for that would be a form of suicide, and potentially biocide. We must ensure that these creations of ours remain safeguarded throughout the long millennia of their dangerous life spans, or until we can develop a safe technology that will render them truly harmless. We are therefore committed, if we wish to protect the Earth and improve the World, to sustaining the development of high technology. To advocate anything else is globally irresponsible.

▲▼▲

Gainesville, Florida
Summer 1976

I am a junior scientist, age sixteen, working in a biochemistry research lab at the University of Florida. Every day I join the professors and graduate students who labor in the lower levels of the medical school, searching for the biochemical lever that will shut down the process of runaway cell growth known as cancer.

I'm proud of my white lab coat, my participation in a noble cause, my newfound knowledge of centrifuges and polyamines and thin-layer gel chromatography. And I'm fascinated by the fate of one Joseph P. McCloud III.

Young Joe was circumcised a few years back, and ever since then, his foreskin has lived on in the university's research labs. We perform our experiments on human skin cells, all of them direct descendants of Joe's former phallic sheathe. Foreskin cells, and Joe's cells in particular, grow extremely well in our clear plastic flasks, and we joke about what a good omen that is for Joe's future sex life. I myself have grown a big batch of these cells, and I'm about to perform my big experiment on them.

The experiment involves watching what happens to certain radioactively tagged compounds as they make their way through the cells' chemical processes. It's a delicate procedure, made a bit dangerous by the radioactivity. Like everyone else, I wear a little badge with X-ray film in it, to monitor my exposure.

Things go well, until the moment they don't, which is the moment when I spill a large amount of radioactive material onto a lab counter. I panic. I imagine sirens going off, skin shriveling off my hands, deformed children. The professor in charge will soon dispel my exaggerated worries, and my badge will later show that my exposure was minimal. But at this moment the thought occurs to me: if a young, relatively careful nerd like me can spill a little of this stuff, what's to stop someone else—or a whole society—from spilling a whole lot more of something a whole lot worse?

▲▼▲

Wisdom, I have always believed, is the only solution to the problem of nuclear waste. For nuclear materials such as plutonium to be safely stored and monitored across the centuries and millennia, humanity must become extremely wise, and design cultural systems that can pass teachings about plutonium down through the generations. Only something like a "Plutonium Priesthood," modeled on the sacred elect of the great religions of the world, could possibly stand the test of time and ensure that future human beings understand the magnitude of the danger we had bequeathed to them.

For reasons I will come to in a moment, I had completely discounted the possibility of a technological solution. "Plutonium will always be with us," I thought to myself. "The only possible safe disposal site would be somewhere off the planet, and rocket launches will not be safe enough for that any time soon, if ever."

But while working on this book, I came upon a new breakthrough in technology, reported in the hip computer magazine *Wired*, that can potentially solve the problem of nuclear waste—cheaply, quickly, and very profitably. A young physicist at the University of Idaho named Paul Brown, putting long-standing theory into practice, has discovered that highly radioactive materials can be transformed into less radioactive materials by bombarding them with gamma rays. The process generates a lot of heat, which can then be used to make electricity. The materials that remain are still radioactive, but their radioactivity dissipates in a matter of months instead of millennia. He's planning a demonstration plant that will cost a mere $5 million to build.

If this technology—or another like it, somewhere down the road—works, and gets widely implemented, it could make possible the eventual disappearance of one of the most dangerous problems on the planet. But it would have one dreadful side effect: it would take from me the comfort I feel in holding a moral and intellectual trump card.

Plutonium, for me, has always been more than a terrible environmental problem or a disaster waiting to happen. Plutonium was my ace in the hole. This element's mere existence (we invented it, after all) was ironclad proof of humanity's fundamentally fallen nature, its spiritual sloth, its need to seek salvation. The non-negotiable nature of its long-term threat to the biosphere would, I believed, eventually slap humanity across the face and wake us up into enlightened stewardship of the Earth. Finally, since relatively few people seemed to know about the problem, or care, my profound concern about plutonium was my badge of membership in a moral and spiritual elite.

This explains the slight twinge of disappointment I felt at learning the problem of highly radioactive nuclear waste might someday be solved, and by a relatively simple technology. The disappearance of plutonium from the list of "insoluble problems" would remove a particularly powerful incentive for the practice of civilizational wisdom. I should have felt nothing but relief at the prospect that the Earth might eventually be rid, through technology, of one of technology's gravest dangers (and if it happens, I will certainly celebrate). But I also felt a certain wistfulness, a certain nostalgia-in-advance for that erstwhile angel of destruction, plutonium. Moreover, the advent of such an easy clean-up technology could reduce the arguments against the proliferation of nuclear power. The net effect would be something like the prophet Lot finding out that God had changed his mind about destroying Sodom and Gomorrah, and that with the distribution of condoms and the emancipation of the sex slaves, the orgies could continue without retribution.

"Gandhi," E. F. Schumacher wrote, "used to talk disparagingly of 'dreaming of systems so perfect that no one will need to be good.'" It is, of course, dangerously naive to believe that technology alone can solve all our problems. But it is in some ways more naive to dream of "making people so good that technologies do not need to be perfected." If we rely for the planet's well-being on the swift ethical enlightenment of humanity, we may hasten the very events we wish to prevent. What's more, we will likely doom ourselves to a lifetime of frustration—a lifetime stuck in Cassandra's Dilemma.

▲▼▲

Washington, D.C.
January 1999

The Worldwatch Institute is releasing its annual State of the World *report, and I happen to be in Washington, so I attend the press briefing. Worldwatch founder Lester Brown is in his trademark bow-tie, vest, and running shoes. Christopher Flavin, the report's principal co-author, dresses more like an accountant and wears a serious look.*

Declaring the 1999 report to be the "Millennial Edition," Brown and Flavin review the century's legacy. Population has tripled, resource use has gone up by a factor of ten, fisheries are collapsing, and so on. Global temperature has shot up so much in the last year that the Institute was forced to recalibrate the graph it publishes annually. Noting that other societies in the past have collapsed, Brown wonders out loud whether they knew what was coming. Did they not see the trends? Or did they see them, but simply not respond?

But it's not all bad news. Brown, especially, wants to put forward his more visionary and hopeful side—he and the Institute are often described as "gloomy"—so he highlights some of the more promising trends. Solar, wind, and hydroelectric energy could together replace fossil fuels. Bicycles and rails could reduce the number of cars. The new CEO of Ford, an actual Ford himself, has vowed to preside over the demise of the internal combustion engine. Brown closes with the usual homily: We know how to convert to a more environmentally sustainable economy. The question is, can we muster the will to do it?

Then we're into the Q&A. At the end of the last century, says one reporter, people worried that mud and horse manure would soon make cities unlivable. They were wrong. What if you're similarly wrong? Flavin notes that we're entering into unpredictable, unstable times. "We know we'll see crises," he contends, "but what crises? Where? We just don't know. History is shaped by surprises, crises, and disasters. Humans seem to learn best from these, unfortunately."

Brown jumps in and reminds the reporter that Worldwatch has, in a sense, already been wrong: "Even we did not anticipate the soaring temperatures caused by global warming." He observes that climate-change–related weather caused more economic damage in 1998 than in the entire decade of the 1980s, and displaced some 300 million people. "Nothing like this has ever been seen before," says Brown. "It's getting harder for us"—meaning, Worldwatch—"to understand the acceleration of history. It's becoming more difficult to anticipate the future."

What, says a less skeptical correspondent, is being done to improve education about these dangerous trends? "Our goal," says Brown, before giving a few examples, "is to provide information about these changes, before disaster becomes the teacher." This, I think to myself, is a prophet's job description, very succinctly put.

Then comes the last question, from a young Eastern European woman. What about the rapid economic growth in my part of the world? she asks. Consumerism is roaring through the region, with little thought for solar energy or reducing waste or these other more positive trends you've mentioned. The education systems are hardly promoting new values. The media is a business that supports the status quo. What could possibly alter the course of those nations?

Brown acknowledges the problem and speaks hopefully about a future "cultural paradigm shift" toward a less consumerist mentality. But then his

tone changes somewhat, becomes more sober, almost regretful. Getting to
that point, he says, "may take some shocks to the system."

▲▼▲

In private conversations with colleagues around the World who are concerned with the dangers of runaway Growth and its consequences, I often hear a disturbing conclusion. For any serious, transformative
change to occur, many say, humanity will have to suffer some catastrophe. What, then, would be the "minimum necessary catastrophe," the
calamity bad enough to shock the World into taking dramatic action
without tearing it apart at the seams?

This is a haunting question, because we have already been witness
to a wide range of calamities that do not seem to meet the criteria. The
decline of many fish stocks, the draining (through river diversion) of the
Aral Sea, the extinction of numerous species, the near-loss of the ozone
layer, the devastation of Central America by a monster hurricane, the
extreme flooding of Bangladesh, the runaway fires in Indonesia that
blanketed all of Southeast Asia in smoke for months . . . none of these
seem to have been sufficient wake-up calls. Should we wish for worse?
Hardly. As I have argued above, to do so would be both immoral and
counterproductive. And given the evidence so far, it appears possible
that even a sudden collapse of the West Antarctic ice sheet and a subse-
quent twenty-foot sea-level rise might simply be taken in stride by the
planet's second most-adaptable animal (I rank cockroaches first). We
will have to find another way out of the trap.

As the long history of prophecy makes clear, human beings—or at
least, their economic and political systems—are strangely averse to
warnings. Warnings, you might say, don't work. When 1,600 scientists
released a statement called the "World Scientists' Warning to Humanity," the American body politic scarcely blinked. When 2,500 U.S.
economists, including eight Nobel prize winners, issued a statement
that endorsed the scientific warnings about climate change and called
for economic measures to address the problem, national leaders—including, paradoxically, some of the drafters of that statement—went on

about their business, and seemed hardly to notice that anything at all had been said.

So if neither well-informed warnings from thousands of respected intellectuals, nor devastating but somewhat contained "shocks to the system," nor even the ever-increasing sales of Worldwatch Institute's *State of the World* report seem to get humanity moving, where does that leave us? Confronting a paradox: We need something more powerful than a minor catastrophe to help prevent a lot of major ones. What could that possibly be?

Since we have reached a point where the prospects for humanity look gloomy indeed, let us turn for advice to two practitioners of the "dismal science"—economics. Our two consultants, drawn from the pages of this century's history, have diametrically opposing views on human nature. One economist came to prominence in the Depression of the 1930s; the other was a beloved figure in the revolutionary 1960s. Not surprisingly, they differ on the best strategy for getting people to tackle very large challenges, like changing the World. (When dealing with consultants, and especially economists, it helps to get two opinions.)

John Maynard Keynes, the chief economic architect of the early twentieth century, foresaw a time when humanity would embrace an ethical sensibility, and "once more value ends above means and prefer the good to the useful." But, he went on to say, don't expect that transformation anytime soon. In his view, progress depended on *delaying* the arrival of ethical enlightenment, because the expansion of the market and the money economy—necessary to create jobs and to break out of the Depression—required the harnessing, even the adulation, of greed, selfishness, and other dependable human flaws. Keynes, therefore, was the quintessential Individualist, ignoring Nature, distrusting ethics, and placing his faith in human beings as they are, with all their warts. "Beware!" he wrote, warning World leaders against too early an embrace of morality in the economy. "For at least another hundred years we must pretend to ourselves and to every one that fair is foul and foul is fair; for foul is useful and fair is not." For Keynes, "foul"—human greed and selfishness—was useful because foul drives Growth, and Growth creates jobs and prosperity. Harness humanity's baser instincts, he seemed to be saying, and phenomenal, transformative amounts of work will get done.

E. F. Schumacher, several decades later, argued for the opposite approach: a more rapid embrace of an ethical and altruistic sensibility and the economics of idealism. Schumacher disparaged Keynes, saying that for him, "The road to heaven is paved with bad intentions." Schumacher went on to write *Small is Beautiful* and *A Guide for the Perplexed*, in which he articulated a quintessentially Egalitarian view of the World. Rather than enshrine a bad thing as a good thing, as Keynes ordained, Schumacher proposed that "The art of living is to make a good thing out of a bad thing"—the bad thing being our present situation, with its abject poverty and ecological devastation, and perhaps our own benighted outlook as well. Unlike Keynes, Schumacher was not directing his thoughts to a power elite, but to all those who have ears to hear and the will to act, just as one would expect from an Egalitarian. He preached economic transformation based on consciousness and compassion. Only by acknowledging our desperate straits, says Schumacher, "can we summon the courage and imagination needed for a 'turning around.'" What follows is one of the most lovely summaries of the Egalitarian vision in the English language:

> This then leads to seeing the world in a new light, namely, as a place where the things modern man continuously talks about and always fails to accomplish can actually be done. The generosity of the Earth allows us to feed all mankind; we know enough about ecology to keep the Earth a healthy place; there is enough room on the Earth, and there are enough materials, so that everybody can have adequate shelter; we are quite competent enough to produce sufficient supplies that no one need live in misery. Above all, we shall then see that the economic problem is a convergent problem which has already been solved: we know enough to provide enough and do not require any violent inhuman and aggressive technologies to do so.

Two economists, two very different perspectives on reality, two opposing prescriptions for motivating humanity to act. The one tells us to harness human greed to the market; the other tells us to unveil the eyes, unchain the heart, and notice that there is already plenty for everyone.

Which view is correct? Can enough Egalitarian souls, moved by facts confirmed by science and their own profound sentiments, muster sufficient courage and creativity to build a new and more enlightened World? Or must we, instead, rely upon humanity's less charitable motivators—the Individualist desire for self-aggrandizement, the institutionalized greed of the market economy—in the pursuit of critical social and environmental goals?

The answer, of course, is yes.

To escape Cassandra's Dilemma and prevent global collapse, we need an idea that is both visionary and profitable, a solution that can appeal to both the ardent altruist and the hardened venture capitalist. We need a source of hope that is also a business opportunity, a hot investment that is also intensely idealistic. We need something that will challenge our higher natures and attract our baser instincts, coaxing us into the game of transformation without polarizing society or fomenting revolution. We need something that has not been seen since humans first began plowing up dirt, building skyscrapers, and messing around with atmospheric chemistry. We need something that has the power to command a lifetime of allegiance, even though it does not truly exist yet in practice, and may never fully exist except in theory. We need something we can barely begin to describe in tangible, concrete terms.

But fortunately, we have a word for it.

PART 2

REINVENTING
THE WORLD

CHAPTER 7

The Future in a Word

Great ideas come into the world as gently as doves.
                                              —ALBERT CAMUS

Dare to be naive.

                              —BUCKMINSTER FULLER

T UCKED INTO THE OPENING
pages of 1972's *The Limits to Growth* is a word that was destined for both
fame and infamy. This was not the first time the word had been used,
nor was this necessarily the defining time. Given the word's ungainli-
ness, its indisputable lack of poetic elegance or euphonious charm, we
could marvel that it went on to claim center stage in a global movement,
and to prompt such vigorous debate. Its first use had been in the fields
of forestry and fisheries; now, it began to apply to the whole World. As
time went on it found both champions and enemies in government,
business, economics, the environmental movement, the press, the
United Nations, and ultimately—maybe this was the best indicator of

its universal reach—among the ranks of large consulting firms. Despite being clearly and meticulously defined, in terms both scientific and social, the word was regularly accused of promoting vagueness, hiding a green political agenda, hiding a pro-business agenda, or attempting to be "all things to all people." Some of its early champions came to abandon it as meaningless; some of its assumed enemies were converted to it as though to a religion. And still the word labored on, in its clumsy but steady way, serving as the political focal point for high-level government commissions, the strategic fulcrum for large corporations, the long-term goal of environmental groups, and the idealistic vision of artists and small journals and tiny villages dedicated to demonstrating a better way of life. All of this transpired over nearly thirty years, while the public was practically oblivious to the quiet revolution forming under its feet and the plans for a new World constellating around this word in a growing network of design schools, research labs, policy institutes, board rooms, government agencies, city halls, retreat centers, and humble vegetable gardens. The word itself, notwithstanding the valiant attempts of many authors and organizations and even public relations professionals to make it part of the common lexicon, refused to attract much attention and remained totally, and modestly, inconspicuous.

The word is: "sustainable."

In *The Limits to Growth,* the word "sustainable" is introduced in the middle of another much-overlooked passage, a paragraph that could be called, "Conclusion Number 2." Conclusion Number 1 spelled out the problem of humanity's runaway exponential growth, which had created the very real possibility of overshoot and collapse, a realization to which the authors had reluctantly come after two years studying a global computer model. That was the bad news. Conclusion Number 2 (which the authors later wished they had listed first) was somewhat more promising:

> 2. It is possible to alter these growth trends and to establish a condition of ecological and economic stability that is sustainable far into the future. The state of global equilibrium could be designed so that the material needs of each person

on earth are satisfied and each person has an equal opportunity to realize his individual human potential.

Conclusion Number 2 was essentially like declaring that Utopia was within our reach. But when *Limits* was released in 1972, the World preferred to ignore this promising notion, and attack the message it (mistakenly) read into Conclusion Number 1: Doomsday is at hand. Three decades later, some kind of Doomsday (or Doomdecade) may be sneaking up on us after all, and some kind of Utopia is still very far away—but the word "sustainable" plods on, gaining steam and accelerating uphill like "The Little Engine That Could."

"Sustainable," from the Latin *sustenare* ("to hold up"), means "able to continue indefinitely." In playing with the computer model known as World3, the authors of *Limits* produced scenario after scenario that was *not* sustainable. Either population outpaced production, production outstripped resources, or pollution overwhelmed Nature. In any case, civilization came to a painful and grinding halt. Finding conditions that *were* sustainable—in the World3 computer model, but more importantly in the real World—thus became the name of the game.

Sustainability in the World3 model, or "dynamic equilibrium" in systems language, was attained only when three things happened: technology drastically improved, the population growth rate dropped to zero or less (about two children per woman), and the growth of industrial throughput stabilized. In other words, Growth stops, but Development goes on. The economist Herman Daly has called this condition a "steady state," but of course there's nothing necessarily steady about it except the total numbers. The more important word is "dynamic." Change continues to happen—radical change, in the direction of radical improvement.

The authors of *Limits* were quite specific about the changes that needed to occur to make the lines on their computer-generated charts level off comfortably at sustainability, instead of turning over and plunging downward toward chaos and destruction. They proposed a scenario where population started leveling off in 1975, and the expansion of industrial capital (factories and machines) stabilized by 1990. Industry got 75% more efficient in terms of throughput, and pollution dropped by at least the same amount. The economy moved from *more stuff* to *more value*, reducing the need for raw materials from the Earth while maintaining or improving quality of life. The things people bought were designed better and lasted far longer. Agriculture and food distribution were greatly improved, resulting in an end to poverty.

That scenario worked in World3. But of course, it did not come to pass in the real World—at least, it hasn't yet. Nonetheless, again, *The Limits to Growth* proved prescient.

Today, senior economic planners in Europe, prompted by the work of leading sustainability researchers and the examples of forward-thinking companies, are talking about attaining "Factor Four" efficiencies—the same 75% reductions in the consumption of energy and materials proposed by *Limits*. (Some are even talking about "Factor Ten," or 90% efficiency gains.) A few countries and many corporations have begun to set, and attain, goals for pollution reduction that in some areas surpass the 75% figure used in World3. The use of wind, solar, hydrogen fuel cells, and other clean forms of energy is on the verge of taking off, to the point where even oil companies envision them replacing our reliance on fossil fuels. Economic growth—meaning, growth in the dollar value of what happens in the economy—is rapidly shifting not just to services, but to *information*, which is even less materials-intensive than services. Information can reduce material flows in other ways, too, as industries learn how to use less and recycle more. Organic farming is now the fastest-growing segment of agriculture in the industrialized parts of the World, and while persistent poverty and hunger are still widespread, the goal of improving distribution to the neediest is increasingly recognized. In some areas, consumer products show signs of becoming much more durable—if not directly in terms of their life spans, then indirectly, by means of utilizing materials that are more recyclable. None of these changes can yet be described as standard practice, but all have long since breached the boundary between theory and reality. These are the early signs of a new World in the making.

But we are getting ahead of ourselves. We were talking about a word.

▲▼▲

Seattle, Washington
March 1991

Today is the third meeting of the group that is starting to call itself "Sustainable Seattle." I've arrived early to arrange the chairs in a circle, to place a printed agenda carefully on each one, and generally to "warm up the room"—I'm a bit obsessive that way as a facilitator. It's a delicate process, forming a group, and I want everything to feel exactly right.

New friends and colleagues including Richard Conlin, Vicki Robin, and Nea Carroll start to arrive. Richard, Nea, and I will soon become the "co-administrators" of the group, and Richard, who runs environmental programs for the YMCA, will some years later get himself elected to City Council. Vicki will co-author the best-selling book, Your Money or Your Life. *Working together on this project will end up creating fast friendships, newspaper headlines, and ultimately global waves. But today, of course, we don't know any of this.*

Instead, we're concerned with definitions. The group that is gathering around this word "sustainable" is unusual: it includes representatives from the Mayor's office, Boeing, the Audubon Society, the Chamber of Commerce, social welfare groups, and others. We're not used to working together, and we're struggling to come to consensus about what we're actually discussing.

It will be a few more months before we find a definition of sustainability we can all live with: "long-term cultural, economic, and environmental health and vitality." The key word is "long-term." The other three main elements (culture, economics, the environment) will be in alphabetical order, to prevent the impression of bias in any one direction. The more dynamic word "vitality" will be added by the business caucus.

And after about six months of debating words and concepts, two changes will have occurred: one, we'll trust each other more, and two, we'll be sick of talking in the abstract. Instead, we'll launch an ambitious project to create a set of indicators for sustainability—a kind of instrument panel, or report card, measuring in very concrete terms whether the city is moving toward long-term health or away from it.

Our report on indicators will link together the fate of endangered salmon, children in poverty, an economic base that is still overly dependent on Boeing for jobs. We'll have fun with this, too, bringing together people from all over the city, doing dramatic readings, throwing parties, giving out awards made of recycled materials. Over the next several years, the Sustainable Seattle "Indicators of Sustainable Community" will get talked about at international conferences, win a United Nations award, and become a model for hundreds of other projects.

But of course, that's all in the future, and completely unsuspected. For now, there's just this ring of chairs, waiting.

▲▼▲

Definitions of "sustainable" abound. In *Beyond the Limits*, the sequel to *The Limits to Growth*, the authors provide five different and complementary versions. The first is both simple and sufficient: "A sustainable society is one that can persist over generations." A society headed for overshoot and collapse is therefore, by definition, unsustainable. Either it survives, or it doesn't. But no society persists forever, just as not even the healthiest person can live forever. Sustainability is therefore an ideal, like health. (Internet joke: "Health is merely the slowest possible rate at which one can die.") There is perfect sustainability, and then there are an infinite number of lesser states that are closer to it or farther away from it. The goal of every society, whether they say it directly or not, is to be as sustainable as possible. The alternatives to sustainability—sudden chaos, rapid or gradual collapse, or slow decay—are unattractive, but that hasn't stopped numerous defunct societies from choosing them.

So, first we acknowledge that sustainability is an ideal, like truth, justice, freedom, democracy, and love. We never completely reach our ideals, but we strive *toward* them—and striving toward them is what defines us as a culture.

Further definitions of sustainability help us by describing the conditions, qualities, and goals associated with achieving this ideal in today's World. In *Beyond the Limits*, Meadows and company defer to economist Herman Daly, who sets three irrefutable conditions for a society's multi-generational survival, which I will reformulate for the sake of succinctness:

THREE CONDITIONS FOR SOCIETY'S SURVIVAL

Condition One. You can't use up renewable resources (such as water, fish, trees) any faster than they actually replenish themselves. Otherwise they run out. (While this principle sounds obvious, humanity consistently ignores it.)

Condition Two. If you are using stuff that will someday run out, and you depend on it utterly for basic necessities including food, water, and energy, you had better be investing some of that *non*renewable stuff into the development of *renewable* stuff that can someday replace it. Fossil fuels fall into this category: long before the oil runs out, better spend a little of that oil on building solar-panel factories.

Condition Three. You cannot dump garbage—whether it's old cars or used chemicals—into Nature any faster than Nature can absorb this refuse without going haywire. For some types of garbage (for instance plutonium, or certain chemicals that act like hormones in the body and cause, even in small quantities, strange malformations of the penis and other unpleasant surprises), that means no dumping at all.

If, in the management of your society, you were to follow these three conditions to the letter, you would achieve *physical* sustainability. But that would not prevent you from organizing your society in some stupid or politically insane ways, so other definers of the word are careful to include the social dimension. Meadows et al. describe a sustainable society as "one that is far-seeing enough, flexible enough, and wise enough not to undermine either its physical *or its social* systems of support." (Italics added.) With the introduction of foresight, flexibility, and wisdom, our sense of the term has expanded beyond the physical to encompass, as a requirement for collapse-free living, some of our finer human qualities. The addition of social systems takes into account that a society without functioning families, schools, and governments is not likely to persist over the long term either, even if all its power comes from solar energy systems.

But that still leaves out morality. Theoretically, you could have an ecologically correct, smart, far-seeing, socially stable society that was also a brutal fascist dictatorship that controlled population by capriciously executing its citizens. While that might be "sustainable" in the purely physical sense, it is hardly worthy of association with the idealism associated with this term. Something more is needed to make the definition complete.

Enter the World Commission on Environment and Development, whose 1987 book *Our Common Future* included a definition of "sustainability" that remains, today, the most widely used and least thoroughly understood formulation on the planet. For poverty to be alleviated, noted the Brundtland Commission (its official nickname), economic development must continue. But we must have a new, nondestructive variety, which they called *sustainable* development, meaning development that "meets the needs of the present without compromising the ability of future generations to meet their own needs." Here we incorporate ethics. It is not enough simply to avoid overshoot and collapse by any means necessary; we must do so while feeding the poor, caring for the sick, and meeting contemporary standards of justice, compassion, and fair play.

But here also is where some perplexing opportunities for vagueness come in. The vagueness gathers not around the word "sustainable," but around the concept of *needs*. What are "the needs of the present"? Lack of clarity on this point has encouraged many companies, governments, and consultants to jump on the sustainability bandwagon without fully considering the challenges this really entails. What stops us from categorizing Bill Gates's mansion as a "need"? What makes genetically engineered food a "need"? Clearly too much room is left for confusion; we need another sorting mechanism. *Beyond the Limits* offers yet another definition, one that forces us toward intellectual honesty by grounding us in the discipline of system dynamics:

> From a systems point of view a sustainable society is one that has in place informational, social, and institutional mechanisms to keep in check the positive [i.e., *trend-reinforcing*, as opposed to trend-reducing] feedback loops that cause exponential population and capital growth. [Capital = "stuff," like cars, factories, and Bill Gates's mansion.] That means that birth rates roughly equal death rates, and investment rates roughly equal depreciation rates, unless and until technical changes and social decisions justify a considered and controlled change in the levels of population or capital. In order to be socially sustainable the combination of population, capital, and technology in the society would have to be configured so that the material living standard is adequate and secure for everyone.

Translation: Do the math. Numbers are the great antidote to vagueness. No matter how you spin the term, sustainability requires that the number of people, and the quantities of stuff they use up and discard, cease their increase. Growth of material consumption must stop, and eventually go down, which means our technologies must be redesigned so that they are vastly more efficient and do no damage to society or the environment. Nature's critical stocks cannot be drawn down to zero, any more than you can keep driving a car with no gas in it. Nor can increasing amounts of garbage flow out from society forever. And we need some way of getting feedback on these trends—that is, a greatly improved system of indicators—together with new social and political methods for turning down the volume on those signals that seem to encourage humanity's lemming-like stampede over the cliffs of history.

The conditions for sustainability are measurable, and measuring them makes you honest about what is sustainable and what is not. Moreover, the phrase "adequate and secure" puts everything through

two more filters: (1) Does everyone have enough? and (2) Are we in any
obvious danger of destroying ourselves? Considering the *security* of our
creations would ultimately eliminate technologies such as nuclear
weapons, and would make us far more cautious about what we do to
the DNA of the life-forms that surround us. The burden of proof
would not be on society, as it often is now, to demonstrate that a new
technology is *not* safe, usually after it has been released to the four
winds. Instead, it would be up to the producer to establish, to the best
of current knowledge, that it *is* safe. Food crops with so-called "termi-
nator genes," which prevent genetically engineered plants from repro-
ducing (not a trait one would want wild plants to "catch"), would surely
not make the cut.

Those are the absolutes; now come the qualifiers. "No Growth"
doesn't actually mean *no* Growth. There would certainly be fluctuations
up and down. (For example, some European nations have, today,
achieved slow or even *negative* population growth rates, and are beginning to consider ways of modestly nudging growth up again.) There
could also be purposeful and harmless expansions, made possible by
new technology. But society "would use material growth as a considered
tool, not a perpetual mandate." At the same time, Development—
qualitative improvement in humanity's technologies, way of life, patterns of governance, economic systems, creative expression,
you-name-it—would bloom. (Indeed, I argue in the final chapter that
it *must* bloom, in a rather accelerated and profitable fashion, for collapse to be avoided.)

And remember, we are not talking here about a dull, earnest,
melancholy, hair-shirt kind of existence, where everyone wears identical
tunics and gives thanks for their daily servings of gruel, content with
the knowledge that Nature has been protected and the Collective equitably served. A sustainable World, properly understood, is not only an
abundant World: it is a wildly diverse and *fascinating* World. This is a
World spilling over with opportunities for personal advancement, business development, creative expression, exploration of the unknown.
Sustainability is beautiful and reasonable and profitable, all at once.
Sustainable solutions come in every imaginable shape and size, reflect

every cultural variation, make possible the highest aspirations of individual human beings. Sustainability itself is not Utopia, but something much more realistic and more interesting: it is the process of trying to approach Utopia from a thousand different directions.

Obviously, at this point in history, little in our industrial societies comes anywhere near the brilliance of true sustainability. But there are examples to which we can point, strategies to pursue, visions to encourage. It's hard to visualize a sustainable society because, as the authors of *Beyond the Limits* admit, "it could hardly be more different from the one in which most people now live." The "collective human imagination," they acknowledge, is too strongly imprinted with the million-year history of human poverty, followed by the relatively sudden splendor of our recent, rapid expansion. Despite the size of the crowd we have already become, we are still responding to what Elias Canetti called "the desire to be MORE."

We can dream of a World where Growth is no longer necessary, where a new conception of Development has reinvented all our systems in ways that are beautiful, intelligent, and environmentally benign. It may be hard to describe this dream in detail. But when someone has made a tangible step in the direction of sustainability, we recognize it when we see it.

▲▼▲

San Diego, California
February 1999

For what may be nearing the hundredth time, I am doing a presentation on indicators of sustainability. Little did I know, when I laid out the agendas for the third meeting of Sustainable Seattle back in 1991, that my volunteer passion would take me around the World and become part of my career.

My bizarre passion for indicators, I now realize, was born out of reading The Limits to Growth *many years earlier. How can society change course if it's not getting the right feedback? We need better measures of progress, to compete for our attention with the Dow Jones Industrial Average and the Gross Domestic Product. We need to get Nature's feedback sig-*

nals faster, and likewise the signals from our own children, our own streets. Apparently a lot of other people share that belief, because I've been asked to give this presentation all over the World.

This one is helping to kick off the latest grandchild of Sustainable Seattle, a project sponsored by the San Diego Natural History Museum. I'm not bored; for me, this is a performance. I throw in jokes, I surprise the crowd with songs, I pretend I'm a talk-show host—and somehow manage to maintain my profile as an expert talking about data, measurement, and public accountability. I explain that the process *of creating indicators is almost more important than the indicators themselves, because of the way the process brings people together and changes their perceptions. Consulting to groups like this is a living, as they say; but it's also a lot more than that.*

For one thing, doing this work brings me to places like this amazing building, headquarters for San Diego's Environmental Services Division. It's a retrofit, which means that it's not a new building, but rebuilt from the inside. It's state-of-the-art sustainability. I had no idea the U.S. mainstream had come this far along, this fast.

I'm working the crowd on a handsome carpet made from recycled soft-drink bottles. In a creative new arrangement, the city doesn't actually own the carpet, but leases it, from a company called Interface. Interface, instead of selling its customers physical carpet, provides "the service of carpeting"; when pieces wear out, Interface replaces them. The city saves money, and the company turns the used materials back into new carpet, at a profit.

The windows, electric lights, heating, and air conditioning have all been redesigned to be so efficient that the building spends two-thirds less on electricity than an identical building right next door. In fact, during our meeting this afternoon, the Director received an "Energy Star" plaque in the mail from the U.S. Department of Energy, the very first building in the country to win that certification.

Everywhere you look you see some lovely and functioning innovation—light switches that turn themselves off, ceiling tiles constructed of stuff that was formerly something else, even the dividers in the men's urinal are made of recycled plastic, in a nice burgundy. Out back are several kinds of composting systems, including my personal favorite, a worm bin. The knowledge that little red worms are eating the scraps from today's lunch tables, and turning garbage into fantastic topsoil, just delights me.

I imagine every building in America being redone like this one, and better: great aesthetics, energy from solar modules on the roof, door-to-door service on a hydrogen-fueled mass-transit system . . . I imagine great worm ranches, billions of worms, composting all the uneaten sandwiches in San Diego . . .

▲▼▲

Sustainability is a deceptively simple word for an extremely complex idea. Complexity, to those who have trouble understanding or accepting a new concept, often gets mistaken for vagueness. But sustainability is anything but vague. It is just very challenging, because it is such a radically new way of thinking. Sustainability wraps economics, ecology, social and personal well-being together in one package. It ties the package up with system dynamics, and mails the whole thing decades or even centuries into the future. No wonder it's had a hard time making it to Main Street.

But the complexity—and the polysyllabic extravagance—of the term "sustainability" does not mean that the word should be abandoned. It may take longer, but eventually, this idea will catch on. History is full of examples of new and complex ideas overturning the old order, often against seemingly long odds. An example is democracy. Today, most people throughout the World take it as a given that governments should be elected by the people. But this is a fairly recent idea, and not a simple one (nor is the word particularly beautiful). Before a rudimentary form of democratic government took hold in the late 1700s in the newly formed United States—inspired, in part, by the ancient Greeks and the Iroquois confederacy of nations—democracy was not exactly a household word. Nor was this form of social organization widely understood, accepted, or practiced. Consider the following; the quotes are in the voice of an imaginary courtier in the service of King George III.

PERCEPTIONS OF DEMOCRACY

Democracy was seen as lost to the ancient world. "Only the ancient Greeks could do democracy, and then not too well: don't forget, they kept slaves, imprisoned their women inside the house, and forced Socrates to drink hemlock. Plato called it 'charming' but 'full of variety and disorder.' You want *that*?" (Apparently, we do.)

Democracy was seen as an unattainable ideal. "It might be a noble and Utopian sentiment to believe in representative government, but as far as the real world of politics is concerned, democracy is for dreamers." (Exactly.)

Democracy was considered too complicated. "It's so much simpler to have the mandate of heaven resting with one person, and royal succession saves us the trouble of having to choose a new leader every time the old one dies. Besides, how would important decisions get made?" (More deliberatively.)

Democracy was considered unworkable in practice. "Voting? By the people, aka, 'the rabble'? You must be kidding. There would be fraud, election-rigging, vote-buying, threats and intimidations, you name it." (Often true, but it hasn't stopped democracy from working.)

Democracy had strong and powerful interest groups allied against it. "If you attempt to revolt and install your precious 'democracy', we will crush you." (Nice try.)

Democracy grew out of the efforts of small groups of social activists. "All this nonsense seems to have gotten started with the publication of a few pamphlets. People seem to be gathering in small groups simply to talk about the idea. What foolishness; where could that possibly lead?" (To transformation.)

Today's examples of democracy are far from perfect. Considering the current state of the art in the United States, country of democracy's modern-day rebirth, the process of self-government is beset with problems and deserving of criticism. But few in the U.S. would argue that today's democracy is not a miraculous advance over the tyrannical monarchy of yesterday. Moreover, democracy in America has steadily improved over time, from the original "one white male property owner, one vote" (in combination with extremely corrupt voting practices) to "one person, one vote." It is sometimes a wild and wacky way to run a nation—Winston Churchill apparently called it "the worst form of government, except for all the others"—but democracy has clearly proven its early critics wrong.

Now, repeat the above exchange in your own mind, replacing the word "democracy" with *sustainability*. Make the skeptical voice that of a hard-line, free-market economist employed by a major oil company— the rough equivalent of yesterday's royal courtier—and rewrite the quotations accordingly. See what I mean? As Yogi Berra said, "It's *déjà vu* all over again."

Just as it has taken some time to work the kinks out of democracy (and that effort is far from finished), sustainability will hardly be perfected, or even perfectly understood, any time soon. This new way of perceiving ourselves, socially as well as politically and economically, faces continuing uphill battles against the forces of inertia, greed, and simple ignorance. Most of the resistance comes, of course, from the mainstream power elite, defenders of the *status quo*, the self-avowed movers and shakers who actually do not want the World to move or to shake, because that might be threatening to their position in society. In the example of the award-winning San Diego city building cited above, the City Council apparently fought against the plan every step of the way—and has yet to acknowledge this extraordinary instance of intelligent, money-saving design right there on its own home turf. (If these city councillors were truly gifted politicians, they would be taking credit for the building by now.)

But sustainability also gets attacked from its left/green flank as well. In an article called "Buzzless Buzzword," no less an environmentalist than Bill McKibben, esteemed author of *The End of Nature*, pronounced the word "doomed" because "it does not refer to anything familiar." He proposed that it be replaced with "maturity," to link it to the cessation of physical growth—and the presumed advent of wisdom and restraint—that we associate with adulthood. Alas, in our youth-obsessed, pizzazz-driven culture, the prospects for galvanizing a transformative social movement around the word "maturity" seem even more daunting.

As a name for the future of our dreams, sustainability may be "the worst word, except for all the others." Like democracy, sustainability has been rudely used and abused; remember that Communist East Germany called itself the "German Democratic Republic." But if perverse misappropriations of idealistic terms are indicators of their symbolic power, sustainability is on the upswing.

Synonyms for "sustainable" in my computer's thesaurus include livable, bearable, passable, tolerable, and sufferable. There are no candidates for a replacement in that bunch, nor are there any credible contenders on the horizon. So it is far too early to abandon the word, and it is also too late: "sustainability" (or its even-less-elegant cousin, "sustainable development") has long since become the global signifier of record, the brass nameplate upon hundreds of doors, agreements, commissions, and initiatives at every level, from the United Nations to the village green. We might as well get used to it.

After all, as many writers have noted, we are "doomed to achieve sustainability" one way or another, at some level of comfort or discomfort, by choice or by Nature's decisive hand. It is far more desirable to attain it by choice, and that means studying it, planning for it, measuring our progress toward it. Choosing sustainability means doing a great deal of education to ensure that everyone understands what sustainability really means, especially those in leadership positions, so that everyone is pulling in the same direction. Failure to do this essential spadework can lead to results that are both comic and tragic.

▲▼▲

Fairfax County, Virginia
Fall 1993

I'm settling into my seat for the opening of a national conference on "sustainable communities." Vice-President Gore has already canceled, and I recognize far too many of the people here—always a bad sign, when you're hoping to expand a movement. But the turnout is pretty good, and a certain buoyant hopefulness hangs in the air.

The welcoming remarks are offered by the president of a local university.' He's happy to see us, and reports that he has long been a champion of "community sustainability." He proceeds to tell an illustrative story.

In the mid-1980s, he was deeply involved in economic development for the local county. "We overbuilt," he confesses. The county was in a state of "hypergrowth," and so bonds were passed and roads were constructed and malls were erected to service the new suburban developments. Alas, new residents did not appear, leaving the county with enormous financial problems.

"We learned our lesson," he assures us. I purse my lips and nod my head, waiting for the punchline. But it's not quite what I expect.

"Then, last year, the Disney Corporation announced that they were planning to build their new theme park here in Fairfax County, which they plan to call Disney's America." The new park is supposed to celebrate American history, and draw millions of tourists out of Washington, D.C., together with new residents, businesses, and jobs. This, he expects, will solve the county's financial problems, and usher them into a new era of "sustainable hypergrowth."

He wishes us well and takes his leave, and the stunned crowd politely applauds him on the way out.

Postscript: *The theme park was eventually quashed by public outcry, in part because local citizens felt the installation of a Disney theme park would amount to a "desecration" of the nearby Civil War battlefields.*

▲▼▲

Having said a great deal about what sustainability is, let us consider what it is not.

FIVE CLARIFYING DECLARATIONS OF SUSTAINABILITY

1. *Sustainability is not environmentalism.* While the former originally grew out of the latter, "sustainability" and "environmentalism" are now very different causes. Many environmentalists distrust the word "sustainable," while practitioners of sustainability (myself included) sometimes distance themselves from the environmentalist label—not because they don't support green causes, but because activism to protect Nature from the ravages of the economy is different from working to redesign the economy itself. We continue to need a strong (in fact a stronger) environmentalism, setting boundaries and protecting society from some people's unfortunate tendency to try to get away with profiteering at Nature's and society's expense. But for environmentalism's "No" to be effective, there must also be sustainability's "Yes." Environmentalism may have given birth to sustainability, but now the offspring needs to be free to grow and mature, departing at times from some of environmentalism's more strident precepts.

2. *Sustainability is not business-as-usual.* To call something "sustainable" does not make it so. Let us be clear: achieving sustainability requires nothing less than a massive reorientation of the global economy and much of society as well. Over the next fifty to one hundred years, that means redesigning and rebuilding virtually everything: cities, transportation systems, cars, power plants, engines of all kinds, materials, educational curricula, patterns of work and leisure, consumer expectations, and especially our systems for handling waste. (If not "Worm bins everywhere!", then something just as good.) This is business-as-very-*un*usual, and looked at correctly, this is also the biggest business *opportunity* since the invention of money. This is "unplanned obsolescence" on a global scale: if virtually everything needs to be replaced, re-

paired, retrofitted, or redesigned, that should translate to millions of new jobs and billions in potential profits (and ultimately planned non-obsolescence).

3. Sustainability is not against economic growth. *Au contraire.* Remember, *economic* growth is measured in *money* (via the GDP). Growth in *money* is not the problem; the problem is Growth, measured in numbers of *people* consuming increasing amounts of *stuff.* A World that is very busy recapturing materials out of the waste stream, replacing and recycling its cars into beautiful hydrogen-powered "Hypercars," retrofitting its buildings with the latest materials and technologies, and continuing to generate more and more economic value by selling *information, wisdom,* and *experience* rather than ever-increasing piles of *stuff*—that World will be making money hand over fist. Its GDP will go through the roof, and for much better reasons than by spending money on the clean-up of oil spills, or on rebuilding after floods, hurricanes, and other climate-change induced disasters (all of which, perversely, currently make the economy look good).

This is the magic of "Development without Growth," which is similar to what the Dutch call "decoupling" (cutting the link between a rising GDP and rising pollution levels). Once you unchain the economy from the shackles of "Growth by consumption and pollution," and set it to work on "Development by learning, improving, rebuilding," only the sky is the limit—and probably not even that, for long. (Flashforward to the future: "Scientists from Moon Colony today released a controversial new report called 'The Limits to Lunar Growth' . . .")

4. Sustainability is neither a religion nor an ideology. Thank the World's various deities for the people who live simply and cultivate non-consumerist lifestyles. Most of them, of course, are in Third World villages; their simplicity is not by choice. But those in the industrialized part of the World who embrace "voluntary simplicity" have set an important and paradigm-busting example: they prove that you don't have to enter the rat race to be happy; that you have more control over your financial life than you realize; and that it's possible to live more sustainably *right now*, without waiting for society and technology to catch up to you. They also set a *moral* example, because while sustainability may be the profitable choice, it is also the *right* choice.

But voluntary simplicity is not everyone's cup of herbal tea, and some people take genuine pleasure—as opposed to the ungenuine kind, induced by the ubiquitous mind-control devices known as "ads"—in shopping. Embracing sustainability does not require a vow of poverty, or a promise to shop only in second-hand stores. If everyone did that, it would be hard to find really great stuff at really low prices. Nor does sustainability require adherence to a creed: "I believe in the coming overshoot and collapse . . ."

Sustainability is the most practical choice for solving some rather disquieting problems. It is also very adaptable. Embrace it in whatever way works for you: as a lifestyle choice, as a business opportunity, or even, if you like, as a religious commitment. That's what freedom of religion is all about.

5. Sustainability is not the end of history. Even sustainability, in the real World, is not forever. Nor is it the final word. Success at sustainability leads not to societal immortality, but to societal *transformation*. Learning how to manage the World in a more elegant and intelligent way is merely the next step on the evolutionary ladder for sentient species like us, who have overrun their respective planets. Similar situations might be as common as dandelions on planets throughout the known (and unknown) universe.

We have no idea what phase in the evolution of conscious organisms comes after sustainability. But it would certainly be nice to give our descendants a chance to find out.

CHAPTER 8

The Proof of the Possible

I believe it to be perfectly possible for an individual to adopt the way of life of the future . . . without having to wait for others to do so.
—MOHANDAS K. GANDHI

Anything that exists is possible.
—KENNETH BOULDING

IMAGINE A VILLAGE WHERE people enjoy all the benefits of modern technology, but create few of the usual problems . . . where virtually all of the energy comes from the Sun, the wind, human exercise, and other clean and creative sources . . . where people of differing languages and ethnicities live together harmoniously, while maintaining their distinct cultures . . . where the once-barren landscape is now growing lush forests, out of which come a steady stream of high-value and renewable products . . . where even the seesaws in the children's playground are disguises for elegant water pumps . . . where everyone has enough, and each person does what they're good at . . . where the sick rest in naturally cool rooms, despite the tropical heat and without air conditioning, while enjoying views of the sky through retractable roofs over their beds (or, if they prefer, while swinging in hammocks, surrounded by their loved ones) . . . and where, in a country long torn apart by war, the continuous stream of inventions developed by this enlightened community is spreading across the land, bringing prosperity, better living standards, and badly needed hope.

This story is not a Utopian fantasy. Such a place already exists.

The village of Gaviotas, on the eastern grasslands of Colombia, has been a testing ground for visionary living for nearly three decades. It's not Utopia, as the residents will quickly tell you; but it's much closer to the ideal of sustainability than the vast majority of the World's communities. Everything in that rosy portrait is true, and more. Gaviotans pride themselves on doing things cheaply, creatively, ecologically—and profitably. They export many products including lightweight windmills (called "gaviotas" now by many Colombians), super-efficient pumps, and pine resin, with minimal impact on Nature, through well-developed marketing channels. They are trying to be a model for village development throughout the so-called Third World (not to be confused with World3, whose villages are virtual), and they are succeeding, despite the fact that civil war is raging constantly around them.

The remarkable story of this community of a couple of hundred people is documented in a recent book by veteran journalist Alan Weisman called *Gaviotas: A Village to Reinvent the World*. Weisman, who has also covered Colombia's civil war and vanishing ecosystems for major newspapers and broadcasting media, is not easily impressed. He's written a number of grim stories about some of the grimmest parts of the World, and he has no illusions about where the dominant trends are heading. But even he finds hope, and inspiration, in the accomplishments of this experimental community whose name means "the river terns." True, it's a small place, a tiny spot on the map in a country best known for drug exports and near-continuous civil strife. But Gaviotas is more than just a village; it is an *example*.

The complex beauty of sustainability is best illustrated by such examples. They shift the argument out of the realm of *Can we do it?* and over to *How can it best be done, today?* Examples prove the possible.

In these times, history is moving quickly, while books live at a slower pace. Any catalog of "best-practice" examples would soon be out of date. Moreover, while an enormous number of small-scale experiments in sustainability are being attempted all over the planet, these are too easily discounted as "marginal" exceptions that will never work at the global scale. Cars, airplanes, and telephones were all dismissed in their early stages of development by knowledgeable people. Innovations associated with sustainability cannot be expected to be any better received, at least initially.

So, in the pages that follow, I briefly offer several time-tested illustrations of sustainability in practice at a *large* scale, secure in the expectation that these exemplars will continue setting the standard for some time to come. I then recount the tale of my own experiments in promoting sustainability, and refer the reader to three books that can serve as springboards into the vast literature on the topic. A more extensive reading list can be found at the end of this book. (As a jumping-off point for the growing Web-based literature on sustainability, please visit www.AtKisson.com. I do not list Web sites here because they change too often.)

First we'll consider examples of true transformation in four very different sectors: national government, business, city planning, and civil society.

National Government: *The Netherlands.* In 1987, more than 11,000 dead seals washed up on the shores of Holland, killed by diseases brought on by high pollution levels in the sea. Holland's Queen Beatrix, in her annual Christmas message, warned the nation that "the Earth is dying." A popular book called *Zorgen voor Morgen* ("Concern for Tomorrow"), published by a government research institute, backed up the message with hard facts, and the practical Dutch swung into action.

Despite having some of the toughest environmental laws in the World at that time, Holland's environment was still killing seals and creating numerous other problems. So environmental and economic planners decided to start over. Instead of issuing even tougher regulations, requiring specific pollution controls and technologies (the approach known as "command and control"), they brought together representatives from every major industrial sector, and began to negotiate.

"Let us agree that we have a serious problem," said the government, and industry, given the undeniable evidence, was obliged to agree. Then the two parties struck some rather unusual voluntary agreements, called "covenants," whereby industry committed itself to achieving drastic reductions in pollution over a twenty-year period—one generation. In return, industry was given free reign to meet those reduction targets in whatever fashion they liked. There would be strict monitoring, and stiff penalties for failing to meet minimum standards; but no government bureaucrats would be hovering over industry, telling them what to do and how to do it.

The results have been remarkable. In the first ten years, reductions in pressure on the environment—with the notable exception of CO_2 emissions—have been largely right on target. Some pollutants are down as much as 90%, while money-measured economic growth has continued. As mentioned before, the Dutch call this "absolute decoupling," and they are now preaching its virtues to the rest of the World. They make key documents available in English, for free, and they even have an "environmental ambassador" in many of their embassies, whose job is to promote the Dutch approach to sustainability. (The Netherlands has an especially keen interest in addressing climate change: rising sea levels could force them to raise their dikes, at a staggering cost to the nation.)

Architects of the Dutch model are leaders in a new international movement, called "Green Planning," which is spreading to countries all over the globe. The Dutch are the first to acknowledge that they have a long way to go to achieve true sustainability, but the nation has three times in ten years renewed its commitment to this path. The goal of "sustainability within one generation," while not likely to be reached exactly on schedule, remains a guiding beacon for the Dutch nation and sets a new standard for national governments everywhere.

Business: *Interface, Inc.* In 1994, Ray Anderson, founder and CEO of the nation's largest supplier of office carpet, was asked to give a speech to his research department on the company's "environmental vision." The company, he knew, didn't actually have an environmental vision, but some customers were starting to ask about such things. So he went looking for a vision, and a vision found him: Paul Hawken's book, *The Ecology of Commerce.*

Reading that book, he says, was like "a spear in the chest." Hawken, himself a former successful CEO, detailed the many ways business was responsible for the planet's environmental problems, as well as the missed opportunities for saving money and making a profit to be found in operating more sustainably. According to Ray Anderson, Hawken's analysis hit him "right between the eyes. It was an epiphany." Anderson dedicated himself, and his company, to a long-term process of transformation with the goal of zero waste, zero damage to the Earth, and ultimately the restoration of the natural systems his company had previously harmed.

Within a few years, drawing on the help of the intellectual leaders in the sustainability movement (including Hawken, energy analyst Amory Lovins, green architect William McDonough, and many more), Interface had drastically reduced its waste per unit while dramatically increasing its sales, breaking the billion-dollar mark. Pumping systems were made far more efficient, new products were developed from innovative recycled materials, and experiments were begun in *leasing* carpet rather than selling (so the old carpet could be reclaimed and remanufactured). Meanwhile, the company's stock tripled in value. As Interface began to attract more attention from both Wall Street and among environmentalists, Anderson was named co-chair of a presidential council on sustainable development, and he began crisscrossing the country preaching the gospel: Sustainability is good for business, and essential for the Earth.

Many other U.S. businesses have taken modest steps in the direction of sustainability, but Interface—which still has a long way to go to reach its ultimate goals—remains in the vanguard. There is an irony to the company's success, because sales growth has outpaced even its accelerated efforts to reduce waste and increase efficiency. Overall, Interface's *total* environmental impact has actually increased, even as its impact *per unit of product* has decreased substantially. Anderson acknowledges this, but notes that his company has captured business from other manufacturers whose practices place much larger stresses on Nature. And Interface's vision of making zero negative impact on the Earth—backed up by major investments in research and training—continues to shape the company's long-term strategy.

Sitting next to Ray Anderson over breakfast one morning, while attending a meeting of the presidential commission he co-chairs, I asked him, "Who are your peers? What other companies and CEOs are moving as aggressively as you are in this direction?" Anderson shook his head ruefully. "No one," he said in his gentle Georgia drawl, "at least not yet, and it's a darn shame, because there's money to be made."

City Planning: *Curitiba, Brazil.* I've met Jaime Lerner, the many-times–elected mayor of this medium-sized city on Brazil's central plateau, only once. He immediately began to sketch on napkins, describing and explaining how, since the early 1970s, Curitiba has transformed itself into one of the World's most livable cities, and the envy of every other city in Brazil. That act of sketching symbolized a restless, improvisatory approach to solving problems: Lerner has helped to instill a sense of perpetual design, creativity, and play in his beloved Curitiba, and an outpouring of innovation has led to widely applicable new models for how humans can live in cities.

This process began with a dramatic act of destruction and reconstruction. In the course of a single weekend, one block of the city's main shopping street was jackhammered up and turned into a pedestrian mall, complete with flowers, trees, and park benches. Shopkeepers, who had been marshaling their forces to protest the idea of closing the street to cars, soon began to request that the mall's car-free zone be extended—in fact, these requests began within hours of its opening on Monday morning.

Since then Curitiba has been a proving ground for new ideas. A space-age–looking bus system moves people in and out of the city on dedicated avenues, with phenomenal speed. Old buses have been converted into mobile schools, which visit the poorer neighborhoods and teach vocational skills. Even slum dwellers (Curitiba has not escaped the Growth dynamics of Brazil) get free consulting time from architects to improve and beautify the construction of their shacks, and they are given a sack of food or a bus token for every sack of garbage they turn in, which keeps the *favelas* (slums and poor shanty towns) clean.

Business has grown on the downwind side of town in a new industrial park that is half green space, and special bus lines connect it to working-class neighborhoods. A federal flood-control program served as an excuse to create many new lakes and parks, and street children are hired as gardeners. The list of new ideas coming out of Curitiba's seemingly continuous *charettes* (brainstorming sessions involving designers from several different disciplines) is a magnificent testament to the practicality of the possible.

All of this has been done on the cheap, without huge federal subsidies. Creativity, ingenuity, and passion have substituted for money. And the result is a less polluted, more convenient, more efficient, more prosperous, and more humane city. The text on a ticket book used by the trash-for-food program repeats to Curitibans a message now being echoed around the globe: "You are an example to Brazil and even to the rest of the world."

Civil Society: *The Natural Step, Sweden (and elsewhere).* In the late 1980s, Swedish cancer researcher Karl-Henrik Robèrt began working on a paper about global environmental problems that he considered to be "the consensus report." Unfortunately, he was a consensus of one. Concerned that society was arguing about the "twigs and leaves" of the environmental debate, while ignoring the fundamental scientific truths—the "trunk" of the tree, which everyone could agree on—he set about to create a much broader social consensus in Sweden.

Robèrt sent copies of his draft report to a large circle of Swedish intellectual leaders and asked them, "What's wrong with this paper?" They were only too happy to poke holes in his thinking and in his prose. Robèrt, also a former national karate champion, did his best to respond to their criticisms, and then sent the draft out again. And again. And again. Each time the criticisms would come back, and each time he would redraft the paper and send it out for another round of review.

Twenty-two drafts later, he had the consensus report that he had originally been seeking. Eventually, the document was endorsed by Sweden's king, and a workbook based on the document—which explains sustainability in terms of basic cell biology and the laws of physics—was mailed to every household and school in Sweden.

From this singular act of intellectual perseverance has sprung an international movement to transform business and community life, known as "The Natural Step." Major U.S. and European corporations have adopted its science-based framework as a way to promote innovation internally, and to reorient their enterprises in the direction of zero emissions, zero damage to Nature's systems, maximum benefit to the community, and enhanced profitability. These companies include furniture giant Ikea, Electrolux vacuum cleaners, Scandia Hotels, and the aforementioned Interface.

The Natural Step starts from a set of four principles, which Robèrt calls "System Conditions," that are the basis for steering innovation and redevelopment within companies, agencies, and communities. Summarized and simplified, these are:

1. you can't dig stuff out of the Earth and spread it around indefinitely;
2. you can't spread human-created stuff around in Nature indefinitely, either;
3. don't erode Nature's capacity to do all the wonderful things Nature does, or you'll be sorry; and
4. do your business efficiently and make sure that everyone has enough.

These "System Conditions" are a quantitatively verifiable definition of sustainability. The science behind them includes the Second Law of Thermodynamics ("stuff spreads out") and basic cell biology ("bad stuff tends to easily accumulate up the food chain"). It's hard to argue the laws of Nature.

While The Natural Step has focused mostly on the transformation of business and the economy, it is firmly rooted in civil society—the self-organizing, nongovernmental sector of society. It is neither a business nor a government program, though some agencies promote it and some businesses profit from it. The organizations that promote The Natural Step are nonprofits, and they make their materials available at modest cost to consultants, community activists, and government agencies. Its continuing dissemination from Sweden to other countries testifies to the power of a good idea clearly and passionately communicated.

▲▼▲

Penang, Malaysia
November 1997

I'm co-facilitating a set of roundtable discussions for the newly launched "Sustainable Penang" project. It's amazing to see how far across the globe this idea of citizens choosing their own measures of progress and sustainability has traveled. I'm grateful for the opportunity to occasionally travel with it; Sustainable Seattle still serves many new projects as a model.

Despite the obvious cultural differences, Sustainable Penang feels very familiar. Over seventy-five civic leaders in health, business, environment, government, cultural heritage, and social welfare have come together to select a new set of indicators for Penang, a prosperous, diverse, and beautiful city. Today, unfortunately, Penang's beauty is shrouded in smoke from the forest fires in nearby Sumatra.

After small group reports on key issues, "votes" for the "most popular" indicators, and the occasional humorous song, a remarkable birth occurs. A local doctor stands up and gives an impassioned impromptu speech on the problem of water quality in Penang. "The streams our children play in are polluted," he says. "No one is even monitoring this issue."

On the spot, he calls for the creation of a new civic group, to be called Penang Water Watch. In the space of a minute, a founding board of directors is formed from among the participants of the roundtable. Within a year, there will be volunteer monitoring teams, and an excellent guidebook for local teachers, officials, and activists.

I've long known that the process of developing indicators—which can seem very abstract—can have very tangible spin-off effects. But it's a rare privilege, and a great joy, to see it happening right here, right now.

▲▼▲

For five years, I was privileged to serve as one of the leaders of a remarkable volunteer initiative in my adopted "second home town," Seattle, Washington. I have alluded to this experience several times in previous chapters; now I would like to tell the story in more detail, because it was through my work with Sustainable Seattle that I came to understand, in a personal way, the power of dedicated people, the potency of a good idea, and the astonishing rapidity with which an abstract concept can become reality and spread across cultures. It was my first genuine experience in helping to change the World.

In 1989, while editing an issue of the journal *In Context* devoted to climate change, I had gotten into a debate with one of our contributing editors, W. R. Prescott. Prescott was convinced that human beings would never respond to Nature's signals in time, and that humanity was essentially doomed to suffer from climatic catastrophe. The problem, he argued, lay in the human "fight-or-flight" nervous system, which is structured to respond to immediate dangers such as a bear at the cave door. Compared to a bear, the slow, invisible change in atmospheric carbon-dioxide levels did not have the same compelling urgency, at least from our brainstem's vantage point. The climate system is just too complicated, the information about it just too abstract, to provoke a response.

I am an optimist by nature and generally unwilling to accept doom as an option. So I argued the case with Prescott in the following way: What about the Dow Jones Industrial Average, or the Gross Domestic Product? The systems they tell us about are extremely complicated, and the numbers themselves are highly abstract. But we have been trained, as a people, to respond to drops in these numbers *as though* they were bears at the cave door. (The phrase "bear market" takes on a different meaning in this context.) Big drops in these measures strike great fear into the hearts of many, and they prompt immediate defensive action, not to mention the occasional jump out the window.

Numbers like these are called *indicators*. They are similar to the gas gauge on your car, or the thermometer that measures your temperature. With training and repeated exposure, the human mind learns to associate signals from indicators with the requirement to take action. When the gas gauge hits "E," you had better buy gas.

What if we found a similar indicator of sustainability? I wondered. What if a number, or a set of numbers, told society whether it was going in the right direction, and did so in a compelling, bear-like way that could touch that primitive part of our brains?

I became enamoured of this idea, and so I was surprised and delighted when, just a few months later, I received an invitation to participate in a one-day forum on creating indicators of sustainability for the city of Seattle. Apparently I was not alone in reaching this conclusion about the power of indicators! I could barely contain my enthusiasm.

The first meeting of what became Sustainable Seattle was hosted by the prominent Washington, D.C.-based Global Tomorrow Coalition, together with a number of Seattle's civic leaders, and it was something of a fortunate disappointment. Failure motivated us to create something even more ambitious. As we came to discover, developing indicators is no easy task, and it is not done in a single day. Moreover, we were a diverse collection of people who mostly did not know each other. We needed time to build trust and common understanding.

Those of us who were the most frustrated by the day's outcome were also the most determined to carry on the work. Six of us became a self-appointed leadership team, and we began to meet regularly in my apartment near Seattle's famous Space Needle. Over carrot sticks and herbal tea, we hatched a quiet revolution.

Through the course of six months in 1991, we and our fellow "Trustees," as we began to call the larger group of active participants, carefully developed an innovative structure and strategy. Sustainable Seattle, at least initially, was not an organization; it was an amorphous network, not tied to any one institution. Our "Board of Trustees" acted as "stewards of the process," a process that would soon grow to include several hundred people. The effort would be almost entirely voluntary, which allowed us to be frugal: $20,000 covered our entire budget for the first three years. Even though Seattle was engaged in a contentious growth-management–planning effort, we were determined to stand clear of divisive local politics; our focus would be on long-term visions and indicators of long-term trends. These choices gave us enormous freedom to try new approaches, a freedom that local government and established organizations did not share.

After agreeing on a structure, a strategy, and a definition of sustainability, we set to work on developing indicators, drawing on the expertise of our members and their friends in various agencies and institutions. We came up with a draft: forty measures that we felt captured the essence of sustainability in all its dimensions. But what would the community think? We decided to find out.

We sent a letter to over three hundred Seattle leaders in government, business, environmental groups, social welfare agencies, the arts, the media, the religious congregations, and more, asking them to participate in an intensive six-month process of review and revision. We expected no more than fifty would be willing to make such a commitment, and so we were astonished when our mailbox filled with over two hundred RSVPs saying, "Yes, I'd like to help."

For the next year, our dedicated core group of around twenty volunteers scrambled to design, facilitate, and process the results from a series of meetings convened to define what sustainability meant for Seattle, and how to measure our progress toward that ideal. Each meeting had at least a hundred civic leaders in attendance, together with interested citizens, reporters, and students. In between the larger gatherings, there were homework assignments, committee meetings, initial data collection. The plenary meetings were popular, in part, because they were *fun*. We spiced up the proceedings with stories, songs, and even—at the end of the process—a dramatic reading of the indicators themselves, complete with excerpts from the works of famous writers and poets that illustrated the human stories behind the abstract numbers and ideas.

One of our favorite stories, related by now–City Council member Richard Conlin, concerned a certain large hall at Oxford University in England. Apparently, one of the massive, three-hundred-year-old wooden beams holding up the ceiling finally began to rot. The young building managers were convinced that finding a tree in modern England that could be felled to replace the old beam was an impossibility— but they were told to go see the university's forester. This gentleman led them through a wood they didn't know about, to a tree whose size astonished them. "There's your beam," said the forester. How could this be? they asked. "Well, three hundred years ago, when our ancestors built that hall, they planted this tree."

After a few more months of research, we released a preliminary report to the media on our indicators, with a press release headlined LONG-TERM TRENDS SHOW SEATTLE'S FUTURE AT RISK. Wild salmon (our most popular new indicator) were disappearing, we told them. More and more children were being born into poverty—an indicator that the economy was less healthy than commonly believed. Some news was good, such as the fact that the local job base was less dependent on Boeing airplanes, and water was being used more conservatively—but Seattle's famous recycling program wasn't working, because the quantity of garbage thrown away was growing faster than the amount of garbage recycled. And all these trends were linked together. In the long run, we reasoned, child poverty was likely to cause a further decline in salmon, since poor children were more likely to turn to crime, which drove people into their cars and out to the suburbs, destroying salmon habitat. The flight to the suburbs reduced support for the city's schools, harming children, and so the cycle would continue unless the community took decisive action.

Certain that our indicator report would be controversial, we stepped back and prepared for a fiery response. But our analysis was met with a thundering silence. "Long-term trends are not news," the newspaper editors told us.

▲▼▲

Seattle, Washington
Spring 1995

A strange thing is happening. Even though we didn't succeed in getting much local attention for the first Sustainable Seattle indicators report, we seem to be becoming famous elsewhere, especially among local-government types. And the farther away people are, the more they think our project is the greatest thing since sliced bread.

It helped that Seattle's city government informally adopted our report. Gary Lawrence, the director of the planning department, even decided to name the city's comprehensive plan "Toward a Sustainable Seattle." Other cities are beginning to ask for help in duplicating our indicators process. City council members who previously didn't know about us are learning about the indicators in the oddest ways, such as by attending conferences in New Zealand or England.

We're currently preparing our second report, this time containing more indicators and even showing a few changes in the trends we high-lighted last time. It looks like we'll get more media coverage, too, since we've picked up a number of very prominent friends and sponsors in the city. We're beginning to understand, at a deeper level, that institutional change of this sort takes place over years, even decades. We're learning patience and perseverance.

It's funny how things work out. We thought we were starting a move-ment in Seattle, and maybe we will in time. But it seems like we've done something unexpected and unintended: we've helped to start an interna-tional movement, the development of indicators of sustainability in cities around the globe.

▲▼▲

Today Sustainable Seattle (S2 for short) is an independent nonprofit organization, led by a team that includes a few veterans of those found-ing days, but staffed mostly by a newer group of volunteers and profes-sionals. (I continue to serve as a volunteer consultant.) Many of the early goals we set have been accomplished: indicators have become part of the mainstream of local government life, and the concept of sustainability is firmly established in civic discourse. The City of Seattle has even created an "Office of Sustainability," spurred by Richard Conlin. S2 is now innovating in other areas, with a course on sustainable living and a guidebook for local sustainability under development, while it continues to redevelop and publish the indicators every two or three years.

What concrete changes have resulted from the effort? It's hard to say. Can the group claim any credit for Seattle's increasing willingness to explore innovative solutions to key sustainability problems, such as efforts to redevelop abandoned industrial sites in ecologically sound ways? Maybe—but the claim would be hard to prove.

Indicators are a very subtle agent of change, because they work in two relatively invisible dimensions: individual consciousness, and social process. When considering the economy, why do we think so much about the importance of unemployment? Because we are regularly exposed to an indicator called the "unemployment rate." It affects our consciousness, and focuses our attention on the issue, almost without our noticing it. The same is true of the stock market numbers; these numbers are most important not because of what they tell us about the market, but because of the fact that they focus our attention on the stock market itself. The mere *existence* of indicators of sustainability is similarly important: it focuses attention on the goal of sustainability, reorienting people's actions in ways they are not likely to notice.

At the same time, the *process* of creating and maintaining indicators changes people, organizations, and communities more directly, but often in ways they did not expect. At the unveiling of New Jersey Future's new indicators for the sustainability of that state, in June of 1999, all of us participating watched as Governor Christine Todd Whitman signed an executive order making sustainability the guiding precept of her administration. She also mandated the development of new indicators for sustainability in the performance of state agencies. Such immediate and *visible* examples of indicators at work are rare, but these "side-effects" are actually some of the principal reasons to pursue the process.

As a strategy for promoting sustainability, developing indicators is a benign version of the Trojan Horse: inside the process are concealed a host of new concepts, values, initiatives, and inspirations, just waiting for the right moment to emerge. I believe this "Trojan Horse Effect" is the real secret behind the spread of the indicators movement to hundreds of communities all over the World, because I have witnessed the benefits of the effect time and time again. Many of these "community indicator projects" (increasingly known as "CIPs") trace their origins directly to Sustainable Seattle; quite a number of them I have been privileged to serve as a consultant. After almost a decade of thinking about indicators, and helping organizations and communities develop indicator systems, my own passion for them is stronger than ever. Experience has proven that they are a very powerful first step on the path to sustainability. The reason is twofold: they are systemic; and they are good vehicles for the diffusion of the sustainability ideal.

"Systemic" refers to our earlier encounter with systems theory, and specifically to the concept of feedback. Indicators fix the feedback loops. When well designed and widely published, indicators provide a warning signal about the status of critical stocks and flows—preferably in time for people to do something about the problems the indicators highlight. Indicator systems are like new, improved "dashboards" for communities and companies, which must operate in an increasingly complex World, facing increasingly tough challenges.

"Diffusion" refers to the ability of indicators to spread from person to person, place to place. Human beings are very comfortable using indicators; they work with them every day, either formally (as with the Dow Jones Industrial Average) or informally (as when you feel your child's forehead to judge her temperature). So *indicators of sustainability* combine the new with the familiar in a very useful way. In some contexts, it is easier to spread the idea of *measuring* sustainability than it is to spread the more abstract idea of sustainability itself. (Understanding this process of diffusion is important; we'll consider it in detail in the following chapter. Also, resources for learning more about indicators are listed in the Notes section at the end of the book.)

Indicators make the concept of long-term, interconnected trends more palpable. (Remember the "gallery tour" from chapter 3.) They make us honest about what sustainability looks like, by translating the concept into a measuring stick and a score card. Indicators are also essential: without them, society cannot function. And without good indicators of *sustainability*, telling us where we're going and what we need to change, society cannot possibly avoid overshoot and collapse.

▲▼▲

Indicators can tell us where we are, and where we need to go, but they are not, by themselves, a solution. Solutions come in the form of *innovations*—new initiatives, new technologies, new ways of solving problems and accomplishing tasks.

If you are new to sustainability, and you want to get more thoroughly introduced to new models and innovations that have the potential to reshape our World, let me recommend three books that are likely to have relatively long shelf-lives. Dozens of books focus on theories of sustainability, and many more detail the problems associated with the World's out-of-control Growth; many of these are listed in the Sources section at the end of this book. But these three books focus on solutions. They are also chock full of detailed examples and descriptions of sustainability in practice, at scales ranging from the very small (households) to the very large (the global automobile industry). Better yet, they have the advantage of being *books*: you don't need "high" technology to access them, and you can take them anywhere. (Note to future historians: Treat these books as vital sources in your research about the transformations that began to occur in the late twentieth and early twenty-first centuries, especially if you've long since forgotten what a "CD-ROM" is.)

Recommendation #1: *Natural Capitalism: Creating the Next Industrial Revolution*, by Paul Hawken, Amory Lovins, and L. Hunter Lovins (Little, Brown, 1999). If every business person, every scientist, every engineer, every economist were to read and heed this book, sustainability would become the norm. The authors are three of the most ingenious minds on the planet, already responsible for catalyzing revolutionary new ways of thinking in business, energy, and the automotive industry. Here in one volume they bring together the results of two decades of experimentation and insight—not only their own, but that of nearly every leading thinker and tinkerer in the field of sustainability. This book will give you a thorough, practical, and conceptual grounding in everything from the reinvention of the automobile (coming soon: the "Hypercar") to the redesign of the market economy. Food, water, materials, neighborhoods . . . it's all here, backed up by numbers and dollar figures and extensive references. *Natural Capitalism* will show you conclusively that a saner, greener, and more profitable World is possible, and that it's already starting to be created. It's an indispensable book.

Recommendation #2: *Eco-Pioneers: Practical Visionaries Solving Today's Environmental Problems*, by Steve Lerner (The MIT Press, 1997). Lerner's other books were collections of wide-ranging interviews with sustainability thinkers and pioneers, but here, he focuses on deeds rather than words. The book serves as a guided tour through dozens of personalities and their inventions, many of whom already are reshaping the World in ways small and large. The cover features John Todd and his Living Machines, biological waste-treatment systems that can take raw sewage or septic-tank waste, replete with cancer-causing chemicals, and turn it into drinking water using only living plants, animals, and sunlight. (The "treatment facilities" look and smell like greenhouses.) Lerner also introduces architect and industrial designer William McDonough ("The only way we are going to get there is to redesign our products. All of our products. Everything. Completely."); City Councilman Dave Crockett ("We now talk about Chattanooga as a defining place for sustainability."); Sacramento municipal-utility manager S. David Freeman ("Our idea is that we will be a solar utility in the future."); and dozens of others, from farmers to global organizers. They're not dreamers; they're making a living at making sustainability work. A great tip-sheet for venture capitalists and idealistic volunteers alike.

Recommendation #3: *Hope, Human and Wild: True Stories of Living Lightly on the Earth,* by Bill McKibben (Little, Brown, 1995). This elegant collection of essays and travelogues is McKibben's antidote to the distressing and brilliant book that made him famous, *The End of Nature.* Here he focuses on three stories of sustainable transformation and renewal: the restoration of the eastern U.S. forests over the last century; the story of Brazil's city of Curitiba; and the remarkable case of Kerala, a large Indian state where quality of life approaches First World standards even though per-capita incomes are among the lowest anywhere. McKibben is a fine writer, with a journalist's devotion to the facts and a storyteller's eye for colorful detail. The book is a pleasure to read, and it is the best documentation available on three classic examples of sustainability in practice at the large scale. It also convincingly makes the case that the World *could* live more slowly, more simply, and more happily, even if it seems hell-bent right now on choosing speed and destructive complication.

These books will get you oriented and start you thinking in pragmatic terms, about sustainability. But of course, the real learning is in the doing.

▲▼▲

Bainbridge Island, Washington
June 1992

After four years of coming to work every day in this suburban basement, riding the ferry over from Seattle and sitting at an editor's desk, I'm leaving. I've been studying and reporting on sustainability long enough; it's time to try to make it happen.

Actually, I don't really want to leave. My departure from In Context *magazine is brought on by a rift that's opened up between myself and the founder. We have different visions of the magazine's future, and competing needs for control. It's his magazine, so I'm the one to go. I feel a bit like a fledgling bird being nudged out of the nest.*

But it's a change I quickly learn to embrace, and ultimately feel grateful for. It's time to find out whether sustainability really means anything in practice, and not just in marginal experiments and small-circulation journals. I spend a day of retreat on Washington's wild beaches, thinking about what to do now. I draw pictures, I sing, I talk to myself (or whoever might be listening in this remote place). And something unexpected happens: I hatch a business.

If sustainability is going to work in the real World, I realize, it's got to work in the market economy. There has to be value added, both perceived and real. People have to be willing to pay for it, to invest in it, to see it as economically sensible and profitable. In a nutshell, sustainability has to make money.

So there it is: the answer I've been looking for on this deserted beach. This is not exactly the mystical sense of wonder I usually come here seeking, but I feel inspired nonetheless. I know exactly what to do. I finally see how to integrate my commitment to sustainability, my knowledge of the field, and even my passion for music and the arts into my work life, as an integrated "practice."

I go home, file for a business license, and become a consultant.

▲▼▲

Since 1992, I have made a substantial part of my living as a consultant on sustainability, helping companies, nonprofit organizations, foundations, and communities create new initiatives and tackle tough challenges. That fact alone is enough to prove to me that sustainability is possible in the market economy; and since I often include music in my speeches and presentations, the work gives me a lot of creative enjoyment as well. But more to the point are the enormous number of *other* people now working in the field, as architects, educators, business consultants, builders, engineers, investment managers, city planners, you-name-it. Universities are beginning to offer degrees in sustainability, or degrees in traditional fields retooled to incorporate the concept, and companies are creating positions for people with those degrees. If I were to reshoot the movie *The Graduate* today, I would rewrite the party scene so that the older fellow with the one-word piece of career advice for Dustin Hoffman—the word was "plastics"—leans over and instead says, "sustainability."

If you want to develop your own practice in the art of sustainability, the pathway can be summed up in the seven principles on the following pages. They are simple, but very challenging. They can powerfully reshape your understanding of reality and your view of the World. Be forewarned that if you take these principles truly to heart, they will change your life irrevocably—yet offer you an enormous sense of purpose and satisfaction.

THE SEVEN PRINCIPLES OF SUSTAINABILITY

1. *Think long term.* Sustainability is not just about next year or next decade, but about generational time-scales. Start by keeping the World of your great-grandchildren in mind.

2. *Understand systems.* Everything is linked together, often in surprising ways. And the dynamics of systems—including feedback loops and exponential growth—are not intuitively obvious. Systems require careful study. Paradoxically, to understand the big picture, you have to step back in order to take a closer look. Use intuition to seek out the missing links, logic to analyze the connections, and science to measure the trends. Otherwise you will continue to miss the surprising ripple effects of various people's uninformed actions and decisions, including your own.

3. *Recognize limits.* Once upon a time the human World was small and Nature was big. Limits to Growth were extremely far away. Exponential Growth has changed all that; we're rocketing past the limits at ever-increasing speed, and must change course. Pretending that limits don't exist doesn't make them less real. In fact, ignoring them gives them the power to determine the future, by forcing us to contend with the inevitable collapse. Working within the limits is the mark of wisdom and the best strategy for maintaining human freedom of action.

4. *Protect Nature.* She provides untold trillions of dollars in services to us, for free. Moreover, she's astonishingly beautiful. We depend on Nature for life—and now a great deal of life depends on our caring for Nature. We cannot afford to let any more of the Earth's species and habitats disappear, or allow any further erosion in Nature's capacity to sustain life in the relatively stable and dependable fashion we humans have come to enjoy.

5. *Transform business-as-usual.* Very little of what industrial societies currently do—whether in business, government, or community life—qualifies as "sustainable." More specifically, very little of this is truly efficient, effective, or elegant based on sustainability's new and demanding criteria. Fortunately, most of humanity's systems are constantly transforming themselves anyway. Your mission, as a practitioner of sustainability in whatever field you choose, is to steer this continuous process of Development in the most intelligent, ecological, and moral direction possible—and to do it in ways that make economic sense.

6. *Practice fairness.* *In Context* founder Robert Gilman used to say that "Sustainability equals fairness over time." If we were truly fair to Nature, to each other, and to future generations, sustainability would happen automatically.

7. *Embrace creativity.* Sustainability requires that humanity make enormous changes, and that means embracing what psychiatrist Charles Johnston calls "the creative imperative." We have to be inventive, creative, and playful—hardly an onerous chore! And yet being playful, for adults, requires practice, because much of our training drums the creativity out of us. For some people, taking up the arts and other seeming digressions into the creative and aesthetic dimensions of life may prove the most direct route to sustainability.

Humanity's mantra used to be, "Grow or die." From here on out, it's "Get creative—or collapse."

CHAPTER 9

The Innovation Diffusion Game

At first people refuse to believe that a strange new thing can be done, then they begin to hope it can be done—then it is done and all the world wonders why it was not done centuries ago.
—FRANCES HODGSON BURNETT

Never doubt that a small group of thoughtful, committed citizens can change the world. Indeed, it's the only thing that ever has.
—ATTRIBUTED TO MARGARET MEAD

THE SECOND OF this chapter's epigraphs (attributed to anthropologist Margaret Mead, though I have never been able to document that attribution in the literature) has inspired thousands of people around the globe working to make the World a better place. Mead's famous quotation describes the first stages

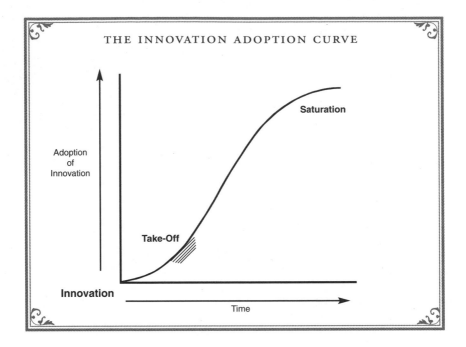

THE INNOVATION ADOPTION CURVE

Saturation

Adoption
of
Innovation

Take-Off

Innovation

Time

of the process of *innovation diffusion*: how a new idea or set of ideas, usually originating with a visionary thinker or inventor, gets adopted by a small number of people who make it their mission to promote these new ideas to the World.

After a new idea is born—whether it's a new concept, a new technology, a new cultural practice, or even an old idea that's just getting reintroduced—it spreads very slowly at first. A junior high school student tries out a new joke with a few of her friends. Amory Lovins describes the idea of a superefficient "Hypercar" to colleagues at Rocky Mountain Institute. Karl-Henrik Robèrt sends a manuscript of his "consensus report" on environmental problems to a few trusted colleagues in Sweden. Only a handful people know about the innovation at this stage, and they carefully test it and assess it to see if it's worth telling other people about.

If the idea is initially a hit, then word of mouth kicks in (and sometimes, of course, a well-funded marketing campaign kicks in as well). The young girl's joke makes the jump to the Internet, auto exec-utives begin to read memos about Amory Lovins and Hypercars, some-one gives Karl-Henrik Robèrt's report to the King of Sweden. Early on comes a make-or-break point, where the innovation has a level of mo-mentum that researchers call "Take-off." From here on out, the graph pictured here turns sharply up, meaning the innovation now spreads very easily and rapidly, sped by exponential growth in the process of one person telling another person. (You see, exponential growth is not in-herently a bad thing; it all depends on what is growing.)

Suddenly we live in a World where everyone with an e-mail ad-dress has seen the joke three times, where primitive prototypes of the Hypercar are beginning to roll off the assembly line, where every household in Sweden has long since received a copy of The Natural Step report. The "something new" becomes old hat. When an innova-tion has been thoroughly integrated into the body of the culture, reach-ing a point the theorists call "Saturation," it's no longer an innovation. It is taken for granted as part of normal life.

Innovation-diffusion theory—first proposed by Everett Rogers in his 1962 book, *Diffusion of Innovations*—is *itself* an innovation, a very powerful one that has been relatively slow to diffuse beyond the borders of academic communications theory. For sustainability's sake, it's high time this theory became common knowledge.

▲▼▲

Seattle, Washington
December 1990

I am watching a small crowd of people milling about, talking intensely to one another, occasionally erupting in giggles of delight or snorts of derision. Once in a while, somebody walks over to an easel off to the side and signs their name. They are greeted with applause from one part of the group, howls of protest from the other.

This is only the third time I've tried this little exercise. It's a simula-tion game based (very loosely) on the work of Everett Rogers. His ideas about how ideas spread through a culture are so exciting to me that I've turned the theory into a workshop. "The Innovation Diffusion Game" is my attempt to diffuse innovation diffusion theory, to make it more popular and accessible.

I'm still working the kinks out. The game puts people into a variety of roles that they may or may not be comfortable playing, from "Change Agents" (who actively promote new ideas) to "Reactionaries" (who staunchly resist them). They play these roles in an imaginary cultural context, such as a community meeting about nuclear power. That's the scene being played out in front of me right now. The anti-nuclear forces, led by the Change Agents, are winning, because they are successfully persuading the group to adopt their innovation: a petition calling for abolishing nuclear power and replacing it with renewables like wind and solar.

But suddenly their progress in the imaginary petition drive comes to a screeching halt. One of the Reactionaries, playing the role of a nuclear power executive, has made a very clever move: she's stolen all the marker pens. No pens, no more signatures, no petition. The Reactionaries win.

During the debrief that follows, the Change Agents express frustration, but everyone reflects that this little exercise was uncomfortably similar to real life. It's hard to organize for change, and all too easy to undermine the process if you can control the resources, especially the media.

But the most surprising reflections come from the successful Reactionary, who in real life is a long-time anti-nuclear activist. She starts to cry. "This was very hard for me" she says haltingly. "All my life I've seen the people I was fighting against as evil, or at least ignorant. But when I was playing this role, I could feel what is must be like to believe in nuclear power, to depend on it for my job and my family's security. I suddenly saw people like me as the enemy. Stealing the pens was an act of desperation. I was protecting my identity and my way of life.

"It's not like I'm going to stop my activist work. But now I want to find a different way to relate to the people on the other side, to see them as human beings.

"I guess most people believe they're trying to do the right thing."

▲▼▲

The process of innovation diffusion is chaotic, because cultures are complex systems. They are creatures swimming in a sea of information that is filled with millions of possible "new ideas." Selected ideas within that sea get eaten, digested, and circulated around, much the same way that a single-celled amoeba takes in a choice particle of food. Very powerful innovations can actually change the *structure* of the cultural system, just as certain chemical compounds can alter the structure of a cell (for good or ill). Sometimes an innovation can completely transform a culture, just as a new concept can completely change the way a large, conscious organism (like you) looks at the World. Given the enormous potential for both positive and negative change that certain innovations carry with them, it's no wonder that cultures are often very cautious about which ideas they take in, and which ones they reject.

▲▼▲

Prague, Czech Republic
September 1992

I'm in Eastern Europe for the first time, marveling at its mixture of Soviet-style apartment blocks and picturesque antiquities. The speech this morning was a risk: for the first time, I tried building songs directly into a keynote address. It went over so well that I've decided to make music a regular part of my presentations. Getting kicked out of a job I loved has turned me into a risk-taker.

It's weird how I came to be here. On the very same day I was first "invited" to leave my job as a magazine editor, I also received invitations to be the opening speaker at two separate international conferences. Amazingly, one was in Hungary, the other here in Prague. They were separated in time by only a few days, so I could easily do them both. Sometimes it feels like the Universe has an uncanny sense of timing, and a bizarre sense of humor.

This afternoon I'm running another workshop using the "Innovation Diffusion Game." This is another first for me: doing workshops for an international audience. I find I have to rely more on non-verbal demonstra-

tions to get the concepts across, including something I call the "Amoeba Game."

I move to the center of the room. "I need a volunteer," I say, and a German fellow stands up and comes forward. "Great, now I need seven more volunteers." A small cluster of somewhat less eager people come forward, and I have them link arms around the German guy. I count the remainder of the group: twenty people. "Okay," I call out, "now I need twenty more volunteers." People smirk and chuckle, but they come up, and I have them link arms in another circle around the central cluster.

Then I move to the person on the edge nearest the door. "Food is this way! Follow me!" I whisper, tugging on a sleeve. The "amoeba" bulges. "Faster, this way, toward the door!"—and now the "nucleus" begins to be caught up in the jostling movement of people. I tug them through the door, around the corner, and suddenly all is chaos, as arm-links break and the group starts to laugh uncontrollably.

"What happened?" I ask, when the group has reassembled. "Change happened too fast," says an Indian businessman. "There wasn't enough communication among the different parts of the amoeba," says a doctor who works in Tanzania. "Maybe going out that particular door wasn't the best idea," says a young environmentalist from the U.K. "It involved too much of a left turn."

Which leads the group to another conclusion: not all innovations deserve to diffuse.

▲▼▲

For people interested in making big change happen, innovation-diffusion theory may come as a comfort, because it underscores the fact that you don't have to change the whole World all at once. In fact, trying to do that is a sure way to fail, as is trying to change right away the people who are most likely to oppose your new idea vehemently. These are just two of the traps you can avoid by getting familiar with the "Amoeba of Culture" and the "Anatomy of Cultural Change."

Cultures are like amoebas: Change starts out at the edge of the pseudopod, on the "cultural membrane," where a new idea has at-

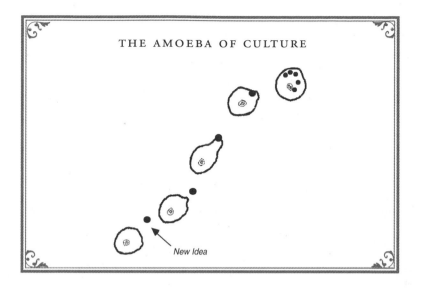

THE AMOEBA OF CULTURE

New Idea

tracted the "amoeba of culture" like a piece of food. Then, if the idea is compelling enough, the entire amoeba follows the pseudopod in that direction. The "nucleus," which symbolizes the power center of the culture, is actually very late to arrive on the scene (and often slows the process down, which can sometimes be good).

Innovations start with an *Innovator*, a person or group who invents, discovers, or otherwise initiates a new idea. But innovators are notorious for having a hard time communicating and selling their ideas. They may be geniuses, or far enough outside the mainstream that people see them as eccentrics—people whose notions may be visionary but are perceived as impractical. And because Innovators are often so enamored of their own concepts, in all their originality and complexity, they may have a hard time explaining them in coherent and convincing terms. They don't fully understand that people need to be *sold* on a new idea, convinced of its benefits, impressed by its features. People need innovations explained to them in comprehensible language, preferably by someone they know and trust, someone who seems more like themselves. That's why Innovators need Change Agents.

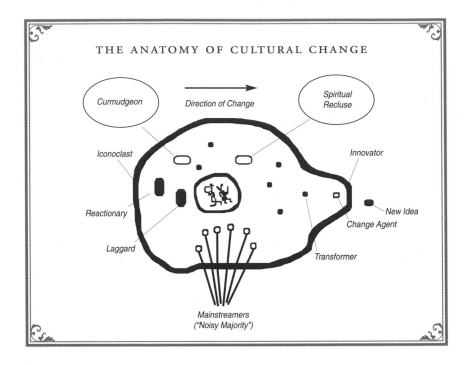

THE ANATOMY OF CULTURAL CHANGE

Curmudgeon

Direction of Change

Spiritual Recluse

Iconoclast

Innovator

Reactionary

New Idea

Change Agent

Laggard

Transformer

Mainstreamers ("Noisy Majority")

Change Agents are people who actively and effectively promote new ideas. Classic examples are sales people and organizers; a champion of new ideas in any profession can take on the role. Change Agents understand that convincing people to try something new is more art than science, and depends more on communication skills than (merely) compelling evidence. As consultant Peter Block puts it, "People don't change their lives based on data. They change it based on an experience, an intimate contact they have with somebody that they trust." Change Agents *are* that point of intimate contact, even if that intimacy sometimes takes the form of the written word or the broadcasted image.

Change Agents are people who know how to move skillfully between two levels: the rarefied atmosphere of innovators and their bold new ideas, and the practical ground of regular people and currently accepted practice. They know how to translate the Innovator's breakthrough into an explanation that other people can understand and buy into. Too much information can overwhelm people, and that's why

Change Agents don't necessarily tell them everything about an innovation all at once: they focus on what is most likely to appeal, to make people want to learn more. (For instance, marketers talk about stressing the benefits first, not the features.) The most effective Change Agents address their promotional activities to people who are predisposed to try a new idea—"early adopters," in the terminology of innovation-diffusion theory.

I call the early adopters *Transformers*, for two reasons: They are the real doorkeepers to the transformation of a culture, and they often work like an electrical transformer, stepping down the voltage of the innovation and easing it into the mainstream gradually, at a speed the system can safely absorb. Transformers are leaders among mainstream people (in the group, the company, or the society at large), who are open to new ideas but cautious about which ones they promote, because they want to maintain their status. If the Transformers embrace an idea, the *Mainstreamers*—the majority of the culture in question, who watch the Transformers for cues on what new ideas to adopt—are almost sure to follow (perhaps at a safe distance). To make sure that the Mainstreamers *do* follow their lead, the Transformers may alter the idea by toning it down, reducing its radicalness, using it in a way the Innovator never intended, or using only part of it.

Here's an illustration: Amory Lovins is an Innovator who dreams up the idea of the Hypercar, a superefficient, aerodynamic, alternative-fuel vehicle that combines the best of every possible current technology. The Hypercar will use new lightweight, composite materials that are stronger than steel but far less heavy; "regenerative braking" systems that recover the energy that in conventional cars is wasted in heat when the vehicle brakes; and perhaps a hydrogen-powered fuel cell that actually adds electricity to the grid when the Hypercar is plugged in at home, turning everyone's personal vehicle into a miniature zero-emissions power plant. Amory doesn't invent these technologies, but he's visionary enough to see how they could all fit together in a new way that would satisfy the needs of the auto industry, its customers, and the planet.

So Amory starts writing and talking about Hypercars, and dozens of other writers, managers, and consultants—Change Agents—pick up on the idea. They promote a somewhat less comprehensive or idealized version to their friends and colleagues who are leaders in the automobile industry. These people are the Transformers, the insiders who determine which ideas get passed on to senior management, or the managers who decide where to invest research money. The Transformers don't want to appear kooky and lose their positions of influence, while the Change Agents don't want to lose credibility with the Transformers. The caution built into the structure of the system tends to slow down the process and dilute the idea increasingly. So by the time a new car incorporating some of Amory's ideas rolls off the assembly line in 1999, elements of the original Hypercar idea are recognizable, but it's far from being the perfect realization of his Innovator's dream. That will take more time, or it may never happen exactly as Amory hopes it will, because he's not in control of the process. Yet the innovation has begun to transform the auto industry nonetheless.

Once the Hypercar enters the market, the cycle repeats itself at a different level. The car manufacturer itself has now assumed the position of Innovator, in relation to its intended customers. Salespeople become Change Agents, trying to sell the car to forward-thinking buyers who act as Transformers. Less adventurous Mainstreamers see their pace-setting, Transformer friends in the new Hypercar, watch to see whether the technology works, and then follow along when a reassuring combination of beauty, safety, reliability, convenience, and price makes it seem sensible for them to do so. (Or they don't follow. Remember the Edsel? Many innovations die before they ever reach the Mainstream.)

Some people may not like the new Hypercars; they are "late adopters," or *Laggards*, satisfied with the status quo and not likely to change until they really don't have a choice. And finally, some people—for example, slow-to-adapt oil companies that aren't happy about the notion that people may need far less of their product—may even fight the idea all the way. People who actively resist innovations, and who have a vested interest in maintaining the status quo, I call *Reactionaries*. This is not to be confused with an insulting term hurled at so-called right-wingers by so-called leftists. Reactionaries can reside at any point on the political spectrum.

Several more roles worth knowing about exist in the Amoeba of Culture. First, the *Iconoclasts*. These are the gadflies, the protesters, the angry critics of the status quo. They are nay-sayers, not idea-generators. "Iconoclast" means someone who attacks cherished images and beliefs. In our Hypercar example, the Iconoclasts would be critics and protest groups who raise objections to the cars currently rolling off the assembly lines, like the gas-guzzling, road-hogging Sports Utility Vehicles. The Iconoclast's role is to highlight the problems with business-as-usual, an activity that helps create the motivation for change within the mainstream. Iconoclasts, when they are very effective, also keep the Reactionaries busy and distracted, so that the Change Agents can do their work without direct interference.

Then there are two roles that have no particular agenda in the transformation process, but they can still exert a powerful influence. *Spiritual Recluses* are contemplatives who withdraw (actually or metaphorically) from the culture to seek, and preach, the eternal truths. They may promote a sense of vision or inspiration, or call for particular values, that affect the atmosphere of the Mainstream and determine its overall openness to particular kinds of new ideas. (Think of the Dalai Lama, whose calls to care for the Earth may encourage more people to try the Hypercar.)

Curmudgeons, in sharp contrast, have given up on the culture. They see change efforts as useless, and they project a nihilistic sense of disappointment and disillusionment. (Does this sound like anyone you know?) Curmudgeons can poison a change process, sapping people's sense of hope or poisoning interest with bitterness. The Serbian language has a great word for this kind of person, the non-stop complainer and party-pooper. It's a word you can hardly say without frowning: *gundjalo*.

▲▼▲

Skopje, Macedonia
November 1995

The entire Innovation Diffusion Game has been translated into Macedonian (with the help of a few Serbian words), and I'm running my workshop, with a translator, for an international development agency. It's a crowd of about sixty, a strange mix of leaders in the environmental movement, members of women's organizations, and businessmen who found out the workshop was free and invited themselves. By attending a day of training, it's explained to me, the businessmen get a per diem from their company.

We're about to run the simulation exercise that's at the heart of the workshop, but it's getting late in the morning, and I want to reassure people that lunch is coming. I also want to try using my very few words of halting, mixed-up Serbian and Macedonian. Unfortunately, I get the pronunciation wrong. Instead of saying "dolazi ručak" ("lunch is coming"), I say "dolaze Rusi"— "the Russians are coming." This sends the crowd into paroxysms of laughter.

After they recover, we run the simulation. I present the fictional situation (involving the promotion of a river clean-up project), and at random everybody draws a role card from a hat. There's one Innovator, a few Change Agents, a handful of Transformers and Reactionaries. The rest of the participants are mostly divided between Mainstreamers and Laggards, but there's a Spiritual Recluse and a Curmudgeon (Gundjalo) thrown in there for fun. Nobody knows who's playing what role; only each person's behavior, as directed by the role cards, provides other players with a clue.

Usually I can walk around and listen to people's conversations as the simulation plays itself out, but this time, all I can do is watch. At first, it's the usual confusing babble of activity—fun to be a spectator, because these folks are really getting into their roles. Then a remarkable thing happens. The fictional innovation sweeps through the crowd like wildfire, becoming almost universally adopted by this simulated culture in a matter of minutes (indicated by signatures on a flip-chart). I've done this Game a lot, but I've never seen anything like this rapid transformation.

What happened? I ask the group. They try to explain, and my translator tries to translate. It's not just that they were hungry; something about what the Change Agents did, some way they effectively boxed out the original Innovator (who can sometimes become a pain in the neck, hurting the cause more than helping with his insistence on intellectual purity) and identified the Transformers quickly, while the Iconoclast kept the Reac-

tionaries busy. I don't quite understand, but my translator sums it up this way: "We Macedonians are very good at politics."

▲▼▲

In real life, of course, any process of change is vastly more complicated than this simulation game. One reason is that the "role players" of the real world may in fact be organizations and institutions as well as individual people. Another reason is that nobody plays just one role: everyone plays *all* of these roles in different contexts. For example, when I cook, I try to be an Innovator, which has its successes and failures. In my various vegetarian phases, I've tried to be a Change Agent, promoting the virtues of a meat-free diet. But when it comes to microwave ovens, I'm a Laggard: I've never owned one. These days, I'm a vegetarian at home, and an omnivore everywhere else.

Also, it's very important to note that *every* role has both a positive and a negative face. Active mainstreamers keep the "amoeba of culture" alive and functioning, but they can be complacent about the need for change. Reactionaries and Laggards may slow down the process of change, but in doing so they might be ensuring that the culture doesn't rip itself apart by changing too fast, or they might prevent a very undesirable change. Innovators and Change Agents are not inherently good; they can be promoting solar cells or personal plutonium power packs. And Innovation theory itself, like many (but not all) technologies, is ethically neutral; it can used for good or ill.

How, then, to apply innovation-diffusion theory to the goal of ending Growth and accelerating Development? By (1) promoting the right kinds of ideas, which I have called sustainability innovations, and (2) promoting them effectively. Assessing which innovations are "sustainable" and which are not can be a complicated business. My firm, for example, performed a sustainability assessment for a city's innovative new water plan. The work required us to employ an engineer, a hydrologist, and a geologist, in addition to doing our own economic, cultural, and political analysis (see our Web site for more information about sustainability assessment). You can start to think about which innovations meet the criteria of sustainability by looking at the Seven Principles at the end of chapter 8. The greater the degree to which an innovation embodies these Principles, the more likely it is to contribute to moving society in the direction of overall sustainability.

A key factor in identifying the most powerful sustainability innovations lies in the application of systems theory. Yes, we need many new technologies that increase our efficiency, decrease our extraction of materials from the Earth, reduce our impact on Nature's complex webs, and lift our societies to higher levels of beauty, prosperity, and equity. But to accomplish those lofty goals, recalling chapter 4, we are in particular need of innovations that *transform the structure of the World-Nature system itself.* New indicators are potentially such an innovation, because they begin to fix the problem of missing feedback loops. (Innovators in all fields, please note: Creative ways of reducing the delay times between when a problem such as climate change starts to occur, when we know about it, and when we start to take action would be very welcome.)

Innovations that correct a problem in the structure of a system are very powerful, because they can have enormous ripple effects. Consider the indicator of carbon dioxide levels in the atmosphere: Were it not for that graph in chapter 3 (and the science behind it), we might not know yet about the danger of global warming. Had that innovative indicator been "adopted" sooner, by more Change Agents and Transformers, the problem of climate change would have been greatly reduced. But even as things now stand, that single innovation—an indicator that helped fix the feedback loop between human beings and the atmosphere—still deserves credit for helping to catalyze other innovations, from solar cells to Hypercars to international treaties. The global CO_2 indicator is now altering the World-Nature system, by motivating people to invent and develop more innovations in response, while giving Change Agents a much stronger case for promoting significant change.

But no matter how brilliant an innovation, how systemically powerful it is in design, or how critical it is to humanity's well-being, nothing happens if the innovation doesn't diffuse.

▲▼▲

Consider the story of scurvy.

In 1601, a British Captain General by the name of Sir James Lancaster discovered a cure for scurvy, a disease that routinely struck sailing crews on long voyages. We now know that scurvy, which involves an outbreak of large and painful sores and other unpleasant symptoms, is caused by a deficiency of vitamin C. Nobody knew the cause then, and Lancaster's discovery was a stroke of luck. By giving lemon juice to sailors and observing the results, he found that the juice would alleviate the sores. He duly reported his discovery to the naval authorities, and recommended that lemons be kept on board as a remedy. But Lancaster was not a man of much standing in medicine. His findings and recommendations were politely ignored.

It would be nearly 150 years before further experiments, by James Lind, a Scottish Naval surgeon more highly placed in medicine, would be conducted along the lines Lancaster first pioneered. Lind's experiments (considered the first clinical trials in medical history) would substantiate Lancaster's claims, but it would be another 48 years before the British Navy adopted citrus as a cure for scurvy, thus giving birth to the term "limey." Absurdly, it would take *yet another 70 years* for the British merchant marine to adopt citrus fruits as common practice, in 1865—adding up to 264 years between the time when the cure was first discovered and the time when any British seaman could go on a long voyage without fear of the disease.

Scurvy's tale is a cautionary one, about the costs to people and society when we delay in adopting good new ideas. Thousands of sailors suffered over hundreds of years because a handful of people, blinded by the privileges of their position, by bureaucratic recalcitrance, and by the lack of a theoretical framework, refused to consider the facts. The sailors themselves—uneducated, and living under conditions that were often equivalent to a brutal dictatorship—were hardly in a position to take matters into their own hands and accelerate the process.

Today our planet is suffering from a variety of forms of "scurvy," ranging from local sprawl to global warming. "Sustainability" is the general name we have given to the cure. But in practice, sustainability consists of a transformation involving hundreds or even thousands of innovations that advance Development while slowing Growth. Whether humanity develops enough of these in time, and adopts them universally, will determine whether our next hundred years are primarily plagued by trial or uplifted with promise. *The key to transformation is the rapid diffusion of innovations.*

▲▼▲

White River Junction, Vermont
November 1998

I'm on my way to a meeting with my publishers, to deliver a signed book contract. Now all I have to do is write a book.

Right around the corner from the Chelsea Green offices, I notice a used book store called The Hundredth Monkey. The name brings a bemused smile to my lips, and triggers the recall of an old story, about a book that was trying to change the World.

In the late 1960s, writer Ken Keyes published The Hundredth Monkey, *which presented the strange and encouraging story of a small group of monkeys on a Japanese island who learned to wash their sweet potatoes. The book was very popular, thousands of copies were distributed free at concerts, and the story of "the hundredth monkey" entered the folklore of the day as a myth about the potential for cultural transformation.*

Those who did not read the book heard about it from their friends, and the story they heard went something like this. A few monkeys started to wash sweet potatoes, apparently having discovered that clean potatoes tasted better. Other monkeys on the island quickly learned to wash their potatoes, and somewhat more gradually, others began to imitate their neighbors, as well. Then, at a certain point—say, after about one hundred monkeys had learned this new skill—an astonishing breakthrough occurred: suddenly all the monkeys, on all the nearby islands, knew how to wash their potatoes. It was as if the knowledge of potato-washing had reached some critical mass

and leaped, instantaneously, from monkey-mind to monkey-mind, jump-
ing over space and time in a new and mysterious way.

And if that could happen, went the punchline, then something simi-
lar could happen with human beings. "The Hundredth Monkey" became a
mantra for social organizers in a variety of causes, from the women's move-
ment to the nuclear freeze campaign. Turn enough people on, some people
believed, and as enthusiasm for a new idea spreads and intensifies, society
will all of a sudden be magically transformed. This vision of instantaneous
and complete transformation was a great solace to thousands of people who
were worried about the fate of the Earth.

Unfortunately, the story about the monkeys wasn't true.

Keyes had borrowed the story from another writer named Lyall Wat-
son, who had derived it from the academic literature, but Watson had re-
ported it, shall we say, inaccurately. The actual story had its origin in
scientific research on learning behavior among the island's monkeys. Yes,
some monkeys did learn to wash the sweet potatoes left out for them by the
scientists who were studying monkeys' behavior (the potatoes were sandy,
and monkeys don't like sand in their food any more than we do). Yes, other
monkeys learned from their example. But the process was hardly mysterious,
nor was it universal. Only the younger monkeys picked up this new potato-
washing trick, and then mothers taught the skill to their young. A few mon-
keys on other islands figured out the same trick independently. End of story.
No magical transformation, no sudden monkey enlightenment.

Thinking about this story, the book that popularized it, and the rea-
son for my visit to White River Junction, I can't help but chuckle out loud.
Which is more important?, I think to myself . . . The truth about the mon-
key story (which is a lower-primate case study in innovation diffusion)? Or
the myth that grew up around it and encouraged thousands of people to
work for peace?

Walking into the editorial offices, I wonder if The Hundredth Monkey
(the store) has any copies of The Hundredth Monkey *(the book). And how*
long, I wonder, before they have a used copy of the book I'm about to write?

▲▼▲

"Transformation" is the process of rapid and complete innovation diffusion, and the consequences that ripple out from an innovation's adoption. Think of the replacement of horses with cars at the turn of the twentieth century, the influence of psychology on twentieth century intellectual life, the advent of television or the Internet and their effects on families, relationships, and society at large. These were all innovations that were so broadly adopted, with such wide-ranging repercussions, that they transformed every culture in which they caught on. Transformation to sustainability is therefore not an empty hope, but is a matter of guiding the processes of invention and innovation diffusion that are going on around us all the time, so that they take us swiftly in the right direction.

Understanding innovation diffusion is therefore critical to spreading the concept and the practice of sustainability, which is an all-encompassing innovation, and to promoting the combination of new ideas, social practices, and technologies that will make the ideal real. For instance, the ideas described in the previous chapter—from the Sustainable Seattle indicators, to the Dutch "Green Plan," to the remarkable creations of Gaviotas—are sustainability innovations, and they have steadily spread to other locales by normal higher-primate methods such as teaching, marketing, and plain old imitating.

What makes an innovation successful? Former astrophysicist Robert Gilman, founder of *In Context* magazine, boiled this question down to a simple equation. I call it the "Gilman Equation," and here's the formula. Change occurs when N – O > CC, meaning when:

$$\text{Perceived Value of the } \textit{N}\text{ew Way} - \text{Perceived Value of the } \textit{O}\text{ld Way} > \text{Perceived } \textit{C}\text{ost of the } \textit{C}\text{hange}$$

In other words, for an innovation to be adopted and change to occur, *the difference in perceived value* between the old and the new way of doing things *has to seem greater than the perceived cost of the switch.*

In even plainer English, for a sustainable solution to be adopted, it has to be seen as *so much better* than what people are already doing that it outweighs whatever additional time, trouble, and money are required to make the change.

The key word in the Gilman Equation is "perceived." It doesn't matter how beneficial the new thing seems to you, how obvious the problems of the old, or how worthwhile the switch. Other people have to *see* the prospect of change that way. Money is a big determinant, but so are many other factors: aesthetics, prestige, convenience, comfort, and that indescribable quality known as "coolness." Either something is cool—sexy, attractive, appealing on multiple levels for reasons hard to describe—or it's not. If an innovation is perceived as cool, that particular factor can outweigh a lot of others, including monetary expense. But without "coolness," the new thing will have a hard time sweeping the World, no matter how cheap it is.

THREE BASIC STRATEGIES FOR MOTIVATING TRANSFORMATION

1. *Promote the new.* Or, in more "technical" lingo, "increase the perceived value of the new idea." Most sales plans are organized around this strategy. The idea is to highlight the benefits of the innovation, note its superior features, design the package for maximum appeal. This is the principal work of Change Agents, but it's also the work of Innovators, who have to make a very cool and highly functional innovation in the first place, so the Change Agents have something to work with.

2. *Critique the old.* This involves decreasing the perceived value of the status quo by attacking it, either directly or subtly, and pointing out its many faults and weaknesses—in short, making the old way of doing things uncool. As an example, think of negative ads in political campaigns that reveal the incumbent's sordid past. In cultural change processes, critiquing the old is generally the work of Iconoclasts, though Change Agents know how to do it as well ("Gas-guzzling SUVs? They're passé, I'm into Hypercars . . .").

3. *Facilitate the switch.* This is the most-important and least-obvious strategy for making change happen. It is also where many change efforts fail, because they forget to *reduce the perceived cost of making a change.* You have to *make it easy* for people to change; that's what "facilitate" means, at its root. You have to lower the perceived expense involved in switching—whether that expense is measured in time, money, status, inconvenience, or coolness—to as near zero as possible. If you can turn even the act of switching into an immediate, perceived net *gain*, so much the better. (This is what car dealers do with rebates.)

For example, if it were cheap and easy to bring in your car and get the engine replaced with a zero-emission one that ran on hydrogen, and refueling was no problem, you'd probably make the conversion. But if it were expensive and a lot of trouble, you would probably *not* do it, no matter how many messages were thrown at you about the benefits of the new fuel and the problems of global warming associated with your old engine. Facilitating the switch makes all the difference.

What factors influence these three elements of the Gilman Equation? What determines whether an innovation gets perceived as having a higher value than the status quo? Innovation researchers have identified five critical characteristics of innovations, factors that greatly affect the rate at which new ideas get adopted.

FIVE CRITICAL CHARACTERISTICS OF INNOVATIONS

1. *Relative advantage.* Does the innovation actually work better than the status quo? More importantly, do people *perceive* it as better? If not, the innovation will not spread quickly, if at all. Lack of relative advantage is what stopped the diffusion of early electric cars in their proverbial tracks.

2. *Complexity.* How difficult is the innovation to understand and apply? The more difficult, the slower the adoption process. Personal computers only began to diffuse rapidly after new operating

systems including the Mac and Windows reduced the complexity factor for the average consumer.

3. *Trialability.* Can people "try out" the innovation first? Or must they commit to it all at once? If the latter, people will be far more cautious about adopting it. You probably wouldn't buy a Hypercar unless you could test-drive it first.

4. *Observability.* How visible are the results of using the innovation? If people adopt it, can the difference be easily seen by others? If not, the innovation will spread more slowly. Low observability is one reason why organic foods have taken a while to catch on; it's hard to see the physical difference in people's health.

5. *Compatibility.* How does the innovation fit with people's past experiences and present needs? Does it require a change in people's values, in their sense of identity? If members of the culture feel as though they have to become very different people in order to adopt the innovation, they will be more resistant to doing so. Consider vegetarianism: for many people, adopting it causes both some inconvenience and even some familial conflict. Compatibility is a critical factor to consider for those promoting sustainability innovations, because too often these innovations require a greater change in personal identity than many people are willing to accept.

Judging from that list of characteristics, the sustainability innovation with the easiest pathway to success will (1) appear highly advantageous (and be cool), (2) be relatively simple to understand, (3) allow people to try it out before they irreversibly commit to it, (4) result in visible improvements to people's lives or to Nature, and (5) be relatively easy to incorporate into a person's (or a society's) existing way of life. All of these factors affect the "Perceived Value of the New Way." Items (3) and (5) also affect the "Perceived Cost of the Switch."

It's not that an innovation *must* meet these criteria; it's just that the probability that it will sweep through a cultural system, and become the newest version of "normal," is greatly affected by these char-

acteristics. Sustainability innovations, and the change efforts associated with them, need to be designed to optimize these factors as much
as possible if the intent is to make change happen swiftly. And remember—we are living in an emergency situation, vis-à-vis global resources
and trends.

The innovation adoption process is not very conscious. Few people sit down to numerically calculate for themselves the pros and cons
of a new idea, the advantages and disadvantages, the costs and benefits.
But the Gilman Equation, and the factors that influence it, are constantly operating in the back of their minds nonetheless. People mull
things over, chat with their friends, notice who's doing what. They read
the signals from the media, the marketplace, and the grapevine. And
they take their cues from the other people in their lives, whether personal friends or public figures, whose judgment they trust.

Your mission, if you want to help create a more rapid transformation in the direction of sustainability, is to become a trustworthy source
of information about the new ideas that can make the concept real, or
even to create those ideas yourself. For sustainability to be achieved "in
one generation," as the Dutch government has challenged us all to attempt, thousands, indeed millions, of new Innovators, Change Agents,
and Transformers must be working on behalf of that goal.

▲▼▲

In the real World's "innovation diffusion game," what role should *you*
play? That depends. Self-assessment is the first step. If you are interested
in the redesign of transportation systems, but you don't know much
about engineering, you are probably not prepared to try to invent a new
kind of car, unless you are so passionate about working on this problem
that you go out and master the relevant skills. You wouldn't be the first
person to follow such a path: many Innovators have fallen in love with
a dream long before they had the skills to make it real.

But if you are good at *describing* and *promoting* new products, you
might make a great Change Agent, perhaps by writing a memo to your
boss about why your company should invest in new, super-efficient Hy-

percars as soon as they actually appear. And if you are uncomfortable with the Change Agent role, or talking about cars just isn't your thing, you can still be the first on your block to buy a new super-efficient Hypercar, thereby becoming a Transformer, and ultimately an object of curiosity, the envy of all your neighbors.

In different contexts you might play different roles—a Change Agent when it comes to broader community organizing, while being an Innovator who thinks up new ideas that move your specific profession in a sustainable direction. To be effective in any such role, you'll need to be well-informed, and you'll also need to be honest with yourself about one important question: How credible do you appear to other people? Assess that, and design your strategy accordingly. If people already look to you for guidance, you are in a very powerful position to make change happen. If you know that you have a reputation for being "out in left field," or you just don't have access to your intended audience, you will need to take another tack, such as reaching out to someone whose credibility with your intended audience you know to be high. If you can motivate these others to become Change Agents (or even convince someone else to convince them to do so), to become the champion of an innovation you believe worthwhile, you will have gone a long way toward accomplishing your goal. Convincing somebody famous and credible to adopt and promote a new idea is often the fast track to innovation adoption. That's why celebrities make so much money pitching consumer products.

Remember that you need never be alone in this enterprise. People are always around who, like you, understand Cassandra's Dilemma. You probably already know such people; and if not, they are not hard to find. Look for the people who know how to cry about the tragedies that life too often serves us, who smile at the beauty inherent in human beings and in Nature, who laugh at the absurdity of our historic predicament. Look for the people with that restless, idealistic hunger in their eyes, that irrepressible desire to change the World.

CHAPTER 10

Accelerate to Survive

All things are possible once enough human beings realize that everything is at stake.

—NORMAN COUSINS

When spider webs unite, they can tie up a lion.

—ETHIOPIAN PROVERB

LET'S CONSIDER THE SHAPE of our global predicament, and try to draw some inspiring conclusions. The search for inspiration requires that we retrace our steps through the bad news. But don't despair: the greatest source of hope for the reinvention of the World lies hidden in plain sight, at the very heart of the predicament.

According to the most credible scientific studies and computer models, the World is heading over a cliff (facing "overshoot"), after which it will probably begin a precipitous decline ("collapse"), propelled by rocketing, exponential Growth in the total number of human beings and the amount of stuff they consume and discard. The complex dynamics of large systems, including long delays in feedback from Nature and slow responses from the World, make the process of Growth extremely difficult to control. Even those occupying the highest offices in the land seem powerless to intervene in any decisive way. The future prospects faced by humanity and Nature at the end of the second millennium appear to be both tragic and absurd.

It is pointless to cast blame in any one direction for what is happening on the planet, and equally fruitless to expect salvation from any single initiative. The problem is not easily attributable to technology, affluence, poverty, population increases, sprawl, economics, human greed, human evil, or human ignorance. The problem shows up in all of the above, because the problem is intrinsic to the dynamics of the global system. The problem gets worse every day, and it gets worse at an accelerating rate, spurred by errant or missing feedback loops and the momentum of exponential Growth. Nature is already suffering acutely from the effects of our predicament, and so are about one billion of the planet's poorest people. In many ways, according to the computer models, overshoot and collapse is already in progress, and we are already "beyond the limits to Growth."

While the problem is not our fault, we are obligated to solve it. Creative action to steer the World in a new direction must come from every direction, every sector of human life, every profession and industry and administration and household, all at once. Over the next generation, it is our responsibility to actually reinvent the World. We must focus on constructing the missing links in the World-Nature system, while learning how to respond quickly to the feedback we already receive. Otherwise, over the course of the next five decades, the World will do a full, slow-motion smash into the evolutionary equivalent of a brick wall.

The cure for overshoot and collapse is *sustainable development*, meaning Development without Growth, in the direction of sustainability. The definition of sustainability is neither vague nor abstract; it is very specific, and is tied to measurable criteria describing how resources are used and distributed. Some of what currently gets called "sustainable development" is no such thing, but that does not mean the concept should be dismissed, any more than the concept of democracy should be dismissed when it is misappropriated by a dictatorship. Sustainability, like democracy, is an ideal toward which we strive, a journey more than a destination.

Embracing sustainability in today's World requires nothing short of a *transformation* in virtually every sector of social and economic life, from technology to town planning. Transformation consists of a *rapid diffusion of innovations*, new ideas that can effectively and speedily replace the status quo with better approaches. Innovations depend for their success on people: the Innovators who create them, the Change Agents who promote them, and the Transformers who set an example for the rest of the culture by adopting them.

Conclusion #1: The World needs an enormous number of new Innovators, Change Agents, and Transformers, all dedicated to turning Development in the direction of sustainability. *People like you.*

Meanwhile, a growing number of people in the World, of all ages and levels of experience, realize that our situation is profoundly dangerous. Some have studied the reports on global trends; some simply feel the danger at an intuitive level. Many are caught in Cassandra's Dilemma, experiencing foreknowledge of a catastrophic future, together with a feeling of powerlessness to prevent the worst from happening.

The emotions caused by Cassandra's Dilemma can be frightening or even overpowering, and most of us hide these feelings within ourselves. Letting them out, through creative expression, spiritual and religious practice, or honest conversation with loved ones, can be tremendously liberating. When we learn that we will not be destroyed by our feelings of fear, anger, and sadness; when we see that we are not alone in those feelings; and when we find we can even laugh at the preposterousness of our situation, we discover a surprising new sense of hope and purpose.

Conclusion #2: There are potentially millions of people who are ready, with support and encouragement, to become Innovators, Change Agents, and Transformers for sustainability, in every walk of life. *People like us.*

Moreover, a boundless number of innovations already exist that promote sustainability in technology, business, government, economics, design, planning, civil society, and personal lifestyle. Many more are being developed. We already know a great deal about how to increase efficiency, reduce pollution, feed the hungry, control sprawl, reduce population growth, transform the energy system. If the solutions are not yet perfect, they are nevertheless vast improvements over current practices.

Not only can we avoid disaster; we can reinvent the World, and make it far more beautiful than the one we humans are currently constructing.

If we engage with our full energy and passion in the creation of new sustainability innovations, and the diffusion of existing ones, and do it in a very accelerated fashion, using every motivational strategy at our disposal, even the computer models suggest we could avoid the threat of overshoot and collapse, stabilize our population and economy, and end poverty. Utopia, or at least a beginner's version of it, is not an idealistic fantasy; it is the only destination worthy of our striving.

Conclusion #3: Transformation is necessary. And possible. *And we can make it happen.*

▲▼▲

Seattle, Washington
October 1995

I'm having dinner with my old friend Darryl Cherney, a long-time Earth First! activist in Northern California. He's on the road, trying to raise money for a non-violent action to save a particularly old and beautiful stand of redwoods. I give him a little money, but ask him to keep my donation anonymous.

I met Darryl in 1982, when we were both struggling songwriters in New York. He had a furniture-moving business, calling himself "The Prime Mover." We worked together for about six months, hauling sofa beds up and down narrow staircases in Manhattan. It was one of my favorite jobs.

Darryl is hardly the same person now. He went from living with his mother in Manhattan, at age thirty, to sitting in trees and trying to organize loggers with his partner, Judi Bari. Their lives were literally shattered in 1992, when a pipe bomb exploded in their car, crippling Judi, injuring Darryl, and getting them both arrested. Believe it or not, the police blamed them for bombing themselves, despite the fact that they had made strong public commitments to nonviolence, and that they had both been receiving death threats for months.

The charges were later dropped, and Darryl and Judi were completely exonerated. However, further investigations were also dropped. The actual bombers were never brought to justice. The whole story still smells bad.

Darryl has always had the edginess of a New Yorker, and there's nothing like an attack on your life to heighten your natural anxiety. His body never seems to stop vibrating, and his eyes tend to dart around the room. But neither he nor Judi have been scared off, though they tend to be careful and watchful now, less strident in their rhetoric. [Judi has since died, of cancer.]

And Darryl, though desperate to save the redwoods, remains committed to nonviolent protest, in the spirit of Gandhi. Like many activists I know, he dreams of catalyzing social transformation with a single, culminating creative act. "My fantasy," he tells me, "is to design the perfect banner, which would be hung at the exact right place, at the perfect moment, so that when people saw it, it started a cascade of events, leading to the preservation of the California redwoods and ultimately saving the world."

It's a noble fantasy—not absolutely impossible, I guess, if you subscribe to the idea (popularized from Chaos Theory) that a butterfly in Brazil can cause an accelerating cascade of ripple effects that ultimately start a typhoon in the Pacific. Darryl tells me how a mountain lake, if the air is very still, can be chilled to freezing temperatures without actually freezing. Then, if you toss a pebble into it, an amazingly fast chain reaction begins, as one wa-

ter molecule aligns itself with another. The lake's surface goes from super-cooled-liquid to frozen-crystal-solid in what seems like an instant, making a very loud "crack!"

"That's the kind of process I dream of starting," he tells me.

I've taken a different path, working with companies and communities and government agencies, trying to introduce them to visionary ideas supported by practical innovations, selling evolution instead of revolution. But I salute Darryl's radical devotion to the forest, and his dream. We raise our beer bottles to the imaginary perfect banner, clink them, and drink a toast.

▲▼▲

The first step in breaking out of Cassandra's Dilemma is to bring it into the open. As business strategists Gary Hamel and C. K. Prahalad noted in the *Harvard Business Review*, "a threat that everyone perceives but no one talks about creates more anxiety than a threat that has been clearly identified and made the focal point for the problem-solving efforts of the entire company." Replace the word "company" with "World" and you have an accurate description of the global situation as well.

Humans have a responsibility for fixing the problems caused by Growth, but that responsibility need not be taken up as a somber burden. The direness of our predicament gives us enormous latitude to try out new responses. The extremity of the emergency invites us to take pleasure in the search for solutions—not to lose sight of suffering, or of the seriousness of the problems we face, but to revel in the creative opportunity. If the World were working perfectly, those of us with restless souls might be tempted to mess it up a little bit; but since it's in a terrible mess, the biggest, most enjoyable challenge is to try to fix it. But we have to work fast—very fast indeed.

Sometimes I get the image of industrial civilization as an enormous airplane, flying blindly through cloudbanks toward the side of a mountain. On board, all is relatively calm and pleasant—with the exception of the disturbance created by a few passengers, who have studied this country, recognized the terrain through a break in the clouds, and comprehended the imminent danger. It has taken them some time to get the Captain's attention, longer still to convince him of their seriousness and credibility. The Captain considers climbing to a higher altitude, but suddenly it is too late to act with calm deliberation, as a wall of mountains appears.

At a moment like that, it does no good for an airplane to slow down. The only solution is to increase the power, and pull up, as hard as possible.

As industrial societies, we face such a moment. Danger looms, directly ahead. We cannot turn around. We cannot slow down. We must accelerate to power ourselves over this gigantic obstacle, with every ounce of economic strength and cultural creativity available to us. This is not a time for pulling back, but a time for pulling ourselves *up*.

Achieving sustainability does not mean slowing down our economy. It means *speeding it up*, and directing its energy toward the redesign and redevelopment of the systems that are the cause of our dilemma. Global sustainability cannot be achieved merely by asking people to drive less, buy less, or live more simply, though these are helpful, admirable, and often satisfying acts of personal dedication. More to the point, we must replace the entire planet's automotive fleet, or at least the engines in all of our vehicles, with a transportation system that does not release carbon dioxide. We must redesign all of our products to be completely reusable, recyclable, nontoxic, and compostable. Almost everything we do, build, and make needs to be redesigned, rebuilt, re-engineered, retrofitted, or simply retired and recycled. The imperatives of sustainability suggest that humanity is facing not a slow-down in economic activity, but a spectacular increase and acceleration.

Paradoxically, by reinventing the World so that it no longer runs on Growth, we can *increase* that strange phenomenon we call "economic growth," now measured by the flow of money. Sustainability is fundamentally a matter of decoupling money from material consumption, so that the *value* within the economy can steadily increase, even as humanity's *throughput* gets drastically reduced. As each new innovation comes on line, and we make switchovers to an array of graceful replacements for today's wasteful products and inefficient services, we will be using up and trashing much less stuff, but growing much richer. This is the long-term objective of Development without Growth: an economically prosperous World that is also much more equitable, creative, and lovely to behold.

As visions go, this is big. Yet it's within our reach. The transformation of social and economic systems is old hat to humanity; over the course of history, we have transformed our societies and economies numberless times. Even the global scale and compressed timeline is not without precedent. During World War II, for example, the World's most powerful nations on three different continents reorganized their economies on very short notice and pointed them in a radically new and transformative direction. Innovation occurred throughout society at a breakneck pace, in every sphere of life. Rockets were invented, the atom was split, women went from being homemakers to airplane builders, all in the space of about five years. Then, in the post-War period, the Marshall Plan redirected huge amounts of capital into a reconstruction effort in both Europe and Japan. We *know* how to do very rapid economic transformation.

We also know how to do extremely rapid social and political transformation, as the fall of the Berlin Wall and its aftermath, and the transition from *apartheid* to democracy in South Africa should never cease to remind us. In the global economy, technological transformation happens as fast as innovation, markets, and capital flows allow—and that speed limit gets higher all the time. Meanwhile personal transformation, as many of us know from experience, can be stunning in its suddenness.

When human systems are *organized* around the purpose of accelerated systemic transformation—complete with increased investments in research and innovation development, well-designed networks of communication and dissemination for the new ideas, and clear channels for feedback to bring corrective signals back to the leaders and innovators—then systemic transformation can quickly occur. At full throttle, it may take us a generation to achieve a reasonable level of sustainability, but it won't necessarily take that long.

All types of transformation are driven by innovation diffusion, happening at extremely rapid speeds. When the innovation involves nothing but *ideas*, the process can look like the lake in the story, which suddenly freezes: people may have held comparable ideas in the backs of their minds for years, but the decision to *adopt* them (such as the idea that the Berlin Wall should no longer stand) can seize thousands of people virtually overnight, prompted by a seemingly small disturbance.

Even the replacement of a fundamental element of infrastructure need not take decades to accomplish. Consider a transition to solar energy from fossil fuels. As Earth Day founder Denis Hayes has pointed out, we could accomplish a near-complete realignment to reliance upon solar technologies in only four years, using methods learned from the development of the first computer chips in the 1960s. The U.S. government, acting through NASA and the Department of Defense, ordered mass quantities of chips, spurring extremely rapid innovation and a swift drop in prices. That intensive act of government purchasing made possible the sudden arrival of the computer era, years or decades ahead of when the market might have produced a transformation on its own. Hayes calculates that by spending $8 billion over the next four years on solar cells—requiring contractors to meet a gradual but accelerated decline in pricing—the government could cause a similar revolution in that market, bringing the price for solar electricity down to levels that could outcompete current sources. Once accomplished, notes Hayes, "the change is permanent," and "after a few years no additional government subsidy is required."

Hundreds of similar strategies are available to us, but we have to recruit the Change Agents and Transformers to champion a steady stream of new innovations to take us down the pathway of sustainability. We do not need to know where that path ultimately leads, but we need to be willing to take the first steps. Likewise, we do not need all the answers; we need only be willing to keep asking the right questions, and listening for the feedback, no matter how strange and puzzling that feedback may at first sound. And the best feedback always raises more questions.

▲▼▲

Batu Caves, Malaysia
February 1982

*I'm living in Malaysia, working as a therapist for heroin addicts, brought
here by an unusual post-graduate fellowship called the Luce Scholars Program. The center where I'm working is, organizationally, a real mess; I've
evolved into a kind of consultant and trainer to senior management, which
is weird, since I'm twenty-one years old. But it turns out I'm much better as
a consultant than I am as a therapist. Managers are easier to deal with than
junkies.*

*Life in the center is stressful, so I get out as often as I can. This time
I'm pursuing my interest in Asian religions; a friend has invited me to tag
along and observe a day in the life of a Satguru, basically the top guy in the
Western hemisphere for his branch of Hinduism. The Satguru is leading a
weeks-long pilgrimage to the sacred temples in Malaysia and Sri Lanka.*

*For some reason, I get seated next to the Satguru at lunch. It turns out
he's an American, a former dancer with the Joffrey Ballet in New York, who
took off to Sri Lanka in his early twenties and spent three years in a cave,
meditating. He's got hair down to his waist, orange robes, extraordinarily
clear eyes, and the absolute devotion and respect of temple-goers here in
Malaysia. It's like eating lunch with the Archbishop of Canterbury.*

*This, I realize, is my big opportunity. I'm on top of a mountain, at a
temple, sitting next to a genuine guru. I know from my academic studies
that Hinduism recognizes the validity of all other religions. So how, I ask
him, can we get people to see that they're all worshipping the same God?
How can we get them to come together as one people? I'm full of yearning
idealism, wishing the world's people could all come together, make peace,
heal the planet, stop killing each other. The question takes me about ten
minutes to ask.*

*When I'm finally done, the Satguru nods thoughtfully. He sips on a
straw, sucking juice from a fresh coconut. Then he clucks and says, "Gee,
that's a tough one."*

▲▼▲

Hope can be found in occurrences that would have seemed entirely unexpected only a few years ago. I find hope in the return of the gray wolf
to North America and the humpback whale to the coastal seas. I find
hope in the sudden drop in the population-growth rate of Bangladesh,
where women are helping each other get access to birth control and
small loans to start miniature businesses. Tremendous inspiration can
be found in the stories of small, experimental "eco-villages" springing
up in various parts of the World, and in the stories of larger political en-
tities such as Curitiba in Brazil, Kerala in India, and the nation of the
Netherlands. And I see enormous hope in the movement toward a new
industrial revolution, fueled by intelligent redesign of the materials and
power sources that drive our economy.

But strangely, I also find hope in the fact that humanity has already changed the planet's atmospheric balance and performed other
amazing acts of ecological destruction. If we can do that, then we can
do anything. Let me explain.

It is sometimes pointed out that young people in criminal gangs
have exceptional organizational and entrepreneurial skills. If you can
turn that innate talent and organizational experience in a constructive
direction, you get remarkable results. I believe the same to be true for
humanity as a whole. If in a mere few centuries, with far fewer people,
using very primitive technology, we have managed to create a huge,
sprawling mess of a World, displacing much of Nature in the process,
then we can certainly create a bountiful and more sustainable World.
If we can expand like a cancerous Growth across the face of the planet,
then we can surely transform ourselves through a benign process of
Development.

There is nothing inherently impossible about learning to live
within critical physical limits, preserving Nature's beauty, and steering
ourselves in the direction of our best dreams. Our demonstrated power
to create havoc on such a massive scale has established an irrefutable
truth: We have the power to *create* on a global scale.

This counterintuitive source of hope is supported by other real-
izations. Just as we know that transformation on a global scale is possi-

ble, because we've already accomplished that, through the process known as "Growth," we know that massive improvements in the quality of Development are possible, because human beings have created thousands of small examples, all over the planet. Now we must redirect Development in the direction of that superior ideal known as sustainability. Making such a collective choice would be an act of consciousness signalling that the World, as we knew it, had indeed come to an end, and a new World was beginning. The new World would be not merely "the age of consciousness" (remember the origin of the word "world," as explained in chapter 1), but the age of *collective* consciousness, the era of humanity's coming to maturity as planetary steward and caretaker of evolution.

▲▼▲

Plainfield, New Hampshire
June 1999

I've been up all night, going over the editor's marks on the final manuscript of this book. Candles are keeping me company. Dawn is just an hour away.

I'm visiting Foundation Farm, the home of Dana Meadows and friends, an assortment of gardeners, musicians, and intellectual acrobats. This time next year all these Cassandras will be living across the river in Vermont, in a new eco-village-and-institute complex called Cobb Hill. For Dana, the move marks a shift away from the "Foundation" era (the farm she is leaving was named after Isaac Asimov's famous 1950s-era science fiction trilogy, which involves scientists accurately predicting a civilizational collapse, and then retreating to prepare for its aftermath) to the "Sustainability Institute" era, a new virtual home for systems modellers who want to make real systems change happen.

I'm watching the moths flitting about near the candles, and thinking about the people who will someday be reading this book. What should I say to them, in these closing pages? I need to say something compelling. I want to tell them to get involved in reinventing the World, and to recruit other people to get involved as well. I want to make them feel both alarmed and inspired. I want to encourage them to take risks, find partners, try new things. But I want to do all this in a way that isn't preachy, or self-righteous, or worst of all, ineffectually earnest.

After all, earnest self-righteousness may have gotten me into sustainability work, but what's kept me going is the polar opposite: fun. Play. Pleasure. Satisfaction. It's more eros than superego. And on top of that, you can earn a darn good living making sustainability real these days, if you know what you're doing.

And of course, there's the question of future generations. People have sex, they make babies, and those babies grow up to inherit the Earth. What kind of World will we leave for them? What changes to the World will they make? Once, at a Balaton Group meeting, I passed around a tape recorder and declared that we were recording a message to our colleagues one hundred years in the future. "We're sorry," said a Russian. "We did our best," said an American. But my favorite message came from an optimistic Austrian: "What's the beer like in your time?"

I'd like to think of our descendants floating around the Anti-Grav bar, drinking locally produced organic ales, enjoying the company of a genetically enhanced sentient dodo bird, watching 3-D holographic teleplays of the early twenty-first century and saying, "Wow, I never realized just how close we came to wiping out civilization as we knew it."

And the dodo bird—whose name, of course, will be Cassandra, and whose species will have been revived and uplifted to human levels of intelligence to make up for two centuries of extinction—will give a little snort and say, "You'd better believe it."

▲▼▲

There can be no question about whether we should or should not transform our society in the direction of sustainability. The question of how we envision it and how we make the transformation to that vision has thousands of different answers, already taking shape around us, all the time. The real uncertainty is whether or not we can summon the collective will, imagination, and intelligence to aim resolutely for sustainability, and whether we can do it before the gathering wave of catastrophe sweeps over us.

The most decisive answer to all such "can or cannot" questions was voiced by one of the great architects of the industrial World, a man whose determination and inventiveness helped to create many of the mind-boggling problems we are now confronting, from global climate change to suburban sprawl. The automobile manufacturer Henry Ford said, "Whether you believe you can or you can't, you are right."

I believe that we can. And I get my sense of hope from believing that you, too, think we can.

Coda

Point Reyes Station, California
February 1999

I'm at Mesa Refuge, a writer's retreat, trying to pour my book into my computer. Poet Philip Klasky is here too, and we've been invited over for dinner with the folks next door.

They have a ten-month old son, Eli. We get to talking about the future. We're all convinced it's going to be mind-boggling, and we worry that it might be horrific, given current trends. What kind of World will Eli live in? What will things be like in 2050, when he's his father's age?

Phil, sitting next to Eli, coos at the baby and says, "Don't worry, I'm sure you'll be having lots of fun."

Eli looks at him, sticks his tongue between his lips, and goes, "Th-p-p-p-p-p-p-p!"

NOTES

Prologue

This version of the myth of Cassandra is synthesized from several different sources, including Edith Hamilton's *Mythology* and *The New Larousse Encyclopedia of Mythology*.

Chapter 1

P. 3   Much of the story of *The Limits to Growth* comes from my long discussions over many years with its principal author, Donella H. Meadows, together with many conversations with Dennis Meadows and the study of press accounts from 1972.

While I focus here on U.S. society's failure to respond to the book's central message, it is important to note that *The Limits to Growth* was a phenomenal publishing success, selling millions of copies in dozens of languages. It was taken much more seriously in Europe than in the U.S., and indeed, Europe continues to lead the U.S. in responding to dangerous global trends.

P. 7   *So a computer model like World3 cannot be discounted simply for being a model . . .*
Donella Meadows notes that everything we know of the real World is also just a model—the model in our heads. We carry a picture of the World in our minds, which we use to interpret what is happening around us. "It's not a choice between World3 and the World," writes Meadows, "it's a choice between World3 and our mental models."

Computer models are not alien things; they are themselves the product of human consciousness. And they are often superior to our mental models in verifiable ways. In our mental models, a growth rate of 2% per year seems like nothing. In a computer model like World3, a 2% growth rate is more accurately represented by its effects: a doubling in 35 years.

The purpose of computer models, says Meadows, "is not to *predict*, but to *warn*, to inspire different behavior from presumably intelligent beings."

P. 11   *The project was, at first, just something fascinating to do. . . .*
Meadows has said both that "We didn't even think about trying to change the world," as I report here, and that "We were just back from [a long road trip through] Asia and *passionate* about changing the world." The common denominator in these opposing accounts is that the authors did not believe anyone would pay attention to their efforts, one way or the other.

P. 20   *. . . becoming aware of the destructive impact of its growth too late to prevent disaster.*
"The too-lateness is the point," Meadows said once. When the collapse begins, plenty of resources are still left. But not enough *time* or *capital* are available to mobilize them before massive disruptions and die-offs begin to occur.

The literature of critique on contemporary development is vast and growing. My allusions here to the work of Wolfgang Sachs and Vandana Shiva reflect years of exposure to their work in a wide variety of media, including speeches, newsletters, videos, and personal communications. A good place to start is Sachs's book *The Development Dictionary*. Other prominent Western critics of development as currently practiced include Ivan Illich, David Korten, and Helena Norberg-Hodge, whose books are listed in the Sources section.

Chapter 2
P. 27   *Attica:*
Plato's description of Attica is found in the dialogue *Critias*, 111b–d. He describes how the "plains" of Attica "were once covered in rich soil, and there was abundant timber on the mountain. . . ." His extended analysis of the terrain's hydrological history reads like a contemporary ecology text, as does his conclusion: "By comparison with the original territory, what is left now is like the skeleton of a body wasted by disease."

Ephesus:
Ephesus, near the contemporary city of Kusadasi, was once the second largest city in the Roman empire. I visited there in 1985, and learned its story from tour guides and historians. The once-lush lands surrounding the city were deforested—as were most of the lands in the Mediterranean basin—for fuel and timber to build ships.

P. 28   *Easter Island:*
The story of Easter Island can be found in any good encyclopedia.

P. 29   *This was Malthus's real agenda; he was a conservative who opposed social programs. . . .*
Nobody seems to like Malthus. The Left, starting with Karl Marx, has always rejected him, largely out of instinct (few are familiar with his political history). The Right has always been equally outraged, despite his friendliness to their political cause, because he seems to limit the potential for the expansion of wealth. The fact that people still seek to refute him some 200 years after the publication of his first small pamphlet suggests that he struck a nerve. I am indebted to Paul Robinson, whose book *The Third Revolution* introduced me to Malthus II.

P. 29   *Green Revolution:*
The phrase "Green Revolution" refers to the development and wide dissemination of new genetic strains of rice, wheat, and other crops designed to produce much larger harvests from the same amount of land. Were it not for these advances, many millions of people would have died of starvation. The "revolution" began with the work of plant biologist Norman Borlaug in Mexico and India, and continues today at numerous research stations all over the World. However, many have critiqued it for creating as many problems as it solved. For an overview, see *The Green Revolution Revisited*, edited by Bernhard Glaeser.

P. 33   *Agenda 21*
Agenda 21 is available directly from the United Nations. Information on the many Local Agenda 21 initiatives is available from the International Council of Local Environmental Initiatives (ICLEI), on the Web at www.iclei.org.

Bush's Secret Service detail was housed . . .
Ruth Sinai, "Rio Motels Offer Unusual Amenities to Media," Associated Press, 13 June 1992.

P. 36   *"I was, in a sense, vulnerable . . ."*
The quotes from Vice President Al Gore, with the exception of those from personal conversation, are all taken from the opening chapter of *Earth in the Balance*. My interview with Gore appeared in *In Context* 32 (Spring 1992), archived on the Web at www.context.org. Gore's comment to Bill McKibben appears in *Hope, Human and Wild*, p. 1.

Chapter 3
When not otherwise specified, data in this chapter come from either *World Resources 1998–99*, published by World Resources Institute, or the Worldwatch Institute's *Vital Signs 1999* by Lester Brown et al. These reports are themselves drawing on the world's most reliable data sources, including a wide variety of international agencies, national governments, and the scientific literature.

P. 45   *As Nobel laureate Elias Canetti wrote in his masterpiece . . .*
Elias Canetti's *Crowds and Power* is, in my view, one of the most important books of the century and essential reading for anyone who wishes to understand why human beings do what they do.

The desire to be MORE grew strong enough . . .
Leontina Albina's astonishing feats of childbearing are documented in the *Guinness Book of Records*.

"But our minds must not go slack . . ."
Annie Dillard, "The Wreck of Time," Harper's, January 1998, pp. 51–56.

P. 46   *Human beings born today can expect to live, on average, nearly* twenty years *longer . . .*
As reported in the *New York Times*, 11 February 1999, p. A19. But this average hides important details. Life expectancies are falling in countries such as Russia, beset by economic and social distress, and plummeting in those countries of Africa where AIDS has become epidemic.

". . . examples of the failures of past population forecasts abound."
The Joel Cohen quote is from his excellent overview study, *How Many People Can the Earth Support?* p. 32.

P. 47 *. . . dramatically reduced growth rates in Bangladesh.*
The surprising success of population policies in Bangladesh is documented in "The Population Slide," by Madhusree Mukerjee, *Scientific American*, December 1998, pp. 32–33.

P. 48 *tonguefish:*
I mention tonguefish and shrimp because of personal experience as a young boy, going out on a shrimp boat, and helping my relatives sort the catch. Even at that age I was astonished by how many other creatures were killed and discarded in order to get the shrimp. Shrimp and other fisheries off the coast of North Carolina have suffered in recent decades and are a small fraction of their previous size.

P. 50 *Gross World Product:*
The Gross World Product is a global aggregate of the Gross Domestic Product, a figure calculated by nearly every nation in the World. For an excellent introduction to the Gross Domestic Product, its history and its problems, see "If the GDP is Up, Why is America Down?" by Cliff Cobb, Ted Halstead, and Jonathan Rowe in the *Atlantic Monthly*. Redefining Progress in the United States publishes the "Genuine Progress Indicator" (GPI), which adjusts GDP for unacknowledged costs and uncounted economic benefits. Call them at 800-896-2100 or visit their Web site (www.rprogress.org), where you can also read the *Atlantic* article. In the UK, the New Economics Foundation publishes a similar measure called the Index of Sustainable Economic Welfare (ISEW). Both indicators had their origin in ideas developed by economist Herman Daly and theologian John Cobb, and documented in their book *For the Common Good.*

P. 51 *. . . a cup of coffee, on its journey to your mug . . .*
The detailed story of coffee and several common consumer products is told in *Stuff: The Secret Lives of Everyday Things*, by John C. Ryan and Alan Thein Durning of Northwest Environment Watch. Be forewarned: you will told that your everyday purchases caused all kinds of havoc. A T-shirt, for example, might include a few tablespoons of oil, the source of polyester. "By buying the T-shirt," write Ryan and Durning, "I helped send an oil derrick's spinning diamond drill bit into the ground near Maracaibo, on the Caribbean coast of Venezuela." You didn't really; you simply responded to the manufacturer placing that kind of shirt in front of you, at a price you could afford. To put the causal blame on you is like blaming the rat for the cheese placed at the end of the race. The solution is to get out of the race altogether, or to reinvent it.

P.52 *. . .the cover for my new CD . . .*
A live version of the song "Whole Lotta Shoppin' Goin On," the title track of the CD mentioned in this chapter, can be seen in the introduction to the excellent 1997 PBS documentary on overconsumption, *Affluenza.*

P. 54 *Americans each consume an average of 260 pounds of meat . . .*
Data on American and Bangladeshi meat consumption is from the *Human Development Report* published by the United Nations Development Program, and reported in the *New York Times.*

Ladakh:
I have heard various versions of the story of Ladakh (and this anecdote) from Helena
Norberg-Hodge over the years. The anecdote is retold from memory, but her experi-
ences are documented in her book *Ancient Futures* and in my interview with her in
In Context 25 (Spring 1990): 28.

Studies have shown that people's sense of satisfaction with their material wealth . . .
Robert Frank, "Our Climb to Sublime—Hold On. We Don't Need to Go There,"
Washington Post, Sunday, 24 January 1999, p. B01. Frank is a Cornell economist, and
the article was based on his 1998 book *Luxury Fever: Why Money Fails to Satisfy in an
Era of Excess.*

P. 59   *"A world community can exist only with world communication."*
Hutchins's essay, "The Atomic Bomb versus Civilization," is cited in *Bartlett's Familiar Quotations,* p. 1014.

P. 59   *. . . the atomic bomb was nothing to be afraid of . . .*
Mao Tse-tung is cited by Annie Dillard in "The Wreck of Time," *Harper's,* January
1998.

The strategy of globalization seems to be succeeding . . .
In the wake of NATO's war against Serbia, and Serbian aggression (and probable acts
of genocide) against Albanians in Kosovo, these remarks about globalization as a
strategy for global peace seem less convincing than when I first drafted them, in February 1999. But in some ways, the war in the Balkans serves to prove the point. Had
the West moved more decisively to build trade ties and economic interdependence
with the former Yugoslavia, the chances for this kind of escalating conflict would
have been greatly reduced.

. . . the diverse babble of languages . . .
Data on world languages is from the *Cambridge Encyclopedia of Language,* p. 360; and
the *1999 World Almanac and Book of Facts,* p. 700.

P. 61   *The Global Brain:*
Peter Russell's *The Global Brain* was both a book and a slide presentation (later translated to video) that presented a provocative synthesis of science and visionary spirituality. He noted that a population stabilized at 10 billion (10^{10}) would roughly equal
the number of nerve cells in the human neo-cortex.

P. 62   *The evidence begins with the fossils . . .*
Information on Steller's sea cow and the ancient Australian flightless bird *Genyornis*
(hunted to extinction 50,000 years ago) are from Peter J. Bryant's excellent Web-
based *Hypertext Book in Biodiversity and Conservation.*

P. 63   *We are killing off our brother and sister creatures . . .*
Estimates on the rate of species extinction vary. This estimate comes from David
Quammen's well-researched essay in *Harper's,* and is on the low end of estimates I've
seen, some of which range up to several thousand times the rate of the "normal" or
"background" extinction rate. There is scientific consensus, however, on the fact of
increased species extinction, and on the extreme speed with which it is occurring.

P. 63   *Fighting animals to the death was particularly popular . . .*
Stories of the training methods of Genghis Khan's armies are told in Lamb's *Genghis Khan.*

Let's start with the birds:
Data on threatened species are drawn largely from tables in John Tuxill, *Losing Strands in the Web of Life.* Tuxill was drawing on surveys done by the International Union for the Conservation of Nature (IUCN). Fish data are from Anne Platt McGinn, *Rocking the Boat.*

". . .a continuation of present trends will lead to widespread fisheries collapses. . . ."
"Fishing Down Marine Food Webs," Daniel Pauly et al., *Science* 279 (6 February 1998): 863.

P. 64   *Not all of the animal news is bad, thankfully.*
Species that have recovered from near-extinction are cited in "Look Who's Back!" *Life Magazine,* January 1999, p. 76.

P. 66   *German insurance magnates to consider . . .*
German reinsurance giant Munich Re is circulating a map that indicates coastal areas of the Caribbean, Pacific, and Indian Ocean likely to be hardest hit by climate change. The company is apparently engaged in private discussion about limiting its liability exposure in such areas, as was reported by Nick Nuttall, or *Times* London, 9 November 1998.

Chapter 4
P. 70   *Systems:*
The past decade has seen an enormous outpouring of good information about systems, from popular business books (like Peter Senge's *The Fifth Discipline*) to simple workbooks (*Systems Thinking Basics,* by Virginia Anderson and Lauren Johnson). These popularizations all grow out of the work of Jay Forrester, the founder of system dynamics at the Massachusetts Institute of Technology. I learned about systems by listening to lectures by Donella Meadows, Dennis Meadows, and Harmut Bossel, three of the world's leading experts in the field, at annual meetings of the Balaton Group in Csopak, Hungary. The idea that the structure of the World system—with its enormous feedback delays and momentum—makes it inherently uncontrollable is an insight I owe to Donella Meadows.

P. 73   *. . .chemicals that mimic the hormone estrogen . . .*
The alarming threat of endocrine disruptors and hormone mimickers is documented in *Our Stolen Future,* by Theo Colburn, Diane Dumanoski, and Pete Myers.

The relentless depletion of our fisheries . . .
The story of the North Atlantic cod is distilled from many sources, including a February 1999 story on National Public Radio. Dennis Meadows, a co-author of *The Limits to Growth,* created an excellent computer-mediated game called "Fishbanks, Ltd." which teaches participants about systems principles by having them manage a fictitious fishery much like that of the disappearing cod. In his experience, few have been able to manage these simulated fisheries sustainably; and professional fisheries managers have often produced the most dramatic collapses. For information on Fishbanks and many other useful systems resources, contact Tracy Botting at IPSSR/Laboratory

for Interactive Learning, University of New Hampshire, Thompson Hall, Room G-01, Durham, NH 03824, or www.unh.edu/ipssr/index.htm.

P. 74 *CFCs:*
The story of CFCs is drawn primarily from Bill McKibben's *The End of Nature*. Projections on future CFC levels are from the U.S. Environmental Protection Agency.

P. 77 *global climate change:*
For the complete history of global climate change, see Gale E. Christianson's *Greenhouse: The Dramatic 200-Year Story of Global Warming*. The story of Svante Arrhenius is particularly intriguing. Arrhenius was a famous Nobel Prize–winning chemist in his day, who also wrote a number of popular books, but his work has been largely forgotten. He spent nearly the entire year of 1895 calculating the effects of CO_2 emissions on the planet's atmosphere, solving thousands of equations on paper. He believed it would take several millennia for humanity to double the carbon dioxide concentration—and that when it happened, it would be a very beneficial thing.

More serious concerns were raised publicly . . .
The authors of *The Limits to Growth* were among the scientists to highlight the problem of CO_2 emissions in 1972, because the data were "incontrovertible evidence of exponential growth" (Donella Meadows).

P. 79 *Another impersonal, systemic, and rather annoying factor . . .*
"The Tragedy of the Commons," first published in 1968, was reprinted as an appendix to Garrett Hardin's book *Exploring New Ethics for Survival*. The quote at the end of the chapter appears in the preface to that book, p. vii.

P. 83 *Money is the single greatest obstacle . . .*
The reflections on the monetary system were greatly aided by Jack Weatherford's *The History of Money*.

Chapter 5
P. 89 *In Context:*
Back issues of *In Context*, which ceased publication in 1996 after a thirteen-year run, are archived on the web at www.context.org. I was its managing editor and then executive editor from 1988–1992. When *IC* ceased publication in 1996, some of its former staff created a similar, but somewhat spunkier quarterly called *Yes! A Journal of Positive Futures*, which can be found at www.futurenet.org.

P. 90 *Global Tomorrow Coalition:*
Global Tomorrow Coalition (GTC) was directed by Don Lesh and Diane Lowrie, former staff of President Jimmy Carter. Lesh had been one of the original partners in Potomac Associates, the U.S. publishers of *The Limits to Growth*. He also worked with project director Gerald Barney on the ground-breaking *Global 2000 Report to the President*, a study of global trends and indicators. This landmark work was completed in 1980 and promptly shelved by the incoming Reagan administration (which also dismantled the solar water heaters installed by Jimmy Carter on the White House roof). During the Reagan and Bush years especially, when global environmental concerns were at a low point, GTC performed an important service by hosting numerous conferences to promote an awareness of global trends, the problems of growth,

and the challenge of developing more sustainably. After the election of the Clinton-Gore administration, it declared its mission accomplished and closed its doors in the mid-1990s.

P. 91 *Scott and Helen Nearing:*
Scott and Helen Nearing, mentioned here only in passing, were perhaps the leading U.S. proponents of "back-to-the-land" living in the twentieth century. They built their houses by hand, grew their own food, refused to use many modern technologies, and attracted thousands of visitors to their homesteads while publishing over thirty books, including *Living the Good Life, The Making of a Radical,* and *Loving and Leaving the Good Life.*

P. 92 *"Pull up and stay and hear my tale of woe . . ."*
"Dead Planet Blues" appears on my seven-song comedy album, *Whole Lotta Shoppin' Goin' On,* produced by Rain City Records and available through Chelsea Green, the publishers of this book. See www.AtKisson.com.

P. 94 *I start to speak the prayer out loud, and it comes out as a song.*
The song alluded to in the Csopak journal entry is "Balaton," which appears on my CD *Testing the Rope,* also produced by Rain City Records, and also available through Chelsea Green.

P. 99 *It had the usual scars across its back from encounters with boat propellers.*
The manatees of Florida live under continuous threat of extinction from the pressures of that state's runaway Growth, but they are still around. In 1997 I went back to visit my family's old marina and learned that a manatee—perhaps a descendant of the manatee we befriended—still spent the summers there.

P. 100 *"For one species to mourn the death of another . . ."*
Aldo Leopold's lament for the passenger pigeon appears in his classic collection of essays on nature and ethics, *A Sand County Almanac.* The passenger pigeon once filled the skies of North America with flocks so enormous they would literally block the Sun. They were killed as pests and consumed for food.

Chapter 6
P. 105 *. . . one strain of the environmental movement would be profoundly disappointed . . .*
My reflections on the strain of environmentalism that essentially wants to "bring on the apocalypse" are the result of years of observation, conversations with movement activists, and readings in the periodical literature (such as the magazine *Earth First!*).

P. 107 *Unabomber:*
The "Unabomber," who waged a solitary campaign of murder and terror by letter-bomb in the United States, killing three and injuring twenty-two, was proven to be Theodore Kaczynski, a former teacher of mathematics with a profound hatred of technology. His extreme tactics, overwrought writing style, and general eccentricity cast an unfortunate shadow over all who have legitimate criticisms of modern technology and its destructive consequences.

P. 111 *TARGETS:*
For a complete description of the TARGETS model—which used the World3 model as a starting point—see *Perspectives on Global Change: The TARGETS Approach,* by

Rotmans and de Vries. The book is dense and academic, but it is also an elegant piece of logic, comprehensive research, and clarity of presentation. The ideas in the book are very useful as a starting point for discussions about the global future among people of very different worldviews, because the TARGETS model presents widely varying future scenarios with equanimity. The quote ("If the world is a place of abundance . . .") is from page 393.

P. 118 *". . . to preserve it through a dark age."*
James Lovelock's worries about the need to preserve our civilization's basic scientific knowledge are recorded in "A Book for All Seasons," *Science*, 8 May 1998, pp. 832–33. David Ehrenfeld's commentary appears in "The Coming Collapse of the Age of Technology," *Tikkun*, January/February 1999, p. 33.

P. 121 *Cesium-137*
The story of the abandoned canister of cesium-137 in Goiana, Brazil, was reported in "Deadly Glitter," *Time* magazine, 19 October 1987, p. 38.

P. 123 *Only something like a "Plutonium Priesthood" . . .*
A version of this idea was first proposed and developed by Joanna Macy and her colleagues in the Nuclear Guardianship Project. For a description, see "Guardians of the Future," *In Context* 28 (Spring 1991): 20.

P. 127 *When 1,600 scientists released a statement . . .*
The Union of Concerned Scientists released the "World Scientists' Warning to Humanity" in 1992. Over 1,600 senior scientists signed the document, which begins, "Human beings and the natural world are on a collision course. Human activities inflict harsh and often irreversible damage on the environment and on critical resources. If not checked, many of our current practices put at serious risk the future that we wish for human society . . ."

"The Economists' Statement on Climate Change" was published by Redefining Progress in San Francisco in 1997. The statement was signed by over 2,500 economists, including such well-known figures as Paul Krugman, Dale Jorgenson, and Kenneth Arrow. The statement endorses the findings of the Intergovernmental Panel on Climate Change and calls for market-based instruments for reducing carbon emissions. For information call Redefining Progress at 800-896-2100 or visit their Web site, www.rprogress.org.

P. 128 *". . . once more value ends above means . . ."*
The quotations from both Keynes and Schumacher are from Schumacher's essay "An Economics of Permanence," in Theodore Roszak's book *Sources*. Keynes is using the word "ends" here in the economist's sense, in the same way that Herman Daly uses it. It refers to the ultimate purpose of life, why we do what we do. To "value ends above means," in economic terms, is to reorient oneself toward the higher values of life—for instance, ethics and enlightenment—rather than valuing economic activity for its own sake (the means to those ends). Daly would agree with Keynes's assertion in the quotation that we currently emphasize the opposite: Nature is the "ultimate means," and God/Enlightenment is the "ultimate ends." The economy is the "intermediate means" and societal goods are the "intermediate ends."

Chapter 7
P. 133   *The Future in a Word:*
Citations of definitions of sustainable development and sustainability are from Meadows, Meadows, and Randers, *Beyond the Limits*, including their citations of *Our Common Future* and the work of Herman Daly.

P. 136   *Factor Four:*
"Factor Four" refers to the goal of achieving 75% reductions in industrial through put (increasing efficiency by a factor of four). "Factor Ten" refers to 90% reductions in throughput (increasing efficiency ten-fold). See Lovins, et al., *Factor Four*.

Chapter 8
P. 155   *Green Planning:*
The official name of the Netherlands' "Green Plan" is the National Environmental Policy Plan. Documents in English are available from the Ministry for Housing, Spatial Planning, and the Environment, or from the Netherlands Embassy in Washington, D.C. Huey Johnson's book *Green Plans* and Barry Dalal-Clayton's *Getting to Grips with Green Plans* also contain basic information. For information on the International Network of Green Planners, write to secr@ingp.org.

P. 157   *Interface, Inc.:*
For the full story of Ray Anderson's and Interface's conversion to the sustainability ideal, see Anderson's book *Mid-Course Correction: Toward a Sustainable Enterprise: The Interface Model*, published by Peregrinzilla Press (1998) and distributed by Chelsea Green Publishing.

P. 158   *Curitiba, Brazil:*
Curitiba's story is told beautifully in McKibben's *Hope, Human and Wild*.

P. 159   *The Natural Step:*
The story of the origin of The Natural Step is told by Robèrt in "Educating a Nation: The Natural Step," in *In Context* 28 (Spring 1991): 10. The U.S. organization has a Web site at www.naturalstep.org. The "Four System Conditions" of The Natural Step are formally written this way: (1) substances from the Earth's crust must not system-atially increase in Nature; (2) substances produced by society must not systematically increase in Nature; (3) the physical basis for the productivity and diversity of Nature must not be systematically deteriorated; and (4) we must be efficient enough to meet basic human needs.

Many other excellent examples of sustainability in action have been documented by ZERI (Zero Emissions Research Institute) in Japan. See, for example, Gunter Pauli's book *Upsizing*.

P. 162   *Sustainable Seattle:*
For more information about Sustainable Seattle and the "Indicators of Sustainable Community," write to them at sustsea@halcyon.com. For a more complete history of the project, see my article in *Environmental Impact Assessment Review*, July–November 1996. For an overview of the community indicators movement, see *The Community Indicators Handbook*, published by Redefining Progress in San Francisco (www.rprogress.org, or 800-896-2100). Also see the excellent *Compendium* published by the International Institute for Sustainable Development, on the Web at http://iisd.ca. Other resources are highlighted at www.AtKisson.com.

Chapter 9

P. 177 *Innovation-diffusion theory:*

The basic principles of innovation-diffusion theory are taken from the books of Everett Rogers, cited in the Sources. Robert Gilman first introduced me to the metaphor of the amoeba, which I have greatly expanded.

The Innovation Diffusion Game:

P. 178 For information on "The Innovation Diffusion Game," see www.AtKisson.com. A trainer's packet with complete facilitation instructions, overhead transparencies, and player instruction cards is available. A simplified version of the original game is archived on the Web at www.context.org, and was first published in *In Context* 28 (Spring 1991): 58.

P. 183 *Hypercar:*

Complete information on the Hypercar idea is documented in *Natural Capitalism*, by Lovins, Lovins, and Hawken.

P. 189 *scurvy:*

The complex story of scurvy and its cure is documented in *The History of Scurvy and Vitamin C*, by Kenneth J. Carpenter.

P. 191 *Unfortunately, the story about the monkeys isn't true.*

The debunking of the "Hundredth Monkey" story was reported by Elaine Myers in "The Hundredth Monkey Revisited," *In Context* 9 (Spring 1985): 10.

Chapter 10

P. 203 *"a threat that everyone perceives but no one talks about . . ."*

Gary Hamel and C. K. Prahalad, "Strategic Intent," *Harvard Business Review*, May/June 1989, p. 75.

SOURCES

Adams, Douglas. *The Hitchhiker's Guide to the Galaxy*. Tenth anniversary edition. New York: Harmony Books, 1989.

———. *The Long Dark Tea-Time of the Soul*. Reissue edition. New York: Pocket Books, 1991.

Adams, Patch. *Gesundheit! Bringing Good Health to You, the Medical System, and Society through Physician Service, Complementary Therapies, Humor, and Joy*. Rochester, Vt.: Healing Arts Press, 1998.

"Adapting to the Inevitable." *Nature* 395 (22 October 1998): 741.

Amidon, Elias, and Elizabeth Roberts. *Earth Prayers from Around the World*. New York: HarperCollins, 1991.

Amis, Martin. "The Janitor on Mars." *The New Yorker*, 26 October and 2 November 1998, 208.

Anderson, Ray C. *Mid-Course Correction: Toward a Sustainable Enterprise: The Interface Model*. Atlanta: Peregrinzilla Press, 1998.

Anderson, Virginia, and Lauren Johnson. *Systems Thinking Basics: From Concepts to Causal Loops*. Cambridge, Mass.: Pegasus Communications, 1997.

"Antarctica: Climate Change and Sea Level." Ice and Climate Division, British Antarctic Survey, Cambridge, April 1998. www.nerc-bas.ac.uk/public/info/antsea.html.

Arndt, H. W. *Economic Development: The History of an Idea*. Chicago: University of Chicago Press, 1987.

AtKisson, Alan. "Barnstorming for Balance: An Interview with Al Gore." *In Context* 32 (Spring 1992): 36.

———. "The Cost of Development: An Interview with Helena Norberg-Hodge." *In Context* 25 (Spring 1990): 28.

_____. "Developing Indicators of Sustainable Community: Lessons from Sustainable Seattle." *Environmental Impact Assessment Review* 16, no. 4–6 (July–November 1996): 337.

_____, ed. *The Community Indicators Handbook*. San Francisco: Redefining Progress, 1997.

Baker, Russell. "The Machine, the Doom and the Fool." *New York Times*, 5 March 1972.

Barjavel, René. *Ravage*. France: Editions Denoli, 1943. Reissued in *Romans Extraordinaire*, an edition of *Omnibus*, Paris, 1995.

Bartlett's Familiar Quotations. New York: Little, Brown, 1948.

Beckett, Samuel. *Waiting for Godot: A Tragicomedy in Two Acts*. New York: Grove Press, 1954.

Berry, Wendell. "Feedback." *In Context* 26 (Fall 1990): 4.

_____. "The Futility of Global Thinking." *Harper's*, September 1989, 16–22.

Bossel, Hartmut. *Earth at a Crossroads: Paths to a Sustainable Future*. Cambridge: Cambridge University Press, 1998.

Brown, Harrison. *The Challenge of Man's Future: An Inquiry Concerning the Condition of Man During the Years that Lie Ahead*. 1956. Reprint. Boulder, Colo. and London: Westview Press, 1984.

Brown, Lester R., Christopher Flavin, Hilary French, et al. *State of the World 1999*. New York: W. W. Norton, 1999.

Brown, Lester R., et al. *Vital Signs 1999*. New York: W. W. Norton, 1999.

Brown, Lester R., Gary Gardner, and Brian Halweil. *Sixteen Dimensions of the Population Problem*. Washington, D.C.: Worldwatch Institute, September 1998.

Brown, Molly Young, and Joanna Macy. *Coming Back to Life: Practices to Reconnect Our Lives, Our World*. New York: New Society Publishers, 1998.

Bryant, Peter J. *Hypertext Book in Biodiversity and Conservation*. School of Biological Sciences, University of California at Irvine, January 1999.
http://darwin.bio.uci.edu/~sustain/bio65/Titlpage.htm.

Caffrey, Andy. "Antarctica's 'Deep Impact' Threat." *Earth Island Journal* (Summer 1998).

Cambridge Encyclopedia of Language. Cambridge: Cambridge University Press, 1997.

"Can the World Survive Economic Growth?" *Time*, 14 August 1972, 56–57.

Canetti, Elias. *Crowds and Power*. Translated by Carol Stewart. New York: Farrar Straus Giroux, 1962. Original published as *Masse und Macht* (Hamburg: Claassen Verlag, 1960).

Carpenter, Kenneth J. *The History of Scurvy and Vitamin C*. Cambridge: Cambridge University Press, 1986.

Carson, Rachel. *Silent Spring*. New York: Houghton Mifflin, 1962.

Christianson, Gale E. *Greenhouse: The Dramatic 200-Year Story of Global Warming*. New York: Walker and Company, 1999.

Cobb, Clifford, Ted Halstead, and Jonathan Rowe. "If the GDP is Up, Why is America Down?" Reprint. *Atlantic Monthly*, October 1995.

Cohen, Joel E. *How Many People Can the Earth Support?* New York: W. W. Norton, 1995.

Colburn, Theo, Diane Dumanoski, and Pete Myers. *Our Stolen Future*. New York: Dutton, 1996.

Conway, Gordon, and Vernon W. Ruttan. *The Doubly Green Revolution: Food for All in the 21st Century*. Ithaca, N.Y.: Comstock Publishing Associates, 1999.

Council on Environmental Quality. *Global 2000 Report to the President*. Washington, D.C., 1982.

Dalal-Clayton, Barry. *Getting to Grips with Green Plans: National-Level Experience in Industrial Countries*. London: Earthscan, 1996.

Daly, Herman, and John Cobb. *For the Common Good: Redirecting the Economy toward Community, the Environment, and a Sustainable Future.* Boston: Beacon Press, 1989.

DeCanio, Stephen J. *The Economics of Climate Change.* San Francisco: Redefining Progress, October 1997.

Dillard, Annie. "The Wreck of Time: Taking Our Century's Measure." *Harper's,* January 1998, 51–56.

Eco, Umberto. *The Name of the Rose.* Translated by William Weaver. San Diego: Harcourt Brace Jovanovich, 1983.

Ehrenfeld, David. "The Coming Collapse of the Age of Technology." *Tikkun* (January/February 1999): 33.

Ehrlich, Paul. "Eco-Catastrophe!" In *Eco-Catastrophe,* ed. by the Editors of *Ramparts.* New York: Harper & Row, 1970.

Ehrlich, Paul, and Anne Ehrlich. *The Population Bomb.* New York: Ballantine, 1969.

Ehrlich, Paul, and John Holdren. *The Cassandra Conference.* College Station: Texas A&M University Press, 1988.

"El Niño/La Niña." National Climatic Data Center, Asheville, N.C., 20 November 1998. www.ncdc.noaa.gov/ol/climate/elnino/elnino.html.

Frank, Robert, ed. *Luxury Fever: Why Money Fails to Satisfy in an Era of Excess.* New York: Free Press, 1999.

Fromm, Erich. *The Art of Loving.* New York: Harper & Row, 1956.

Gelbspan, Ross. "This Story Is About the End of the World." *The Village Voice,* 9 March 1972.

Glaeser, Bernhard, ed. *The Green Revolution Revisited: Critique and Alternatives.* London and Boston: Allen & Unwin, 1987.

Gore, Al. *Earth in the Balance: Ecology and the Human Spirit.* New York: Plume, 1992.

Guinness Book of Records. Dublin: Guinness Publishing Company, 1999.

Hamel, Gary, and C. K. Prahalad. "Strategic Intent." *Harvard Business Review* (May/June 1989): 75.

Hamilton, Edith. *Mythology.* New York: New American Library, 1942.

Hamilton, Kendall, and Kimberly Martineau. "The 100-Year Forecast: Very Hot, and Stormy." *Newsweek,* 18 August 1997, 12.

Hammond, Allen. *Which World? Scenarios for the 21st Century: Global Destinies, Regional Choices.* Washington, D.C.: Island Press, 1998.

Hardin, Garrett. "The Tragedy of the Commons." 1968. Reprinted in *Exploring New Ethics for Survival: The Voyage of the Spaceship Beagle* (New York: Penguin, 1972).

Harrison, Paul. *The Third Revolution: Environment, Population and a Sustainable World.* London and New York: I.B. Tauris & Co. Ltd., 1992.

Hawken, Paul. *The Ecology of Commerce: A Declaration of Sustainability.* New York: HarperBusiness, 1993.

Hawthorne, Nathaniel. *House of the Seven Gables.* Boston: Ticknor, Reed and Fields, 1851.

Hayes, Denis. "How to Create a Solar Economy in Four Years." *Green Living* (Winter 1998–1999): 39, 46.

Hertsgaard, Mark. *Earth Odyssey.* New York: Broadway Books, 1998.

Himmerlfarb, Gertrude, ed. *On Population: Thomas Robert Malthus.* New York: Random House, 1960.

Hull, Fritz, ed. *Earth and Spirit: The Spiritual Dimension of the Environmental Crisis.* New York: Continuum, 1993.

Hyams, Edward. *Soil and Civilization.* London: Thames and Hudson, 1952.

Illich, Ivan. *Deschooling Society.* New York: Harper & Row, 1971.

Innes, Judith E. *Knowledge and Public Policy: The Search for Meaningful Indicators.* Revised edition. Piscataway, N.J.: Transaction Publishers, 1990.

"January 1995 Events in the Northern Larsen Ice Shelf and Their Importance." National Snow and Ice Data Center, World Data Center-A for Glaciology, Boulder, Colo., 24 March 1998. www-nsidc.colorado.edu/NSIDC/LARSEN/#intro.

Johnson, Huey. *Green Plans: Greenprint for Sustainability.* Lincoln: University of Nebraska Press, 1995.

Johnston, Charles A. *The Creative Imperative: A Four-Dimensional Theory of Human Growth and Planetary Evolution.* Seattle: Ten Speed Press, 1986.

Kahn, Herman, et al. *The Next 200 Years: A Scenario for America and the World.* New York: William Morrow, 1976.

Kerr, Richard A. "Warming's Unpleasant Surprise: Shivering in the Greenhouse?" *Science* 281 (10 July 1998): 156.

Korten, David. *The Post-Corporate World: Life After Capitalism.* San Francisco: Berrett-Koehler, 1999.

———. *When Corporations Rule the World.* West Hartford, Conn.: Kumarian Press, 1995.

Lamb, Harold. *Genghis Khan: The Emperor of All Men.* Garden City, N.Y.: Garden City Publishing Co., 1927.

Leopold, Aldo. *A Sand County Almanac.* 1949. Reissued. New York: Oxford University Press, 1987.

Lerner, Steve. *Eco-Pioneers: Practical Visionaries Solving Today's Environmental Problems.* Cambridge: The MIT Press, 1997.

Lewis, Anthony. Telephone interview, 9 February 1999.

Living Planet Report 1998. WWF International, Gland, Switzerland, 1998. www.panda.org.

"Look Who's Back!" *Life Magazine,* January 1999, 76.

Lopez, Barry. *The Rediscovery of North America.* Lexington: The University of Kentucky Press, 1990.

Lovelock, James. "A Book for All Seasons." *Science* (8 May 1998): 832–33.

Lovins, Amory, Hunter Lovins, and Paul Hawken. *Natural Capitalism.* Boston: Little Brown, 1999.

Lovins, Amory, Hunter Lovins, and Ernst Ulrich von Weizsacker. *Factor Four.* London: Earthscan, 1997.

McGinn, Anne Platt. *Rocking the Boat: Conserving Fisheries and Protecting Jobs.* Washington, D.C.: Worldwatch Institute, 1998.

McKibben, Bill. *The End of Nature.* New York: Doubleday, 1989.

———. *Hope, Human and Wild: True Stories of Living Lightly on the Earth.* Boston: Little, Brown, 1995.

Meadows, Donella H. "The Limits to Growth Revisited." In *The Cassandra Conference,* ed. Paul Ehrlich and John Holdren. College Station: Texas A&M University Press, 1988.

———. "Sometimes It's Hard for an Environmentalist to Remain Upbeat." *Valley News* (Lebanon, N.H.), 9 January 1999.

———. "Ways to Intervene in a System (In Increasing Order of Effectiveness)." Unpublished manuscript; condensed version published in *Whole Earth Review,* Fall 1997.

Meadows, Donella H., Dennis L. Meadows, and Jørgen Randers. *Beyond the Limits: Confronting Global Collapse, Envisioning a Sustainable Future.* White River Junction, Vt.: Chelsea Green, 1992.

Meadows, Donella H., Dennis L. Meadows, Jørgen Randers, and William H. Behrens III. *The Limits to Growth.* Second edition. New York: Potomac Associates/Universe Books, 1974.

Mukerjee, Madhusree. "The Population Slide." *Scientific American,* December 1998, 32–33.

Myers, Elaine. "The Hundredth Monkey Revisited." *In Context* 9 (Spring 1985): 10.

Nearing, Helen, and Scott Nearing. *Living the Good Life*. Harborside, Maine: Social Science Institute, 1954.

Netherlands, Government of the. Ministry of Housing, Spatial Planning, and the Environment (VROM), Ministry of Economic Affairs, Ministry of Agriculture, Nature Management and Fisheries, Ministry of Transport, Public Works and Water Management. *National Environmental Policy Plan 3*. February 1998.

————. *Policy Document on Environment and Economy: Towards a Sustainable Economy*. January 1998.

New Larousse Encyclopedia of Mythology. London: Hamlyn Publishing Group, 1968.

1999 World Almanac and Book of Facts. Mahwah, N.J.: World Almanac Books, 1998.

Norberg-Hodge, Helena. *Ancient Futures: Learning from Ladakh*. San Francisco: Sierra Club Books, 1991.

Norgaard, Richard B. *Development Betrayed: The End of Progress and a Coevolutionary Revisioning of the Future*. London: Routledge, 1994.

Nuttall, Nick. "Climate Disaster Map Pinpoints 'No-Go' Areas for Insurers." *Times* (London), 9 November 1998.

Osborn, Fairfield. *Our Plundered Planet*. Boston: Little, Brown, 1948.

"Panel Warns of World Growth." *Boston Record American* (AP), 4 March 1972.

Pauli, Gunter. *Upsizing: The Road to Zero Emissions: More Jobs, More Income and No Pollution*. Sheffield, UK: Greenleaf Publishing, 1998.

Pauly, Daniel, et al. "Fishing Down Marine Food Webs." *Science* 279 (6 February 1998): 860–63.

Perkins, John H. *Geopolitics and the Green Revolution: Wheat, Genes, and the Cold War*. Oxford: Oxford University Press, 1997.

Peterson, John L., Margaret Wheatley, and Myron Kelner-Rogers. "The Year 2000: Social Chaos or Social Transformation?" Unpublished manuscript. Arlington Va.: Arlington Institute, September 1998.

Pirages, Dennis C., ed. *Building Sustainable Societies: A Blueprint for the Post-Industrial World*. Armonk, N.Y.: M. E. Sharpe, 1996.

Plato. *Critias*. Translated by A. E. Taylor. In *Plato, Collected Dialogues*. Princeton: Princeton University Press, 1963.

Plato. *The Republic*. Translated by Allan Bloom. New York: Basic Books, 1968.

Platt, Charles. "Nuking Nukes." *Wired*, February 1999, 72.

"Population Growth Problems Debated." *Denver Post* (AP), 22 April 1972.

Quammen, David. "Planet of Weeds: Tallying the Losses of Earth's Animals and Plants." *Harper's*, October 1998, 57–69.

Rapoport, Roger. "Catch 24,400 (or, Plutonium is My Favorite Element)." In *Eco-Catastrophe*, ed. by the Editors of *Ramparts*. New York: Harper & Row, 1970.

Roberts, Callum M. "Ecological Advice for the Global Fisheries Crisis." *TREE* 12, no. 1 (January 1997).

Robin, Vicki, and Joe Dominguez. *Your Money or Your Life*. New York: Viking Penguin, 1992.

Rogers, Everett. *Communication of Innovations: A Cross-Cultural Approach*. New York: Free Press, 1971.

————. *Diffusion of Innovations*. 1962. New York: Free Press, 1995.

Roszak, Theodore, ed. *Sources: An Anthology of Contemporary Materials Useful for Preserving Personal Sanity While Braving the Great Technological Wilderness*. New York: Harper & Row, 1972.

Rotmans, Jan, and Bert de Vries. *Perspectives on Global Change: The TARGETS Approach.* Cambridge: Cambridge University Press, 1997.

Rowe, Jonathan, and Mark Anielski. *The Genuine Progress Indicator: 1998 Update.* San Francisco: Redefining Progress, March 1999.

Russell, Peter. *The Global Brain: Speculations on the Evolutionary Leap to Planetary Consciousness.* Los Angeles: J. P. Tarcher, 1983.

Ryan, John C., and Alan Thein Durning. *Stuff: The Secret Lives of Everyday Things.* Seattle: Northwest Environment Watch, 1997.

Sachs, Wolfgang, ed. *The Development Dictionary: A Guide to Knowledge as Power.* London: Zed Books, 1992.

Saul, John Ralston. *The Unconscious Civilization.* New York: The Free Press, 1995.

Schumacher, E. F. "An Economics of Permanence." In *Sources: An Anthology of Contemporary Materials Useful for Preserving Personal Sanity While Braving the Great Technological Wilderness*, ed. Theodore Roszak. New York: Harper & Row, 1972.

Senge, Peter. *The Fifth Discipline: The Art and Practice of the Learning Organization.* New York: Doubleday/Currency, 1990.

Simon, Julian. *Theory of Population and Economic Growth.* Oxford: Basil Blackwell, 1986.

_____. *The Ultimate Resource.* Princeton: Princeton University Press, 1981.

Solomon, Andy. "Big Melt May Bring Big Freeze." Reuters/America Online, 23 January 1999.

Sterling, Claire. *Washington Post*, 5 January 1972.

"The Ultraviolet Index." U.S. Environmental Protection Agency, 22 May 1998. www.epa.gov/docs/ozone/uvindex/uvover.html.

Thomas, Lewis. *The Lives of a Cell: Notes of a Biology Watcher.* New York: Viking Press, 1974.

"The Top 10 El Ni–o Events of the 20th Century." National Climatic Data Center, Asheville, N.C., 4 June 1998. www.ncdc.noaa.gov/ol/climate/elnino/elnino.html.

Tuxill, John. *Losing Strands in the Web of Life.* Washington, D.C.: Worldwatch Institute, 1998.

United Nations. *Agenda 21 Earth Summit: United Nations Program of Action from Rio.* New York: United Nations Publications, 1992.

United Nations. *Human Development Report 1998.* New York: United Nations Development Program, 1998.

"UN Lauds Longer Life Span Worldwide." *New York Times*, 11 February 1999, A19.

"UN: Ozone Layer at All-Time Thinnest by 2001." Reuters, 22 June 1998. www.epa.gov/spdpublc/mbr/mbrsci62.html.

Vogt, William. *Road to Survival.* New York: W. Sloane Associates, 1948.

Waldman, Peter. "Taste of Death: Desperate Indonesians Devour Country's Trove of Endangered Species: Global Efforts to Preserve Rare Animals and Plants Overwhelmed by Panic: Brains, Served Fresh and Raw." *Wall Street Journal*, 26 October 1998, A1, A8.

Ward, Peter. *The End of Evolution: A Journey in Search of Clues to the Third Mass Extinction Facing Planet Earth.* New York: Bantam, 1994.

Weatherford, Jack. *The History of Money.* New York: Three Rivers Press, 1997.

Weisman, Alan. *Gaviotas: A Village to Reinvent the World.* White River Junction, Vt.: Chelsea Green, 1998.

"What is Club of Rome, the Doom Prophet?" *Cleveland Plain Dealer*, 19 July 1972.

World Commission on Environment and Development. *Our Common Future.* Oxford: Oxford University Press, 1987.

World Resources Institute. *World Resources 1998–99.* Washington, D.C., 1998.

INDEX

CHELSEA GREEN produces books that educate and entertain while providing information relevant to the ideas and practices of sustainable living. Once in a great while, however, a project comes along that accelerates this mission beyond the printed page. Music sustains us too!

We are proud to introduce BELIEVING CASSANDRA —The CD by Alan AtKisson.

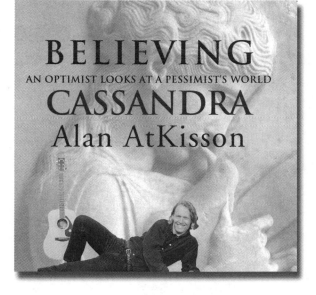

Songs included:

1. Cassandra's Lyre
2. Dead Planet Blues
3. Trying to be Happy in a Crazy World
4. What Kind of World Do You Want
5. The System Zoo
6. Extinction Blues
7. I Volunteer
8. (Beware of) Exponential Growth
9. Iona
10. I Love, Therefore I Am
11. If the Trees Were the People
12. Sustainability
13. Balaton (We'll Carry On)

This compact disk is a collection of Alan's original songs about living in dangerous times. By turns inspiring and funny, entertaining and educational, these songs come in wildly diverse styles ranging from traditional to pop-rock to big-band swing.

The lyrics are full of wordplay, poetry, and creative intelligence, and deal with everything from system dynamics to voluntary simplicity.

Enhance your enjoyment and understanding of BELIEVING CASSANDRA by experiencing it in its musical form, too. The book and compact disk are perfect companions.

You'll be singing along in no time!

Also available from Chelsea Green are two other CDs by Alan AtKisson: "Whole Lotta Shopping Going On" and "Touching the Rope."

For ordering information call 1.800.639.4099 or visit our Web site at www.chelseagreen.com

CHELSEA GREEN

Sustainable living has many facets. Chelsea Green's celebration of the sustainable arts has led us to publish trend-setting books about organic gardening, solar electricity and renewable energy, innovative building techniques, regenerative forestry, local and bioregional democracy, and whole foods. The company's published works, while intensely practical, are also entertaining and inspirational, demonstrating that an ecological approach to life is consistent with producing beautiful, eloquent, and useful books, videos, and audio cassettes.

For more information about Chelsea Green, or to request a free catalog, call toll-free (800) 639-4099, or write to us at P.O. Box 428, White River Junction, Vermont 05001. Visit our Web site at www.chelseagreen.com.

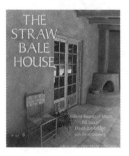

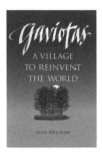

The Straw Bale House
The New Independent Home
Independent Builder:
  Designing & Building a
  House Your Own Way
The Rammed Earth House
The Passive Solar House
The Sauna
Wind Energy Basics
Wind Power for Home &
  Business
The Solar Living Sourcebook
A Shelter Sketchbook
Mortgage-Free!
Hammer. Nail. Wood.
Y2K and Y-O-U:
  The Sane Person's Home-
  Preparation Guide
Stone Circles

Sharing the Harvest
Passport to Gardening:
  A Sourcebook for the
  21st-Century
The New Organic Grower
Four-Season Harvest
The Apple Grower
The Flower Farmer
Solar Gardening
Straight-Ahead Organic
The Contrary Farmer
The Contrary Farmer's
  Invitation to Gardening
The Bread Builders:
  Hearth Loaves and Ma-
  sonry Ovens
Whole Foods Companion
Keeping Food Fresh
Good Spirits

Gaviotas: A Village to
  Reinvent the World
Beyond the Limits
Loving and Leaving the
  Good Life
Scott Nearing: The Making
  of a Homesteader
Simple Food for the
  Good Life
Who Owns the Sun?
Global Spin:
  The Corporate Assault
  on Environmentalism
Hemp Horizons
Seeing Nature
The Man Who Planted Trees
The Northern Forest
Genetic Engineering, Food
  and our Environment